Do you know . . .

. . . where Qwilleran's fortune comes from?

. . . when Chief Andrew Brodie made his first appearance?

. . . what the term "Down Below" refers to?

. . . what Polly Duncan calls her cat?

. . . why Lilian Jackson Braun decided to make her star detective a man instead of a woman?

At last—a companion volume for fans of the multimillion-selling mystery series—filled with tantalizing trivia, inside information, and more!

THE CAT WHO . . . COMPANION

THE CAT WHO . . . COMPANION

Sharon A. Feaster

BERKLEY PRIME CRIME, NEW YORK

THE CAT WHO ... COMPANION

A Berkley Prime Crime Book / published by arrangement with
the author

PRINTING HISTORY
Berkley Prime Crime trade paperback edition / December 1998
Revised edition / November 1999

The Penguin Putnam Inc. World Wide Web address is
http://www.penguinputnam.com

ISBN: 0-425-17425-5

PRINTED IN THE UNITED STATES OF AMERICA

10 9 8 7 6 5 4

Acknowledgments

Thanks to Lucile Estell, who introduced me to *The Cat Who* . . . Thanks to my mother, Dorothy Feaster, and my sisters and brother—Mary, Fran, and Bill—who encouraged me. Thanks to Donna Owens, who wouldn't let me give up. Thanks to Neely Beaty, my favorite English teacher, who taught me to write.

Thanks to the people Down Below and the residents of Moose County, who share their lives with us.

Thanks most of all to Lilian Jackson Braun, "The Lady Who" gives us such wonderful stories of Koko and Yum Yum and their sleuthing companion, Qwilleran, and who allowed me the honor of visiting with her and meeting Koko the Third.

Contents

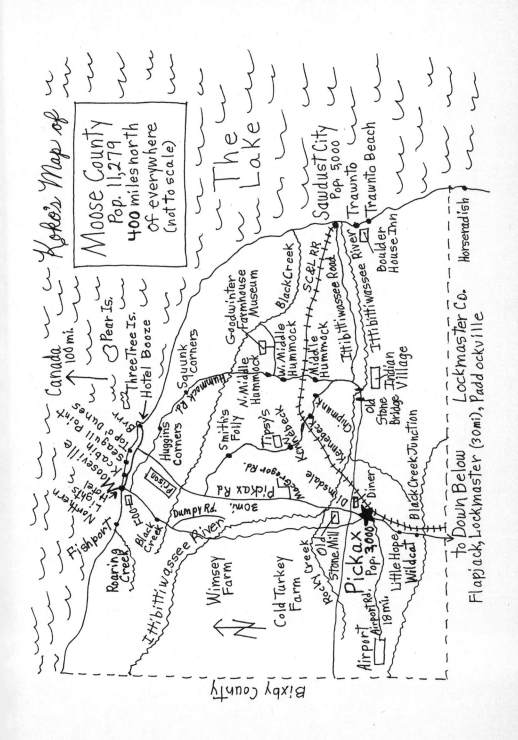

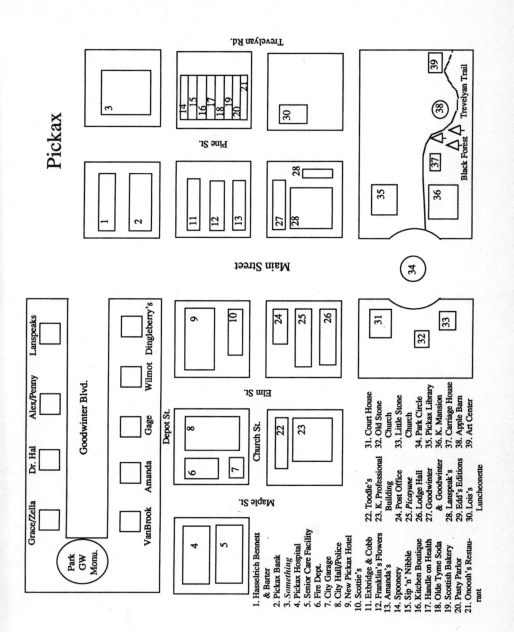

Pickax

Trevelyan Rd.

Pine St.

Main Street

Trevelyan Trail

Black Forest

3

14
15
16
17
18
19
20
21

30

1
2

11
12
13

27
28
28

35

36
37
38
39

34

Grace/Zella
Dr. Hal
Alex/Penny
Lanspeaks

Goodwinter Blvd.

VanBrook
Amanda
Gage
Wilmot
Dingleberry's

Park
GW
Monu.

Maple St.

Depot St.

Elm St.

Church St.

4
5

6
7
8

9
10

24
25
26

31
32
33

22
23

1. Hasselrich Bennett
   & Barter
2. Pickax Bank
3. *Something*
4. Pickax Hospital
5. Senior Care Facility
6. Fire Dept.
7. City Garage
8. City Hall/Police
9. New Pickax Hotel
10. Scottie's
11. Exbridge & Cobb
12. Franklin's Flowers
13. Amanda's
14. Spooney
15. Sip 'n' Nibble
16. Kitchen Boutique
17. Handle on Health
18. Olde Tyme Soda
19. Scottish Bakery
20. Pasty Parlor
21. Onoosh's Restau-
    rant
22. Toodle's
23. K. Professional
    Building
24. Post Office
25. *Picayune*
26. Lodge Hall
27. Goodwinter
    & Goodwinter
28. Lanspeak's
29. Edd's Editions
30. Lois's
    Luncheonette
31. Court House
32. Old Stone
    Church
33. Little Stone
    Church
34. Park Circle
35. Pickax Library
36. K. Mansion
37. Carriage House
38. Apple Barn
39. Art Center

Introduction

M_y *introduction to the incomparable Koko, the luscious Yum Yum, and the Qwintessential reporter came in 1992 when, while I was* recovering from surgery, a friend gave me *The Cat Who Wasn't There.* I was hooked by the cats' sharp, dainty claws! I couldn't wait until the next book!

Then I discovered there were earlier books. I didn't rest until I had collected them all. Although each book is a complete story in itself, I found myself reading them in sequence and enjoying the way the recurring characters developed over the years.

Lilian Jackson Braun spins a yarn about a world-famous newspaper reporter, and the threads run from a large Midwestern city to Junktown to Moose County to Breakfast Island to the Potato Mountains and back. And early in the tale, James Mackintosh Qwilleran becomes entangled first with Kao K'o-Kung, then with Yum Yum—two intelligent, beautiful, and witty Siamese cats. The independent bachelor becomes the "willing slave" of his two feline partners, and the trio sets about unraveling mysteries and crimes.

Lilian knows how to imbue the Siamese with just enough magic to make them incredible sleuths, but not so much that they become unbelievable. They don't do anything "uncat-like." They are very curious cats who are highly sensitive to emotions in people and changes in the atmosphere. They sniff here and there, pilfer a letter or a pen, push books off a shelf, scratch at this and that, push dominoes off a table, hiss at this person, talk to that person—and Qwilleran's finely tuned intuition and reportorial skills go to work.

One day the idea for a companion book catapulted into my brain, as a way of organizing information about Qwilleran, the cats, the characters, and the crimes.

"Koko and Yum Yum and Their Catly Behavior" describes the two lovable and precocious Siamese and their shenanigans—from racing on crossbeams to using technology to forecasting weather to pilfering glittery objects to communicating with Qwilleran and his acquaintances. "The Cats' Games and Tricks" explains Dictionary, Book!, Scrabble, dominoes, and other catly pastimes.

"Qwill: The Man and His Career" provides snapshots of Qwilleran's life, as well as a description of the contents of his writing portfolio. "Cast of Characters" contains an alphabetical listing, coded with book titles, of all the people and animals Qwilleran and the Siamese have encountered Down Below, in and around Moose County, and in the Potato Mountains.

"The Cats' Pages" is a listing of businesses, clubs, groups, and buildings—should you decide to go shopping when you visit the places Qwilleran, Koko, and Yum Yum have lived. Designed to assist you on your vacation is "The Cats' Geography Book," which lists important points of interest.

"Crimes and Clues" contains summaries of the investigations that Qwilleran and the Siamese have conducted, including clues Koko and Yum Yum have provided. "The Women in Qwill's Life" has descriptions of the women to whom Qwilleran has been attracted over the years, especially his up-and-down relationship with Polly Duncan.

Should you want to visit some of the apartments and houses Qwilleran and the cats have lived in, "Gracious Abodes" provides highlights of what to look for during your tours. And when you're hungry, "A Companion's Guide to Dining" will tell you which eating establishments to avoid and which restaurants to enjoy.

The tales of Down Below and Moose County wouldn't be complete without a look at *The Cat Who Had 14 Tales*, a collection of short stories that includes early information on some of the characters Qwilleran meets. Through stories featuring a variety of cats, you'll see a foreshadowing of some of the talents of Koko and Yum Yum.

How did Lilian Jackson Braun get started in her writing career? Is there a real Koko who provides catspiration? Just where is Moose County? Lilian discusses these and other questions in "The Lady Who . . ."

I hope you enjoy *The Cat Who . . . Companion* as you read and reread the tales of the world-famous Siamese sleuths and their partner, Qwilleran.

The Cat Who . . .

Could Read Backwards
Ate Danish Modern
Turned On and Off
Saw Red
Played Brahms
Played Post Office
Knew Shakespeare
Sniffed Glue
Went Underground

Talked to Ghosts
Lived High
Knew a Cardinal
Moved a Mountain
Wasn't There
Went Into the Closet
Came to Breakfast
Blew the Whistle
Said Cheese
Tailed a Thief
Sang for the Birds
Saw Stars
The Cat Who Had 14 Tales (short story collection)

How talented can one cat be?

Thanks to those of you who have communicated to me that you're enjoying *The Cat Who . . . Companion!* I'm glad it has found a place on your bookshelf, next to *The Cat Who . . .* books.

I hope that you enjoy this update, which includes information from Lilian Jackson Braun's *The Cat Who Saw Stars*. It has updates on Qwill, the cats, and the crimes they solve, plus your favorite old and new characters, places, abodes, and dining. The update also has a new quiz, so check your knowledge!

October 1999

THE CAT WHO . . . COMPANION

1

Koko and Yum Yum and Their Catly Behavior

Koko is a fascinating character who becomes smarter with each book. His repertoire of games and clues grows with each mystery. Although Yum Yum joins the family after Koko, she definitely makes her own place in Qwilleran's heart.

The Cat Who Could Read Backwards

Qwilleran's first meeting with Koko takes place in Mount-clemens's apartment when the art critic invites the art writer for dinner. Kao K'o-Kung is named after a thirteenth-century artist of Turkish descent who lived as a Chinese gentleman. Koko is a "long, lean, muscular cat with light-colored sleek fur and an unbearable amount of assurance and authority." He is "somewhat of a hermit and suspicious of outsiders."

Koko, as his name was shortened by Qwilleran, has the "dignity and grace of Chinese art." He has "quite a nose for printer's ink" and reads newspaper headlines, tracing the words backward from right to left. He also has an appreciation for modern art and favors biographies.

Koko's voice can sound like an ambulance siren, which he turns on whenever his meals are late. He likes white grape juice and refuses to eat raw meat. He flies, too. When he wants to sit on top of an eight-foot bookcase, he "puts his ears back and zooms up like a jet."

The Cat Who Ate Danish Modern

Koko's slanted eyes are brilliant blue. He enjoys eating spiderwebs and has started licking the glue from stamps and envelopes, but he loves lobster and anything else that's expensive. Qwill thinks Koko reads price tags.

Koko changes his diet—to the green wool of the expensive Danish chair in Noyton's apartment. Qwill realizes it is Koko, not moths, who's taking bites out of his wool ties. Qwill immediately calls a psycatatrist, Dr. Highspight. She says it's "just like Gilbert and Sullivan . . . 'For he's going to marry Yum Yum, te dum.'" The psycatatrist tells Qwilleran to find another nickname for Alacoque "Cokey" Wright because Koko thinks Qwill is using his name and he's very jealous.

Qwilleran first meets Yum Yum when the cat is in the lap of Mrs. Tait, who calls her Freya. Her husband insists that the cat's name is Yu—the ancient Chinese word for jade. After Koko and Freya/Yu capture Mr. Tait, when he attacks Qwilleran, Qwill adopts the young female Siamese and changes her name to Yum Yum.

Yum Yum is "dainty and sweet," her face "a poignant triangle of brown, and her eyes enormous circles of violet-blue." Her brown ears cock at "a flirtatious angle," and there's a cowlick on her white breast. She has a kink in her tail.

Because of his work in solving crimes, Koko is presented an

honorary press card complete with an identification photo—his eyes wide, ears alert, and whiskers bristling.

The Cat Who Turned On and Off

Koko and his new companion Yum Yum have a new sleeping place—inside the springs of Qwilleran's bed in the Medford Manor.

Yum Yum likes to keep an eye on the contents of the wastebasket. When Qwill tries to amuse Yum Yum with a rubber mouse, she turns her back on it and picks a crumpled paper handkerchief out of the trash can.

Yum Yum's "normal speaking voice [is] a soprano shriek." She likes to sit on Qwill's chest while he's asleep. She stretches out her paw and gently touches his moustache, then uses the stubble on his chin to scratch her head. She and Koko sometimes awaken Qwilleran by playing hopscotch on the bed.

Yum Yum has a "nice understanding of protocol; she's always on Koko's left." Koko is self-assured, but Yum Yum's "as nervous as a cat." She "sits on laps and catches mice—all the things cats are supposed to do."

One evening Mrs. Cobb brings hot, frosted brownies with walnuts to Qwilleran's apartment, and she offers to read his palm. Koko and Yum Yum stage a catfit to encourage Mrs. Cobb to leave.

During the Block Party meeting in the attic, there's "a sudden blast of noise from the floor below." It's a torrent of popular music from a radio in the Cobbs' apartment. Koko turned it on by "scraping it with his hard little jaw."

The Cat Who Saw Red

On a trip to the veterinarian to have his teeth cleaned, Koko turns into a "fur tornado." With three people hanging on to him, Koko still turns around, leaps off the table, and runs into the kennel room. He lands on top of the air conditioner—eight feet off the floor—and cusses at everybody.

Qwilleran calls Yum Yum "little sweetheart" and speaks to her with "an unabashed gentleness that his cronies at the Press Club would not have believed and that no woman in his life had ever heard."

At his new home at the Maus Haus, Koko investigates the bathroom, where he "crowed in exultation, enjoying the extra resonance that tile walls gave to his normally loud and penetrating voice."

Qwilleran says that Koko and Yum Yum can "smell through the refrigerator door." If there's lobster, they won't eat chicken; and if there's chicken, they won't eat beef. Koko rings for his breakfast by stepping on the tab key of the typewriter.

The next time Qwilleran returns home, he is greeted by a "scene of incredible beauty." The cats have taken a ball of gray yarn and "spun a web that enmeshed every article of furniture."

After returning from an overnight visit to Rattlesnake Lake, Qwill is told by Mrs. Marron that the cats "took sick" and the Sanitation Department took them away because they were dead. Qwill is devastated. He sits down at the typewriter to write a "requiem for two lost friends." Then he hears a crying and scratching at the window. It's Koko and Yum Yum, who jump to the floor and trot to the kitchen, "looking for their dinner."

The Cat Who Played Brahms

Koko's portrait hangs in the lobby of the Press Club. He's the only cat in the history of journalism to have his own press card signed by the chief of police. It is commonly understood at the Press Club that "the brains behind Qwilleran's success belongs to a feline of outstanding intelligence and sensory perception."

Although Qwilleran starts out for his north country vacation "with a light heart," the Siamese feel otherwise. Yum Yum howls "in strident tones whenever the car turned a corner, rounded a curve, crossed a bridge, passed under a viaduct, encountered a truck, or exceeded fifty miles an hour." Koko scolds her and bites her hind leg, "adding snarls and hisses to the orchestrated uproar."

Upon arrival, the two cats waste no time. Yum Yum leaps around overhead from beam to beam while Koko "sits imperiously on the moose head" above the fireplace.

Yum Yum likes to untie the shoelaces of visitors. She awakens Qwilleran by sitting on his chest, "her blue eyes boring into his forehead, conveying a subliminal message: breakfast."

Koko and Yum Yum become weather forecasters. One evening they begin to prowl restlessly. Yum Yum emits "earsplitting howls" and Koko butts his head against the legs of tables and chairs. Within minutes a high wind rushes in and trees begin to sway. Several days later, Koko throws himself at the legs of tables and chairs, while Yum Yum emits "an occasional shriek." By nightfall, a storm is overhead.

Rosemary Whiting buys tulips of various colors from the prison gift shop. Koko pulls out all the black tulips and scatters them over the floor. The second time he does it, Rosemary locks him in the bathroom. Qwill opens the door slowly to a blizzard-like scene. Paper towels are now confetti. A fresh box of two hundred facial tissues is empty, and the toilet tissue has been unrolled. Bath salts and scouring powder are everywhere.

Koko engages in "one-upmanship." He follows Rosemary around the cabin and repeatedly maneuvers his tail under her foot. His "bloodcurdling screeches" unnerve her. She goes home.

The Cat Who Played Post Office

At the Klingenschoen mansion, Koko and Yum Yum like to sit on the cool marble and watch envelopes dropping through the door's mail slot. Koko scoops a letter from the pile, and Yum Yum bats it around the slick floor. They jump into the pile "like children in a snowbank." Yum Yum tries to push letters under the Oriental rug because she likes to hide things.

Koko sorts the mail and takes Qwilleran the letters he thinks are important. Koko grips a pink envelope in his jaws and parades around "with an air of importance." It's a letter from Lori Bamba, whom the cats like. Koko takes off with another letter, one from Qwilleran's former landlady, Iris Cobb, who's an excellent cook.

Koko personally delivers an envelope addressed in red ink from Hixie Rice, who used to speak French to Koko when they lived at Maus Haus. He also delivers a card about a new seafood restaurant and a letter from Mildred Hanstable. After the dinner party, the mail-cat delivers Penelope Goodwinter's thank-you note, which has a "faint but heady suggestion of Fantaisie Féline" perfume from Paris.

Yum Yum jumps onto Qwilleran's lap and touches his moustache "with an inquisitive paw." Accustomed to stealing brushes, she can't understand "bristles attached to a face."

Koko heads for the antique piano and plays four notes: G,

C, D, E. Qwill hums the tune Koko played: "How Dry I Am!" Qwilleran pours Koko a jigger of white grape juice.

Qwilleran admits that "the cat is ten pounds of bone and muscle in a fur coat, with whiskers and a long tail and a wet nose, but he's smarter than I am."

The Cat Who Knew Shakespeare

The cats' parlor in the remodeled carriage house is carpeted and furnished with "cushions, baskets, scratching posts, climbing trees, and a turkey roaster that served as their commode." There's also a collection of secondhand books, which Koko enjoys pushing off the shelf.

Koko likes to have telephone conversations with Lori Bamba.

At the opening ceremony for the Klingenschoen Museum, Koko rides up the elevator carrying a dead mouse. Qwilleran is sure that Koko pressed the elevator button himself, because of Koko's mechanical abilities.

At the wedding of Iris and Herb, Koko speaks up with a "Yow!" He has no intention of holding his peace forever. Qwilleran has the ring, which slips out of his hand and rolls across the rug. Yum Yum bats the ring around until she finally pushes it under a rug and Qwilleran catches up with her.

After Qwilleran leaves for the program at the Old Stone Church, Koko starts "carrying on like a banshee." Mr. O'Dell carries the cats over to the apartment because of the "divil of a row that he was making." Koko sensed the danger and thus saved Yum Yum and himself from the devastating fire.

The Cat Who Sniffed Glue

Koko has a "high-decibel yowl," and Yum Yum's shriek can be duplicated "only by a synthesizer." Either of them can be heard for blocks if the windows are open.

Koko is the "inspector general," who insists on "screening everyone for security reasons." Koko walks "with a resolute step" while Yum Yum minces along "with graceful, pigeon-toed steps, a few paces behind him."

Yum Yum has a "lightning-fast paw like a steel hook." She "opens doors, unties shoelaces, and steals anything small and shiny." She likes to leap onto Qwilleran's lap, "landing as softly as a cloud and turning around three times before settling down." Once when Qwill arrives home, he finds the cashew nuts have been "fished out of the bowl and batted around the room." Yum Yum is licking her right paw.

One evening Qwilleran comes home to discover his writing studio with signs of vandalism: "desk drawers open, papers scattered about the floor, desktop ransacked, and paper clips everywhere." Yum Yum is crouched on the wall shelf in her "guilty position—a compact bundle with elevated shoulders and haunches." Yum Yum opened the drawers with her famous paw and Koko licked all the glue from the gummed flaps of the envelopes. Once before he had ungummed a whole sheet of stamps and "paraded impudently around the apartment with an airmail stamp stuck on his nose." Now Koko is sitting with a "fazed expression in his eyes and a peculiar splay-legged stance—he's high on glue!"

Koko "doesn't like anyone to touch his tail, pry open his mouth, or apply his name to any other entity—animal, vegetable, or mineral." That's why Qwill has "only ginger ale and not that other popular beverage."

Koko is learning how to turn the television off.

The Cat Who Went Underground

When Qwilleran takes the Siamese to the log cabin, the cats are soon both overhead, "leaping across the beams, landing on the mantel, swooping down to the sofas, and skidding across the polished floor on handwoven rugs." Koko likes to sit on the moose head, between the antlers.

The Siamese like to help Qwilleran while he's writing. They play "toboggan" on the papers that land on the floor, "skidding across the oiled floorboards in high glee." They also like to sit on his notes and "catch their tails in the carriage of his electric typewriter."

After Qwill returns from dinner one evening, he finds Yum Yum darting insanely about the living room while Koko sits "with magisterial calm on top of the moose head." Qwilleran pursues Yum Yum around the cabin until she finally drops a dead mouse in his typewriter.

When Lori calls Qwill, Koko senses who is on the line, jumps on the bar, and purrs throatily. Qwill holds the receiver to the cat's head, and there are "yowls and musical yiks and cadenzas that Lori seemed to understand."

Koko and Yum Yum are camera shy. Every time Qwilleran tries to grab a picture while they are "in a delightful pose," they suddenly change to an undelightful pose. Qwilleran takes them to Bushy's studio for a formal picture, but they refuse to leave their hamper. They firmly attach their claws to the open weave of the basket and remain "riveted to their travel coop for the remainder of the evening."

The Cat Who Talked to Ghosts

While Qwilleran listens to the opera *Otello*, Koko sits on the coffee table, swaying slightly. Opera puts him in a trance. Yum

Yum sits curled up on Qwill's lap with her paws covering her ears, "a feline commentary on Verdi."

Koko's reaction to the loud Vince Boswell is to lay back his ears. No one has ever called him "kitty" before. When an electrician comes to the farmhouse, Koko keeps a wary eye on him, and Yum Yum inspects his shoelaces.

Qwilleran takes one of his favorite dishes out of Iris Cobb's freezer and thaws a large portion of lamb shank cooked with lentils. He turns his back to make a phone call, then returns to find that the Siamese have enjoyed their portion of lamb—and his. All that remains on his plate is "a mess of lentils and a shank bone, gnawed clean."

Koko and Yum Yum don't react well to a visit from Bootsie, Polly Duncan's Siamese kitten. Bootsie has a running fit and then eats their food. Koko and Yum Yum sit on top of the seven-foot wardrobe and won't come down, not even to eat.

The Cat Who Lived High

Koko can "see the invisible, hear the inaudible, and sense the unknowable." Yum Yum captivates Qwilleran with "shameless wiles." They don't react well to the news that they are moving to the Casablanca apartment building Down Below for the winter. Koko burrows under the hearth rug and Yum Yum hides under the rug in front of the sofa.

When Qwilleran returns to the Casablanca apartment on the first night, he notices that the foyer and other rooms are lighted, although he distinctly remembers leaving the apartment in darkness. He discovers that most of the lamps have touch-switches, and the Siamese had apparently run from one to the other, making them light up.

Crumpled paper is "like catnip" to Yum Yum, and she retrieves it from the trash can in three seconds. When Qwilleran crumples up a newspaper clipping, Yum Yum awakens from her sleep and retrieves it. She also likes the sensation of the water-bed.

Qwilleran arrives home after a dinner party to find the bedroom floor wet and the bathroom floor flooded. The sink is overflowing, the faucet is running full force, and Koko is sitting on the toilet tank "surveying his achievement."

The Siamese like ice cream, but not chocolate or strawberry. When Qwilleran gives them Neapolitan ice cream, they carefully lap up the vanilla but ignore the other two flavors and paw the air in sign language saying, "Take it away!"

The Cat Who Knew a Cardinal

Qwilleran has to be cautious when driving with the cats. Any "sudden start or stop, or any turn in excess of twelve degrees, upset Yum Yum's gastrointestinal apparatus and caused a shrill protest—or worse."

Yum Yum likes to pilfer small objects. Her law is, "If anything can be unhooked, untied, unbuckled, or unlatched, DO IT!" Her voice is changing. Frequently she delivers a "very assertive contralto yowl that sounds suspiciously like 'N-n-n-NOW!' "

The Siamese like to race over the beams and up and down the ramps in their new home, the renovated apple barn. When they reach the lower balcony, they swoop down to the main floor "like flying squirrels, landing in a deep-cushioned chair."

When Qwilleran puts Yum Yum in a harness, she rolls over into a "leaden lump of uncooperative fur." She lies in a simulated coma until the harness is removed. Another time when he puts the harness on her, she ends up on one of the radiating beams that meet in the center of the barn, her harness snagged on a bolt. Qwilleran has to ease himself out on the twelve-inch beam until he can dislodge her and then back up all the way to the catwalk. Koko helps by crouching on Qwill's back.

When Bushy comes to photograph the house for insurance purposes, the Siamese try to get in every picture. This is a radical departure from their behavior when Qwilleran had taken them to Bushy's studio for photographs and they had stubbornly refused to leave their carrier.

The Cat Who Moved a Mountain

When Qwilleran announces to the cats that they will be spending the summer in the Potato Mountains, Koko seems excited. But when Qwilleran packs the car, the cats become invisible. Koko hides on a bookshelf behind the biographies—the end of his tail visible as a clue. Yum Yum, however, is very serious. She huddles on one of the beams under the roof, which is "accessible only by a forty-foot ladder." Qwilleran resorts to the "T-word": Treat! After a feast of canned cocktail shrimp, the two Siamese hop into their carrier.

While traveling to the Potato Mountains, Qwilleran stops for a quick burger and fries, leaving the Siamese in the car. As he leaves the restaurant, he hears the continuous blowing of his car horn. Koko is standing behind the wheel "with his paws planted firmly on the horn button." Qwilleran is upset, until he sees a bent coat hanger on the passenger side—car or cat thieves had tried to break in, but Koko had foiled their plot!

At Tiptop, Yum Yum discovers the staircase and runs up and down "like a pianist practicing scales." Koko likes the painting of mountains and rubs his jaw against a corner of the frame, moving the mountain.

Qwilleran sleeps well his first night on the mountain, until about 5:30 A.M., when he is jolted awake by what sounds like gunshots. The Siamese have explosively raised all four shades in their bedroom.

When Dolly Lessmore says she has always had dogs, Koko and Yum Yum walk out, "their long, lithe bodies making U-turns in unison."

When Qwilleran arrives home one night, he hears human voices upstairs—coming from the radio. Koko is up to his old trick of turning things on and off.

The Cat Who Wasn't There

Qwilleran holds intelligent, though somewhat one-sided, conversations with Koko and Yum Yum. The Siamese are "sophisticated companions whom he treats as equals."

When Qwilleran is trying to think of a suitable cat-sitter for the Siamese while he's in Scotland, Koko suggests Mildred Hanstable by staring pointedly at his empty plate when it's time for his midday snack. Qwilleran gives them a handful of crunchy cereal that Mildred makes.

Mildred reports that she and the cats are getting along just fine. Yum Yum sits on the quilting frame and watches the needle go in and out, and Koko helps read tarot cards. When Koko figures out that Qwilleran's voice is coming from the telephone, he insists on talking to him.

Whenever the Bambas visit, the Siamese make themselves "highly visible, walking back and forth languorously, pivoting and posing like models on a fashion-show runway."

Koko and Yum Yum have taken up "wet cleaning." They lick the streak of melted butter from the suede surface of Qwilleran's new coat.

Qwilleran takes Yum Yum, but not Koko, to the Pets for Patients program at the Senior Care Facility. Yum Yum is reluctant, and Qwilleran has to "install the squirming, clutching, kicking" cat into the carrier. Yum Yum strikes the "dead-cat pose" she always assumes after losing an argument. But she behaves nicely with Mr. Hornbuckle and sits "in a contented bundle on the blanketed lap, purring gently."

Qwilleran is alarmed when he comes home and finds "a pair of debilitated animals lying on the rug in front of the sofa." Their fur is hot! Lori Bamba says the cats "probably slept on top of the dryer until they were half-cooked."

The Cat Who Went Into the Closet

Koko has a "degree of intelligence and perception" that is "sometimes unnerving to a human with only five senses and a journalism degree." All Yum Yum has to do to make Qwilleran capitulate is to "reach up and touch Qwilleran's moustache with her paw."

One of their favorite catly pleasures is listening to Qwilleran read to them. Koko likes to choose the books.

Mrs. Fulgrove accidentally shuts Koko in the cleaning closet, where he activates the can of foam carpet cleaner, filling almost the whole closet with a white cloud.

One night Qwilleran is being prevented from sleeping by a constant ringing of the phone. After a few more rings, there's silence. The cats had also been annoyed and had "taken matters into their own paws."

When Qwilleran orders the Siamese out of the room for poor manners, they leave the room, but not immediately. "First they thought about it, then scratched an ear and licked a paw, then thought about it some more, then sauntered out."

The Cat Who Came to Breakfast

Yum Yum has the "instincts of a safecracker and a shop-lifter" and, when frustrated, screams like a cockatoo. When Yum Yum fusses, she can work "industriously and stubbornly for an hour without any apparent purpose and without results." She finds a rusty nail in a crevice, works to get it out, then pushes it back into another crevice.

The cats' daily grooming is accomplished with a walnut-handled brush given to them by Polly. Koko likes to be brushed while walking away, "forcing his human valet to follow on his knees." But Yum Yum fights the brush.

According to Elizabeth Appelhardt's numerological analysis of Yum Yum's name (also her original name of Freya), the female Siamese is "patient and independent, with strong will-power." Koko, on the other hand, is "aristocratic, scientific, and mentally keen, but rather secretive."

The Cat Who Blew the Whistle

Koko and Yum Yum stalk into the living area at eleven o'clock one evening, staring at Dwight Somers and telling him it's time to go home. He leaves.

When the Siamese sing for their supper, it's a "duet of baritone yowls and coloratura trills, the latter more like shrieks." Yum Yum demands her own plate.

Koko has a "sense of right and wrong." When Mrs. Ful-grove lines up the duck decoys facing west instead of east, Koko throws a fit. Yum Yum, however, once tried to steal the police chief's badge off his chest.

When Koko sits inside the portable pyramid set up in Qwil-leran's house, there's a power outage in the whole county.

When the cat comes out of the pyramid, the power comes back on!

When Qwilleran is trying to collect his thoughts, he walks around his barn-house in a large circle. Whenever Qwilleran does this, both cats "fall into line behind him, marching with tails at twelve o'clock."

The Cat Who Said Cheese

Koko is the master of one-upmanship, proving his title more than once with John Bushland. Bushy tries to take pictures of the cats for a calendar competition. While Bushy and Qwill are talking, the Siamese rehearse "every pose known to calendar cats." The instant Bushy raises his camera, they change to uncalendarly positions.

Qwilleran buys an old cheese basket that used to belong to Mrs. Cobb. Yum Yum claims it, curling into it with contentment. However, Qwilleran returns home to find her in desperate straits—her tiny head is caught in one of the holes of the basket. He has to break the wicker strands to free her.

Koko goes into a "grasshopper act" when there's a message on the answering machine. He jumps in "exaggerated arcs from floor to desktop to chair to bookshelf." The faster he jumps, the more urgent the call.

Lori tells Qwilleran that cats have twenty-four whiskers on each side, which may account for their ESP. When Qwilleran counts, he finds that Yum Yum has twenty-four, but Koko has thirty!

The Cat Who Tailed a Thief

Koko always eats "with his rear end pointed north" and Yum Yum "always approaches her food from the left."

The cats and Qwilleran are enjoying a new activity: chasing the lone housefly that came with the condo. Qwill stands ready with folded newspaper, and the cats futilely leap and crash into each other as the fly, named Mosca, swoops playfully around the two-story living room.

The Siamese fight over Carter Lee's Russian fur hat, rolling in it and kicking it. This results in the departure of Carter Lee and Danielle from Qwilleran's apartment—for which Qwill rewards the Siamese.

Yum Yum has lots of toys in a drawer of a hutch: things that bounce, rattle, roll, glitter, or smell like catnip. She entertains herself for hours with these toys.

The Cat Who Sang for the Birds

While Koko tries to communicate his suspicions to Qwilleran, Yum Yum hides her evidence under the sofa or rug. They like to stand on their hind legs and gaze out the "low-silled windows that flanked the front door." They're watching a "congregation of seven black crows" just outside. The crows are strutting "in unison like a drill team."

Qwilleran uses a white canvas tote bag with the logo of the Pickax Public Library to carry the Siamese back and forth to the new gazebo. Birds come to the bird feeders and birdbaths—the cats are entranced. They now get Qwilleran out of bed at dawn when the birds come, one cat "yowling in an operatic baritone" and the other "uttering soprano shrieks." Yum Yum likes to bat insects on the screens, but Koko likes to listen to all the songs of the birds. He makes friends of the crows and sings for the wrens and the robins.

Koko has begun a new bleating sound: *aaaaaaaaaaaaaaa*. He also answers back the pileated woodpecker: *kek-kek-kek-kek*. Koko mimics the birds' evensong, although not in the right key.

Koko sometimes gives Qwilleran a headache through efforts at thought transference. One day Qwilleran decides to write a column on "the ample moustache," as exemplified by Mark Twain, Einstein, Groucho Marx, and others. Koko was sitting on a large book, *Mark Twain A to Z*, a man with a great moustache.

While Qwilleran is trying to think of a new format for the spelling bee, Koko sits on *Baseball, An Illustrated History*, then runs around in circles. Qwilleran realizes that what he needs is a whole new ball game! A Pennant Race!

Yum Yum picks a yo-yo out of the wastebasket and uses it as a hockey puck.

After a noontime treat of Kabibbles, the two cats wash up in unison: "four licks of the paw, four swipes over the mask, four passes over the ear—all repeated with the other paw. The choreography was remarkable."

Koko and Yum Yum like to chase each other up and down the ramp inside the apple barn. Koko chases Yum Yum up, then they slam on the brakes and Yum Yum chases Koko down. Time: sixteen seconds.

The Cat Who Saw Stars

The sleek, muscular Koko "simply moved in" with Qwilleran at a time when Qwill was getting his life back together.

Qwill and Koko have a special kinship, one with a "feline radar system" and the other with "an intuitive moustache." Koko's perception of right and wrong goes "beyond catly concerns." He can sense answers to questions that humans can't. Koko enjoys a brushing with the "dignity of a monarch being robed for a coronation."

Yum Yum was "a poor little rich cat abandoned in a posh neighborhood" when Qwilleran rescued her. He named her Yum Yum because of "her sweet expression and winning ways." She has a "vested interest in shiny objects, cardboard boxes and crumpled paper." Yum Yum considers a brushing a game of "fight-the-brush."

The Siamese like to go to Mooseville for sounds and sights: "squawking gulls, peeping sandpipers, cawing crows, chipping chipmunks! And everything moves: birds, butterflies, grasshoppers, waving beach grass, splashing waves." The cats like to roll on the concrete floor of the kitchen porch, but not the lakeside porch because of the sand from the beach. They also like to listen to Qwilleran read, especially books with sound effects such as bleating of sheep, barking of dogs, meowing of cats, and mooing of cows.

Koko likes to sit on large books, such as *Mark Twain A to Z.* He takes possession of the pedestal for Qwill's copper sailboat, posing "like an ancient Egyptian cat" and staring at the night stars. Qwilleran says Koko "studies the constellations at night" and "does graduate work in crow behavior during the day." One day a hummingbird gets its long beak caught in the porch screen. Yum Yum gently pushes the beak with her paw and frees the bird, saving its life.

Koko chooses a book from the shelf, Mark Twain's *A Horse's Tail,* about an army horse named Soldier Boy. The cats enjoy Qwilleran's sound effects. Koko, who likes to deliver mail, scatters Polly's postcards all over the floor, leaving teeth prints on two.

Elizabeth urges Qwilleran to buy stuffed Kalico Kittens for the cats, but Qwilleran knows they ignore "velvet mice, rubber frogs, and tinkling plastic." They prefer "a necktie with a man on the other end." But he takes one named Gertrude.

Koko has a catfit during a strong squall on the lake. He topples a lamp, scatters books and papers, crumples rugs, and unrolls several yards of paper towels. He also displaces the two postcards with teeth marks on them. During the pounding rain, which lasts most of the night, Yum Yum crawls under Qwilleran's bedclothes, and Koko soon follows suit.

Yum Yum adopts Gertrude, the Kalico Kitten which Qwilleran has purchased. She gives Gertrude a few licks, then carries it to her favorite seat on the sofa. While sitting on the porch table, Yum Yum nestles Gertrude between her forelegs with a "contented look of fulfilled motherhood." For years, Bushy has been trying to take pictures of the Siamese, to no avail. He tracks down an old lens that takes pictures of subjects without their knowledge. He sneaks a perfect picture of Yum Yum with Gertrude.

Late one night Koko is studying the stars from his pedestal on the porch. The sky seems to be getting lighter, and the cats are becoming nervous. Yum Yum runs indoors. Suddenly there's a blast of wind and a large, round object floats downward. Koko's fur stands on end, then he paws open the screen door and runs toward the beach, with Qwill close behind. Qwilleran sees small creatures with four legs and long tails coming out of the round object. Qwilleran catches Koko, then he sees stars and blacks out. When he awakes, he's on his chair on the porch, but Koko's fur is sandy and Qwill's clothes are, too.

Qwilleran wonders if Koko's superior intelligence is that of "an alien race who were not little green men but little green cats!" Qwill is willing to concede that Koko wasn't seeing stars, but "fuzzy green blobs," during his stargazing on the porch.

2

The Cats' Games
and Tricks

The first cat toy Qwilleran encounters is Mintie Mouse, a bunch of dried mint leaves tied in the toe of a sock (Backwards). *Made by* Mountclemens, it's a "rather free abstraction of a mouse that appealed to Koko's artistic intellect." Koko likes to bat Mintie under furniture, an action that gives clues to crimes Qwilleran is investigating.

The first game Qwilleran invents is Sparrow (*Backwards*). It's like tennis, except there's only one player and no net. Qwill makes a paper sparrow tied to string that Koko bats with his paw. If Koko hits it, he gets a point; if Koko misses, Qwill gets a point. After four days of play, the score is 471 for Koko, 409 for Qwilleran.

Dictionary is a game at which Koko excels (*Danish*). Qwill uses the tattered unabridged dictionary, on which Koko sharpens his claws, and he and Koko play a word game. Koko digs his claws into the pages, and Qwill opens the book, reading aloud the guide words at the top of the columns. He uses the right-hand page if Koko uses his right paw, but Koko usually plays southpaw. If Qwill can define the words, he gets a point for each word. If not, then Koko gets the points. The cat usually wins, unless Koko is trying to get across a message to Qwill, in which case Koko has been known to use the same words more than once.

Because Koko is jealous of the phone, he often reacts negatively when it rings, especially if it's a woman (*Danish*). Once when Fran Unger calls Qwilleran, Koko cuts the connection by planting a foot on the plunger button.

Qwilleran endures Siamese Whisker Torture (*Danish*). When Koko decides it's time for Qwill to get up, he hops onto the bed and lightly touches his whiskers to Qwilleran's nose and chin. If Qwill doesn't respond, Koko applies his whiskers to his cheeks and forehead, then to his eyelids, in order to accomplish his mission.

While trying to talk the managing editor into another week on a case, Qwilleran uses a trick he learned from Koko: He stares the editor in the eye and waits for an affirmative (*Danish*). It works.

Koko's new achievement is turning out the light (*On/Off*). He leaps up to the footboard, "balancing like a tightrope walker." With forepaws against the wall, Koko stretches his neck and scrapes his jaw against the light switch, turning the light out. Satisfied, he settles down on the bed, curling up for sleep.

Koko likes to watch Qwilleran's typewriter—"the type flying up to hit the paper, the carriage jerking across the machine." Koko "rubs his jaw against a button, flipping the carriage or resetting the margins."

One night Qwill is awakened while dreaming about Niagara Falls. He staggers to the bathroom and there is Koko, with "one paw on the porcelain lever of the old-fashioned toilet, watching the swirling water with an intent, nearsighted gaze." Yum Yum is sitting in the marble washbowl.

Koko uses his on/off skill to open the latch on the potbellied stove and uncovers Andy's unpublished manuscript. The next day, Koko wakes Qwilleran before dawn by standing on the bed, rubbing his teeth on the wall switch, and turning the lamps on and off.

Koko enjoys his newfound mechanical abilities (*Red*). He steps on the tab key of the typewriter and resets the left-hand margin. He's fascinated by the typewriter with "its abundance of levers, knobs, and keys." When Qwill sits down at the typewriter to make a list of restaurants to visit, he discovers that Koko's already typed a capital T. Qwilleran adds "oledo Tombs." Koko also tampers with Qwilleran's weigh-in. The cat stands behind him with "front paws planted solidly on the platform of the scale." Koko's newest typing effort produces B W, which Qwilleran interprets as an order for beef Wellington. His final typing effort is K V R—phonetically requesting *caviar*—something for which he has acquired a taste while at Maus Haus.

Koko uses his mechanical skills at the cabin in Mooseville (*Brahms*). He wakes Qwilleran shortly after dawn to the opening chords of the Brahms *Double Concerto* by placing one paw on the power button of the stereo and another on play. When the phone rings, Koko nudges the receiver off the cradle and sniffs the mouthpiece. Qwilleran has to put the phone inside a cabinet.

After moving into the Klingenschoen mansion, Koko and Yum Yum take on a new duty: delivering the mail (*Post Office*). They wait by the mail slot, rummage through the envelopes, and then Koko delivers letters he thinks are important to Qwill.

Koko discovers a hidden talent: playing the piano. He plays a descending progression of four notes: G, C, E, G. Qwilleran recognizes the opening phrase of "A Bicycle Built for Two."

At other times he plays the opening notes of "Three Blind Mice," the opening of Beethoven's "Fifth," and "How Dry I Am."

Koko enjoys another game—pulling books off the shelf (*Shakespeare*). Koko pulls out a title, and Qwilleran reads aloud, "accompanied by purrs, iks, and yows." Koko has been on a Shakespearean kick. On one occasion Koko's selection is *The Life of Henry V.* While Qwilleran reads the king's pep talk to his troops, Koko assumes his "listening position, sitting tall and attentive on the desktop, his tail curled around his front paws." As Qwill reads, Koko interjects his own, "Yow" and "YOW-OW!"

Koko turns into a message machine (*Glue*). His "mad racing back and forth" tells Qwilleran the phone has been ringing in his absence. Ordinarily the cats assist Qwilleran's "creative process by sitting on his notes, biting his pen, and stepping on the shift key of the typewriter."

Koko's Tarzan act (*Underground*) is a deep, continuous, rumbling moan that rises louder and angrier and ends in a high-pitched shriek. It's usually reserved for stray cats.

Koko can predict the phone is going to ring a full ten seconds before it does (*Ghosts*).

Koko learns a new game: Scrabble (*High*). Koko quickly learns to withdraw several tiles, and Qwilleran tries to make a high-scoring word. Qwilleran earns the points from the word; Koko gets the leftover points. Qwilleran quickly spells WHIPS from Koko's first try. After Qwilleran explains to Koko that he needs to choose consonants like X and Q and not too many vowels, Koko improves his game. The score is nearly tied at quitting time.

The next game, Koko wins the first few draws so handily that Qwilleran changes the rules to permit proper nouns, slang, and foreign words. Even with a handicap, the cat wins.

Koko learns to play dominoes (*Breakfast*). He enjoys "moving any small object around with his paw, whether bottle cap or wristwatch," so dominoes is a natural for him. To play this adapted game, Qwilleran spreads the dominoes facedown on a small oak table. Koko places his forepaws on the table and studies the black rectangles, finally knocking one off the table. It's 6–6, or Double-Six, the highest-scoring domino. Qwilleran tries to get Koko merely to draw four dominoes, but Koko enjoys "shoving a small object from a high place, peering over the edge to see it land." Qwilleran counts the spots on the dominoes that he drew and that Koko knocked on the floor. Koko's score is ninety pips; Qwill's is seventy-eight.

While Elizabeth Appelhardt is visiting, she introduces Qwilleran to numerology. Koko knocks off 0–1, 1–2, 1–4, 3–4. Elizabeth translates the numbers into letters, which spell Cage, her middle name. The next time Koko yowls to play dominoes, he sits on the dominoes "like a hen hatching eggs," then pushes several pieces off. By adding the pips on each domino, Qwill got B, D, G, H, and K. He complains to Koko that he needs "*vowels*, the way we did when we played Scrabble." Koko's next three dominoes correspond to A, E, and I. From Koko's pieces, Qwilleran spells words like: *field, beach, baffle, lake* or *leak, fable, dice, chalk, chick, cackle, hijacked, jailed, ideal, deface, flea* or *leaf, lice, bike, feed,* and *Beadle.*

Whenever Qwill shouts, "Book! Book!" that's Koko's cue to dislodge a book from the shelf (*Whistle*). Koko nudges *The Swiss Family Robinson*, an odd connection between the Swiss novel and Celia Robinson, the inventor of Kabibbles snack food.

Whatever book the cat chooses, the man is obliged to read aloud (*Cheese*). Koko's choice is *Stalking the Wild Asparagus*. Qwilleran entertains the Siamese with sound effects on the chapter about wild honeybees. He's also reading *The Birds* to them.

Koko and Qwilleran play Blink. They stare at each other, and the first one to blink pays a forfeit. Koko always wins and gets a toothful of cheese.

Koko wins. Koko always wins.

3

Qwill: The Man and His Career

James Mackintosh Qwilleran's name has confused newspaper staff for two decades, but the Qw *is a true Scottish spelling. His career* "traced a dubious curve": sports writer, police reporter, war correspondent, winner of the Publisher's Trophy, author of a book on urban crime. Then came a "succession of short-term jobs on smaller and smaller newspapers, followed by a long period of unemployment—or no jobs worth listing." He gets his career back together by taking a job as a reporter with the *Daily Fluxion.*

Qwilleran stands six-foot-two, with more black than gray hair. He has a large pepper-and-salt, luxuriant moustache, which is more than face decoration. Qwilleran believes his moustache makes him more sensitive to events and people, signaled by a "tingling sensation on his upper lip."

As a newspaperman, Qwilleran's job is to interview people and write features, in between solving crimes. He never takes notes; his mind is "a videotape recorder." He has had amazing success in interviewing criminals, old ladies, politicians, and cowboys by using the Qwilleran Technique. He has asked no prying questions, but just "smoked his pipe, murmured encouraging phrases, prodding gently, and wore an expression of sympathetic concern." His approach is composed of "two parts sympathy, two parts professional curiosity, and one part low blood pressure."

He doesn't give up his writing, even after he receives the Klingenschoen inheritance.

QWILLERAN'S YOUNGER DAYS

Qwilleran was born a Cub fan in Chicago on May 24th, and grew up with his friend, Archibald Riker. As the only child in a single-parent household, Qwill played dominoes with his mother. The game was his "boyhood *bête noir*, along with practicing the piano and drying the dishes."

Qwilleran never knew his father; Arch Riker's father, Pop Riker, was "as good a father as he had ever known." Qwilleran had never known his grandparents, which is probably why he is drawn to octogenarians and nonagenarians, and enjoys meeting and talking with older people of both sexes.

Qwill's mother used to call him Jamesy. She was Anne Mackintosh Qwilleran, born in Massachusetts, making him a "second-generation codfish." His father's family came from the Northern Isles. His mother died when he was in college. Her advice included: "Give more than you get. . . . Be yourself; don't imitate your peers. . . . Always serve beverages on a tray."

Qwilleran's mother insisted that he write thank-you letters to his mother's friends who sent gifts that were too young for him. "We accept gifts in the spirit in which they were given." His mother's favorite maxim was, "Keep your eye upon the doughnut and not upon the hole." That bit of repeated advice made him "a doughnut addict" who likes "the traditional fried-cake with cake-like texture and crisp brown crust."

She also told him, "It's common courtesy to tell your family where you're going and when you expect to return." Now Qwilleran follows that advice by telling Koko and Yum Yum about his plans. Another favorite saying was, "When there's nothing to say don't say it."

Qwilleran's mother was reading Spenser's *Faerie Queene* when he was born, so she named him Merlin James, which resulted in endless heckling in high school. When he went to college, he had his name changed to James Mackintosh Qwilleran.

Arch and Qwill used to be in scouting together. Qwill was the only kid who "hated camp outs and cookouts." Qwilleran's friends called him Snoopy because he was "always snooping into other kids' lunch boxes." As a child, Qwill received a model train, but what he really wanted was a baseball mitt. He acted in school plays, participated in spelling bees, and reluctantly practiced the piano. Arch said Qwill wouldn't let anybody else use his baseball bat. Once Qwilleran and Arch were sent to the principal's office for putting glue on the teacher's chair pad. Each blamed the other! In high school he played baseball and edited the school paper, the *North Wind.*

In college Qwilleran had planned to be an actor, until a professor steered him into journalism. In his first dramatic appearance, he played the butler and "dropped a silver tray with a whole tea service." He acted in *The Mikado* and played the lion in *Androcles and the Lion.* He played Tom in *The Glass Menagerie,* and Dionysus in Aristophanes's play, *The Frogs.* He also wrote student shows while in college. Qwilleran tended bar and worked in a nursing home during college. He spent some time in the army and came out with a trick knee.

Arch and Qwill both went into journalism, but Qwill got the "glamour assignments." He was a top crime reporter and

was sent to "cover hot spots overseas." He was a foreign cor-
respondant in Italy. When Arch married Rosie, Qwill was his
best man. Qwilleran was in Scotland when he met and married
Miriam, but they were divorced about ten years ago.

Now his whole life is structured around the "humble rou-
tine of feeding the Siamese, brushing their coats, entertaining
them, doing lap service, and policing their commode" (*Whistle*).

The Cat Who Could Read Backwards

The *Daily Fluxion* is a newspaper "Down Below," with a
circulation figure of 427,463. The publisher's slogan is *Fiat
Flux.* Qwilleran is offered a desk in the Feature Department—
as the art writer! Percy, the managing editor, assures Qwilleran
that an ignorance about art is exactly what he wants: "The less
you know, the fresher your viewpoint." Qwill discovers that his
longtime friend, Arch Riker, is feature editor. Arch gets the
"crusader's blood" flowing through Qwilleran's veins with stories of the paper's controversial art critic, and Qwill takes the
job.

Qwilleran's first assignment is to interview popular artist Cal
Halapay, but he has trouble getting the young millionaire to
answer his questions. He views an exhibition of schoolchil-
dren's art at the Board of Education Building. He hopes to
write "something tenderly humorous about the crayoned sail-
boats, the purple houses with green chimneys, the blue horses
that looked like sheep, and the cats—cats—cats."

His first profile of an artist is Uncle Waldo, the elderly artist
who paints primitive pictures of livestock. Qwilleran writes a
brief, humorous piece about a graphic artist who changed to
watercolors after a hundred-pound lithograph stone landed on
his foot. Next Qwill dashes off an inspirational story about a

"prizewinning textile weaver who was also a high-school math teacher, author of two published novels, licensed pilot, cellist, and mother of ten." His next feature focuses on a poodle who paw-paints pictures for a show at the humane society shelter. Butchy Bolton, a metal welder artist, is the subject of yet another feature story.

The Cat Who Ate Danish Modern

To Qwilleran's surprise, Percy has a new assignment for him—a weekly supplement in magazine format. But the topic is interior design, not crime, his preferred beat. Qwilleran is challenged to take on *Gracious Abodes*, the weekly magazine, by Percy's encouragement to beat the *Morning Rampage* to the punch, and by a promotion and an increase in salary.

The focus of *Gracious Abodes* is design and *decorating*, another area Qwilleran knows little about. His first feature is about George Verning Tait's expansive and expensive jade collection, worth $750,000. The collection is stolen the day after the magazine article comes out.

Qwilleran writes about a remodeled stable, but the article is killed because the car-dealer owner is worried the publication might encourage theft. He finds his next feature in Mrs. Allison's residence for career girls. Cokey Wright says it looks like "an Early American bordello," which it actually is.

For the next magazine issue, David Lyke offers to let Qwilleran write about his apartment. Although Qwill makes the visit, the article doesn't make it into the magazine because Lyke is murdered.

The Cat Who Turned On and Off

It's almost Christmas and time for the annual writing competition. Besides $3,000 in cash prizes, there are twenty-five frozen turkeys for the honorable mentions. Qwill decides to write a heartbreaker about Christmas in Junktown. He longs to get out of the Feature Department and write about "con men, jewel thieves, and dope peddlers." Junktown is full of antiques. Qwilleran hates antiques.

Mary Duckworth's father discovers that Qwilleran had been a "crime reporter in New York, Los Angeles, and elsewhere," and that Qwill had won national journalism awards. Qwilleran had "some lean years as a result of an unhappy marriage and a case of alcoholism."

Qwill writes a "pseudo-serious essay" on the subject of his cats' proclivity for climbing inside the bedsprings, writing: "For a cat it is a matter of honor to enlarge the opening and squeeze through."

Qwilleran writes about Christmas in Junktown and becomes involved in influencing City Hall. The city often doesn't pick up the trash. Junktown asks for better streetlights, but the city says no. The residents try to put up old-fashioned gaslights at their own expense, but the city says no. Qwilleran explains the problems to Arch Riker, who gets their boss to talk to City Hall and convince the mayor to cut through all the red tape.

The Cat Who Saw Red

Qwilleran wins the $1,000 prize in the *Daily Fluxion*'s contest for his features on Junktown. Now he has a strict diet and a new assignment—the new gourmet beat. He has to write a regular column on the "enjoyment of good food and wine" under the heading of "Prandial Musings." When he complains about the column's title, Arch tells him that it could have been "Swill with Qwill."

Qwilleran looks at himself in the full-length mirror and doesn't like what he sees. His face is fleshy, his upper arms are flabby, and "where he should have been concave, he was convex." He now needs reading glasses, his moustache and hair are at the "pepper-and-salt stage," and his "beefy waistline another reminder of his forty-six years."

He interviews Robert Maus on his cooking philosophy over dinner at the Toledo Tombs, accumulating plenty of material on the man's "pride and prejudices." Qwilleran covers a "Choose Cheese" press party. He survives a luncheon to introduce a new dog food and writes a "mildly witty piece about it, comparing the simplicity of canine cuisine with the gustatory demands of catdom."

He writes a colorful story about dining at the Petrified Bagel in Junktown, but Arch says it can't be printed. Qwill visits the farmers' market with Robert Maus, collecting material for a column. He writes up a "standard piece" about the statewide cake-baking contest at Rattlesnake Lake and a column on the whimsical theories of Max Sorrel: "If you want to test a guy's sincerity, serve him a bad cup of coffee. If he praises it, he's not to be trusted."

The Cat Who Played Brahms

Qwilleran is in shock because of changes at the *Fluxion*. They give the staff "unisex restrooms," then move in new desks in green and orange and blue. They take away Qwill's typewriter and give him a "video display terminal that gives him a headache." He decides to go away for three months. He wants to "go up north and get away from city hype and city pollution and city noise and city crime." He plans to write a novel while up north.

Qwilleran inherits the entire Klingenschoen fortune from Francesca, whom he calls Aunt Fanny although there's no blood relation. Under the terms of the will, the funds are held in trust for five years, with Qwill receiving the income—provided he agrees to live in Pickax for five years and maintain the Klingenschoen mansion as his address. After five years, the estate will be transferred to Qwill in toto.

When Arch Riker calls to tell him that Percy wants him to come back and start an investigative reporting job right away, with "double your salary and an unlimited expense account," plus a car, Qwilleran has to give it some serious thought. He decides to resign from the *Fluxion* and move to Pickax.

The Cat Who Played Post Office

Everybody in Pickax City seems to like Qwilleran—he's an "affable companion, a sympathetic listener, and the richest man in the county." All his neckties were woven in Scotland. They're full of holes because Koko chews on them.

Qwilleran is unsure about what to do with all the money. He decides to establish a Klingenschoen Foundation to "distribute the surplus income within Moose County." Everyone is delighted and calls it "the best news since the K Saloon closed."

Qwill's new position requires several assistants. He receives a letter from Lori Bamba, who asks whether he needs a part-time secretary. He does. She can answer his letters at her home, and the cats like her.

He also needs a housekeeper. He interviews several before receiving a letter from his former landlady Down Below. Iris Cobb has sold her antique business to Rosie Riker and asks

Qwill if he needs a housekeeper, cook, and antique appraiser. He does.

The Cat Who Knew Shakespeare

Qwilleran is dealing with a "unique midlife crisis." After years of getting by with a modest salary, he's now a millionaire—or billionaire. Now his chief concern, "like that of every other Moose County adult," is the weather, especially in November because of the snow the residents call The Big One.

People ask Qwilleran how he's coming along with his book. He says okay, but thinks of "his neglected typewriter and cluttered desk and disorganized notes." He decides he would like to write a history of the local newspaper, the *Pickax Picayune.*

Polly Duncan suggests that Qwilleran interview the Old Timers on tape so their stories can be preserved. He interviews Amos Cook and Hettie Spence, who worked for the *Pickax Picayune* around 1920. He also interviews Euphonia Gage, Junior Goodwinter's grandmother, who tells Qwill about her grandfather's medical practice.

Homer Tibbitt, former teacher and principal, enlightens Qwill about education during the seventy years since he started teaching. His next interviewee is Sarah Woolsmith, who has spent all her life on a farm.

The Cat Who Sniffed Glue

Qwilleran decides to participate in the Theatre Club's production of *Arsenic and Old Lace.* He's destined to be the "hit of the show" when he roars "Bully!" and "Charge!"

Hixie Rice suggests an "original revue" for the grand opening of the new playhouse. It will be a "spoof of contemporary life" with "humorous skits, witty parodies, a chorus line, and comic acts"—all written by Qwilleran! He starts singing the first line of a few parodies as he walks home, one for each town in Moose County.

At Qwill's suggestion, the Klingenschoen Fund makes possible a newspaper "of professional caliber." Arch Riker comes up to run it. When Arch suggests that the new *Moose County Something* can use Qwilleran's skills as a feature writer of "meaty, informative stuff," Qwill agrees. He decides he's "miscast as a novelist" and is indeed a journalist. Qwill realizes that he's "not geared for producing fiction." He has been talking about a novel for two years, but he's gotten nowhere. He plans to write a column about "interesting people who do interesting things."

His first featured person is Eddington Smith, owner of Edd's Editions, a bookstore in Pickax. Edd sells old books and has a hand bindery in the back. He also does library care— dusting books and treating leather bindings in peoples' homes. Another interview is with Wally Toddwhistle, the county's best taxidermist and "an artist at reconstructing animals." He and Hixie Rice write an original revue for the Theatre Club.

The Cat Who Went Underground

Qwilleran decides to spend the summer at the log cabin on the lake. He has three reasons: "Pickax is a bore in warm weather; Polly Duncan is away for the summer; and we're out of ice cubes." He becomes a building subcontractor. He spends much of his time calling Glinko's for numerous repairs to the old log cabin. Then, against advice from his friends, he decides to have a carpenter make an addition to the log cabin.

Qwilleran has a writing commitment: two features a week for his column "Straight from the Qwill Pen" for the *Moose*

County Something. His first article is about a dog named Switch, assistant to an electrician in Purple Point. Switch assists his owner by "selecting tools from the toolbox and carrying them up the ladder in his mouth."

Qwill has another column idea about the "infamous Mooseville antique shop called The Captain's Mess, operated by the bogus Captain Phlogg." But the man is almost impossible to interview because he's "inattentive, evasive, and rude." The next column is about Old Sam, the gravedigger, who has been digging graves with a shovel for sixty years.

Tourists are being told that a shipful of gold bullion had sunk a hundred years ago and was still in the lake. Qwilleran makes a "mental note for his column." Another idea is the restoration of abandoned cemeteries by the student history clubs. The students are cataloging the family graveyards around the county. Qwilleran meets Young Jake Armbruster, a young man studying pre-med who is planning to go into surgery, like his father, at the Pickax Hospital.

Qwill attends the Wimsey reunion and hears Emma Huggins Wimsey's incredible story of her orange cat, Punkin. Emma gives her mementos to Qwill, including a valentine candy box and school notebooks filled with stories of her life. She was a north-country farmwife who attended teacher's college, taught school for a while, and then retired to raise a family. Qwilleran has an idea that her stories can be published in the *Something* and the Klingenschoen Fund can publish them in book form, with royalties establishing an Emma Wimsey Scholarship.

Qwilleran, Roger MacGillivray, and John Bushland go to Three Tree Island to look for signs of a UFO landing for a story for the paper. They don't find any clues, but are stranded during a severe storm and have to be rescued by helicopter. Qwilleran has never experienced a flood, but as he rides near the swollen river, he makes enough firsthand observations for a possible subject for the "Qwill Pen."

The Cat Who Talked to Ghosts

Qwilleran has a simple life in Pickax City: writing his column for the *Something*, "driving an energy-efficient car, dating a librarian, and ignoring the fact that he owns half of Moose County and a substantial chunk of New Jersey." He has never been "the acquisitive type." If he can't eat it or wear it, he doesn't buy it. But he retains his interest in crime, possessing "a journalist's cynicism that [can] scent misdoing like a cat sniffing a mouse."

After the death of Iris Cobb, Qwilleran and the Siamese move to the Goodwinter Farmhouse Museum until a new manager can be hired. In his past, "he had interviewed kings; he had been strafed on a Mediterranean beach; and briefly he had been held hostage by a crazed bank robber." But he had never raked leaves until he moved to the farmhouse.

Needing a topic for the "Qwill Pen," Qwilleran remembers the English teacher, whom he called Mrs. Fish-eye, who taught him how to write a thousand words on any topic. Qwill looks around and sees fences—his next topic. Moose County is "crisscrossed with picket fences, hand-split snake fences, barbed wire, four-bar corral, and even root fences," stone walls, and "six-foot grapestake stockades."

Qwilleran writes a column about Kristi Waffle and her goat farm, but has to cancel it because her ex-husband poisons all of her female goats. Qwill's next column is about the Goodwinter Farmhouse Museum's new disaster exhibit. He plans to write a column about the Goodwinter collection of old printing presses, but the so-called expert who is cataloging them disappears—and will be going to jail when he's found.

Qwill visits ninety-eight-year-old Adam Dingleberry at the Senior Care Facility. Adam tells about the early family business, which was making mine shaft houses, coffins, and furniture. When Adam's grandfather opened the furniture store, he gave free funerals to folks who bought his coffins.

The Cat Who Lived High

Qwilleran is going back Down Under to the Casablanca apartment building, to determine whether the K Fund will refurbish it. His time spent in Junktown "whetted his interest in preservation."

While talking with Jerome Todd, Qwilleran comes up with two ideas: writing a book about the historic Casablanca and renovating the old apple barn in Pickax as a residence. However, he soon begins to miss his favorite friends in Moose County. The Casablanca is a disaster, and the Countess won't agree to sell it to the Klingenschoen Fund. Writing the book about the Casablanca loses its appeal.

His car, the Purple Plum, is stolen, crashes, and burns, causing extreme agitation and grief when Moose County residents hear inaccurately that Qwilleran died in the accident. Qwill has no living relatives, but "his extended family included the entire population of Moose County."

Qwilleran reveals to Isabelle Wilburton, an alcoholic, a horrifying accident that made him realize he needed help. While he was living like a bum in New York, one night he was so drunk he fell off a subway platform. Onlookers hauled him out of the way of the train just in time. That was a "sobering experience" and the turning point that enabled him to rebuild his life.

The Cat Who Knew a Cardinal

After "twenty-five years of chasing the news in the United States and Europe," Qwilleran has "succumbed to the attractions of rural living." He's living in a renovated apple barn, which scandalizes the people in Pickax City. Thrifty by temperament, he drives a used car, fills up his car at the self-serve pump, scrutinizes price tags, and buys used books.

Qwilleran is always on the lookout for *City of Brotherly Crime*, the bestselling book he wrote eighteen years ago. He didn't save a single copy. But Eddington Smith finds a copy for him.

Qwill's desire to write a book surfaces once again. Following the mystery surrounding Hilary VanBrook and his death, Qwilleran determines to write the biography of the Mystery Man of Moose County. Once again, he's distracted from his goal and doesn't produce the book.

Qwilleran expects his experience at the steeplechase in Lockmaster County to provide worthwhile material for his column. He decides "it would be a better show with more horses and fewer people." He writes from a "Moose County point of view: factual, descriptive, politely complimentary, and not overly enthusiastic."

The Cat Who Moved a Mountain

Qwilleran develops a sudden desire to head to the mountains. Moose County is more than a "thousand miles away from anything higher than a hill." He has completed his five years of life in Moose County, so now he's a "certified billionaire with holdings from New Jersey to Nevada." Everyone is wondering what he will do and where he will live. In celebration of his inheritance, more than two hundred people gather in the ballroom of the "seedy old hostelry" named the New Pickax Hotel.

But now Qwill wants to "get away from it all for a while" and rethink his purpose in life—and his future. He doesn't like golf or fishing, or expensive cars or custom-made suits. When Moira and Kip MacDiarmid talk about their vacation in the Potato Mountains, Qwilleran decides that that's the place he and the Siamese need to go for the summer. The mountains "sounded appetizing, and he enjoyed what he called the pleasures of the table." Arch Riker extracts a promise from Qwill that he will write a column for the *Moose County Something* "whenever a good subject present[s] itself."

At Potato Cove, Qwilleran buys four mugs from Otto the potter, a seven-foot iron candelabrum, and three dozen handmade beeswax candles. He also buys five woven batwing capes: a bright blue one for Polly, royal blue for Mildred, green for Fran, violet for Lori, and taupe for Hixie. In his younger days as an underpaid journalist, "generosity had been a luxury beyond his means, but now he was enjoying the opportunity to be munificent."

Qwilleran is documenting the exploits of Koko and Yum Yum, and plans to write a book one day about their adventures. Feeding the cats is "the one constant in his unstructured life." His other activities pivot around this ritual.

He sends Arch Riker his travel notes, spoken into his tape recorder as he traveled to the Potato Mountains. Qwill tells Arch that he might write about the "local conflict between the environmentalists and the proponents of economic growth."

Qwilleran knows he has to investigate J. J. Hawkinfield's murder and Forest Beechum's conviction. As a cover, he decides to spread the word he wants to write a biography of Hawkinfield. After solving Hawkinfield's murder, Qwilleran calls Polly Duncan and learns of her very unnerving experience of being followed by a strange man. He quickly leaves Spudsboro and heads for Pickax and Polly.

The Cat Who Wasn't There

Qwilleran as a journalist "had been content to pound a beat, churn out copy, and race deadlines" for the *Daily Fluxion*. He enjoyed "semicelebrityhood" while writing for major newspapers Down Below, but that was nothing compared to "his present status as a billionaire frog in a very small frog pond."

When Qwill finds out about the Bonnie Scots Tour, he's relieved that Polly Duncan will be out of Pickax and out of harm's way—and he agrees to go with her. Qwilleran plans to write about the trip to Scotland for his "Qwill Pen" column. He promises Arch Riker to "write a thousand words on castles" for his first column.

Arch asks Qwill to write an article about Grace Utley and Zella Chisholm and their teddy bear collection. Grace wants someone to write and edit a book about the collection, and Arch suggests Qwilleran. Qwill's story and Bushy's photographs are picked up by the wire services and are published in several major newspapers around the country.

Qwilleran agrees to work in the box office for the Theatre Club, selling tickets for *Macbeth*. "He had sold baseball programs at Comiskey Park and ties at Macy's, but he had never sold tickets in a box office."

The Cat Who Went Into the Closet

Qwilleran's "casual way of dressing and lack of pretension" belie his status as a multimillionaire. He's "happier than he had ever been in his entire life." He's happy living in a small town, writing for a small newspaper, "loving an intelligent woman of his own age," and living with two companionable cats.

Qwilleran finds notes written by Euphonia Gage's father-in-law about the disastrous Moose County fire of October 17–18, 1869. Hixie Rice persuades him to write a one-man show, pretending there was radio at the time of the fire and taking the role of a radio announcer "broadcasting on-the-spot coverage of the disaster." Qwilleran did some acting in college and had enjoyed working before an audience. He's tempted and gives in. He writes and performs a docudrama based on historic facts. The *Moose County Something* sponsors Qwilleran in the one-man show, which is produced and directed by Hixie.

After meeting Nancy Fincher, Qwill decides to write a column on dogsledding. He announces to Polly that he is planning "an in-depth profile of Euphonia," but Polly is "familiar with his ambitious writing projects that never materialize."

Another first for Qwilleran is playing Santa Claus in the first Pickax Christmas parade. He agrees because he thinks it might make an interesting topic for a column. Qwill writes a column about his experience of being snowed in at Purple Point and being taken by dogsled over the frozen bay.

The Cat Who Came to Breakfast

Qwilleran has found "middle-aged contentment" in Moose County, where he walks and bikes and fills his lungs with country air. He has a "fulfilling friendship with Polly Duncan."

Qwilleran tells Polly that he may do some freelance writing during the summer. He jokingly describes a "cat opera for TV." Polly wants Qwill to write a "literary masterpiece," but this idea is hers, not his. Qwill tells her he knows his limitations. "I'm a hack journalist, but a *good* hack journalist."

While on Breakfast Island, Qwilleran writes a column about the "island with four names and four cultures": the natives, the mainlanders, the summer residents, and the tourists.

The Cat Who Blew the Whistle

Qwilleran has a "unique distaste for money," particularly so since he is someone whose net worth is recorded in twelve digits. He's the wealthiest man in the northeast-central United States. Friends call him "Qwill," with affection. Everyone else calls him "Mr. Q," with respect. Women refer to him with words such as "tall and good-looking" and "romantic." The men say things like, "fits in with all kinds of people," "he lives with a couple of cats," and "always with that woman from the library."

He finds a topic for his "Qwill Pen" column about an owl in his orchard, whom he calls Marconi. When Qwilleran visits Floyd Trevelyan and sees his extensive model train collection, he has an "old familiar urge" to write a book, this time about hogs and wildcats (engines and runaway trains), doing research and interviewing retired railroad personnel. He does manage a column about Floyd's trains.

Junior gives him his next assignment: Qwill is to write a "miniature think-piece on the actor's perception of both the role and the theme of the play" for each of the nine or ten characters in *A Midsummer Night's Dream*.

He senses a source of material in "Scottish Night" at the lodge. He also writes a thousand words on the aurora borealis, the "colorful phenomenon in the midnight sky" that the tourists enjoy but the locals take for granted. He's also trying to "find something different to say about baseball" for his column. He dashes off a column on the sweet corn of August, of which farmers produce only enough for local consumption.

Qwill decides to write a book on the Steam Age of railroading. He interviews Ozzie Penn, an old engineer. He writes a pseudoserious column on the history of sunburn, inspired by a painting that depicts a beach scene at the turn of the century. He also writes a review of the Pickax Theatre Club's production of *A Midsummer Night's Dream.*

Qwilleran tries his hand at writing a folk song about Ozzie Penn's wildcat train, "The Wreck of Old No. 9," and gives it to Derek to perform.

Junior asks when Qwilleran might plan to get a word processor. Qwilleran declares, "I like my electric typewriter and it likes me!" Qwilleran "could do his best thinking with his feet elevated, a legal pad in his left hand and a black felt-tip in his right."

The Cat Who Said Cheese

Dwight Somers talks Qwilleran into being one of the celebrities who will be "auctioned off" for charity for an evening. Qwill will offer a complete makeup and hair styling at Brenda's Salon, then dinner at the Old Stone Mill. Qwill agrees when he realizes the adventure would be material for the "Qwill Pen."

Arch Riker gives Qwilleran an assignment to cover the opening session of Mildred's series of cooking classes for men only. A Friday column is dedicated to a treatise on "nobodies."

Qwilleran becomes interested in another topic for a book: the New Pickax Hotel, a landmark for more than a hundred years. He interviews Gustav Limburger, the owner. While there he meets Aubrey Scotten, a beekeeper who sells honey. This is another possibility for the "Qwill Pen." He's excited that he has met two more "characters" for a book he'll write someday.

He writes about food during the Great Food Expo week.

One column is on eating in the "good old days," asking the question, "Where are the foods of yesteryear?" After the cheese-tasting party, he writes a thousand words.

One Sunday afternoon, Qwilleran visits Elaine Fetter for an interview about mushrooms she grows, especially shiitake. There are three strains of shiitake, one called *Koko*.

The Cat Who Tailed a Thief

People admire Qwilleran's "amiable disposition and sense of humor," as well as his "sympathetic way of listening." He believes that "money is less interesting than the challenge of deadlines, exclusives, and accurate reporting." His motto is "late to bed and late to rise," although he is nevertheless healthy, wealthy, and "at least witty."

Qwilleran finally gets up the nerve to wear his new kilt to Scottish Night. Bootsie gives him a sporran, a fur pouch worn with the kilt. Mr. MacMurchie lends him a knife to wear in his sock. The Mackintosh dress tartan is mostly red, while the hunting tartan is mostly green for camouflage in the woods. His full-length photo appears on the front page of the *Something*.

Qwilleran and Mildred Riker are working on the project to publish the late Iris Cobb's cookbook, but only about a dozen recipes are original. Hixie Rice's solution is to make a coffee-table book with large color photos on slick paper, containing only Iris's own creations.

Qwilleran again decides to write a book: a "compilation of Moose County legends, anecdotes, and scandals," to be entitled *Short and Tall Tales*. He plans to collect stories on tape and possibly produce a print edition as well as the recorded book. His first tale is the "Dimsdale Jinx," as told by Homer Tibbitt. The next tale is "Hilda the Clipper," about an "eccentric woman who had terrorized the entire town of Brrr" seventy years earlier, according to storyteller Gary Pratt. Qwill's next tale is the "Mystery of Dank Hollow," recounted by Silas Ding-wall. He plans to go to Horseradish to listen to Wetherby Goode's great-uncle Joe's tale about a man who claimed the power to de-haunt houses.

On December 23, Qwilleran turns in a thousand words on Santa Claus. After the New Year, he straps on his snowshoes and writes a column on the joys of snowshoeing. Another idea for a column is "comfort food": What do people eat in times of exhaustion, sadness, or frustration? Another column is on "February," which includes the story of his own "seven-year valentine feud" that had begun in high school. He plans to write a dissertation on breakfast cereal, but delays it after Lynette Duncan's death. Qwill writes a column about Lynette instead.

He writes a "trenchant treatise on the specialized art of naming cats," and invites readers to mail in names of their own cats. He's overwhelmed with the responses.

The Cat Who Sang for the Birds

There's "nothin' highfalutin about Mr. Q!" Except he's bought a car phone for his brown van so he can call the city desk of the *Moose County Something* whenever a hot story breaks. He has a collector's item, a "skinny bike"—a British Thanet, circa 1950, called a Silverlight—which he rides on Sandpit Road.

Qwilleran "would have given anything to be a jazz pianist," and regrets his "boyhood choice of batting practice over piano practice."

While Qwilleran is trying to think of a new format for the spelling bee, Koko sits on *Baseball, An Illustrated History*, then runs around in circles. Qwilleran realizes that what he needs is a whole new ball game! A Pennant Race! Ten teams of all-star spellers! A World Series between Moose County and Lockmaster! Baseball caps in team colors! "Take me out to the spell game!"

Someone leaves two cats on Qwilleran's doorstep, and he takes them to the library to live. Patrons are excited about the cats and the contest to name them. One is an orange cat; the other is brown and black with tortoiseshell markings. Qwilleran draws the winning names: Katie for the brown-and-black and Mackintosh for the orange. The young woman who submitted the name says her family has an apple orchard, and she thought they could call him Mac.

Qwilleran has recently written a column on dowsing, also known as waterwitching, in which natives use a forked stick to locate underground water. He's also written about the Handy Helpers, a group of volunteers who help their neighbors in times of crisis. He attends the open house for the Goodwinter Farmhouse Museum. It was held in the metal storage barn and was boring, but Qwilleran manages to write a tongue-in-cheek account of the event.

He's writing a column on pencils—the fat, yellow kind with thick, soft leads that he used on his first newspaper job. Qwilleran tends to draft his copy in pencil while sitting with his feet up. "Words and ideas flow more easily in that position."

Qwill receives a recumbent bicycle in appreciation for dreaming up the Pennant Race. Since he likes to ride a bike, and he can do his best thinking while sitting with his feet up, now he can do both at the same time.

Qwilleran interviews Phoebe Sloan, the Butterfly Girl, about butterflies. He has an unusually difficult time drawing her out. He's raising a crop of butterflies in a box, "hoping to write something intelligent on the subject." After Phoebe is murdered, he sets the butterflies free with a sense of desperation.

Qwill writes a thousand words about Duff Campbell and his

watercolors. He writes another column on the common hen's egg. Thornton suggests a column on "old tombstones and how the old cemeteries reflect changes in our culture."

He writes a long-promised tribute to Mrs. Fish-eye, the English teacher who taught him to write a thousand words on any topic. Soon afterward, he receives a letter from Martha V. Snyder—Mrs. Fish-eye—who has been following his column, sent to her by a granddaughter who trains racehorses in Lockmaster.

Qwilleran decides to start another Pasty War by writing a column about an old pasty recipe that calls for "pig's liver."

The Cat Who Saw Stars

After establishing the Klingenschoen Foundation to manage the fortune and distribute it "for the betterment of the community," Qwilleran was free to "write, read, dine well, and do a little amateur sleuthing." He has "a Sherlockian interest in solving mysteries." Qwill's friends think of him as "amiable, witty, willing to do favors, and fond of taking them to dinner." They describe him as, "Swell fella! Not stuck up at all." "That's some moustache he's got! M'wife says it's sexy, 'specially when he wears sunglasses." "You'd think he'd get a proper house—and a dog—even if he doesn't want a wife." His moustache is "a virtual landmark" in Moose County.

Qwilleran decides to move up to the cabin in Mooseville since Polly will be gone the whole month of July. After finding Koko sitting in the bucket seat of Qwill's recumbent bike, "looking wise," Qwill decides to take the bike to Mooseville. He agrees to bring up the rear of the Fourth of July parade with his high-tech bike.

After dinner at the Rikers' beach house, Qwilleran dreams that Moose County has become an independent principality ruled by a royal family—all cats! The royal cat family is "intelligent, entertaining, and inexpensive to maintain." In a later dream, he has lunch and a discussion with Mark Twain, who is Qwilleran's newest interest. Eddington Smith says his father told him that Twain had lectured in Moose County once. Lisa Compton confirms that Twain had come through on a lecture tour and that her great-grandmother had a crush on Twain. Her old diary is "full of fascinating stuff." (He makes a note for the "Qwill Pen.")

One day while Koko is sitting on the Mark Twain reference book, staring intensely at Qwilleran, Qwill has an idea to promote the city of Pickax: an annual Mark Twain celebration, with proceeds going to the county's literacy program. Hixie Rice says that Qwill would win a Mark Twain Look-Alike Contest.

When he hears that an elderly widow is making a sampler for him, Qwilleran is apprehensive. But Rebecca Hawley stitches words from one of Qwill's columns: "Cats are cats . . . the world over! These intelligent, peace-loving, four-footed friends—who are without prejudice, without hate, without greed—may someday teach us something." The yarns are Siamese colors. He's overwhelmed!

Qwilleran enjoys reading the work of Christopher Smart, a journalist who lived in the eighteenth century. Smart wrote a poem about his cat, Jeoffrey, that Qwill likes to quote. He also likes to read the *New York Times.*

Qwill is keeping a personal journal in which he records the cats' antics. He should have started when he was younger, but he was always busy "growing up, playing baseball, acting in plays, sowing wild oats, discovering the work ethic, hanging around press clubs, and making life-threatening mistakes." At last he's a journalist with a journal. He's also making a collection of local stories for a planned book, *Short and Tall Tales.*

"The Qwill Pen" column rates ninety percent readership,

better than the horoscope. Qwilleran recently interviewed Magnus Hawley and other commercial fishermen, even spending time on the lake with a fishing crew, and wrote a column about the blessing of the fleet in the spring. A recent reader-participation stunt was a question: "Why do your cats squeeze their eyes?" Hundreds of subscribers mailed in their replies. Qwilleran used the results for his column. The most popular thoughtful explanation was, "They're smiling."

He writes a thousand words about the Fourth of July from the point of view of Benjamin Franklin ("How would Poor Richard react to backyard barbecues and high school majorettes in silver tights?") Qwilleran invents another "reader-participation stunt": He runs a picture of an antique pressed-back dining chair with cane seat and spindles, then asks readers who own that type of chair to send him a postcard.

He reviews the summer theater production of *Visit to a Small Planet,* in which Derek steals the show. The purpose of a review of a small-town play is to tell the "stay-at-homes" what opening night is like: the people, the setting, the audience, and the unexpected.

His next column is on the diary of Lisa Compton's great-grandmother, who had a crush on Mark Twain. One entry was about strange objects in the sky prior to the 1900s. He's working on a column about the construction and operation of antique spinning wheels, and interested in the possibility of spinning cat hair into yarn. He decides it would take forty years to collect enough hair from Koko and Yum Yum for a vest. While in Cecil's hardware store, he has an idea about a column on nails: Why is a three-inch nail called a three-penny nail? He dashes off a thousand words on the dogcart races, which he announces. He listens to people's "worst-ever rain stories" for his Friday column.

Dr. Teresa Bunker, Wetherby Goode's cousin, is looking for a collaborator for an animated feature about crows, and Qwill has said he might be interested. He's definitely interested in her story about her great-grandfather Captain Bunker and the unusual way he overpowered lake pirates. Qwilleran tries to steer talk toward the crow feature so she can be on her way. But he doesn't find anything in his research to suggest a workable scenario. Finally he suggests that a scarecrow might make friends with crows and start an "underground movement in their behalf." The scarecrow is condemned to death for his plot.

Qwilleran is secretly writing the "Ask Ms. Gramma" column in which Ms. Gramma comments on common grammatical errors made by Moose Countians! Only Junior Goodwinter knows who's actually writing the column.

4

Cast of Characters

Al (*Cheese*) — Counterman at the Dimsdale Diner.

Allison, Mrs. (*Danish*) — Owner of residence for professional girls Down Below. She's a "haggard woman" with a colorless face.

Alstock, Virginia (*Whistle*) — Polly's assistant at the Pickax Library. She's the "main fuse in the Pickax gossip circuit." She's a contralto soloist at the Little Stone Church. (*Sang*) — Her husband is on the spell team for the Oilers, sponsored by Gippel's Garage.

Alvola (*Cardinal*) — Waitress at Lois's Luncheonette in downtown Pickax.

Amberina (*On/Off*) — One of the sisters who runs The Three Weird Sisters antique shop in Junktown. She's a "brunette with luscious blue eyes and dimples" and a voice "with musical intonation." (*High*) — Amberina is working for an auction house and living at the Casablanca. Her brunette hair is "lighter, redder, and frizzier." Divorced, she now goes by the name Amber.

Amberton, Lisa (*Cardinal*) — Wife of Chase. She's a good bit younger than her husband and is interested in Steve O'Hare.

Amberton, W. Chase (*Cardinal*) — Owner of a horse farm and the horse Son of Cardinal. He's "pushing sixty" and wants to move to a warmer climate.

Amy (*Mountain*) — Owner of Amy's Lunch Bucket in Potato Cove. A "plump and pretty woman with the healthy radiance of youth," she and Forest Beechum had planned to marry, but Forest was imprisoned. They have a two-month-old son, Ashley.

Anderson, Mr. (*Danish*) — Church editor of the *Fluxion*.

Appelhardt, Elizabeth Cage (*Breakfast*) — A twenty-three-year-old woman with long, lank hair who lives at The Pines on Grand Island. She's very thin and wears unusual clothing. She decides to move to Pickax City. See *Elizabeth Cage*.

Appelhardt, Jack (*Breakfast*) — Youngest son, age twenty-six. A very handsome man, he has been married and divorced three times. He "appears to have no serious calling."

Appelhardt, Richard (*Breakfast*) — Elizabeth's brother Ricky. He's "a perfectly wonderful vet" who has always loved animals.

Appelhardt, Rowena (*Breakfast*) — Mother of Elizabeth and three sons. She's "buxom, regally handsome, and dramatically poised like an opera diva on stage" and speaks with a powerful contralto voice.

Appelhardt, William (*Breakfast*) — Oldest son, who was supposed to become a lawyer. He finished law school, but can't pass the bar exam. William restores carriages.

Armbruster, Dr. Jake (*Underground*) — Surgeon at the Pickax Hospital.

Armbruster, Young Jake (*Underground*) — Big, blond young man in Moose County. Jake is in pre-med, planning to go into surgery like his father.

Arnold (*Stars*) — Owner of Arnold's Antique Shop in Mooseville. He's an "ageless man with tireless energy," with a weathered face sporting rimless glasses.

Ascott, Mrs. (*Underground*) — Very large, old clairvoyant from Lockmaster, godmother to Mildred Hanstable's grandchild. When she starts predicting the future, she sounds "like a drill sergeant."

Avery, Lois (*Danish*) — Former girlfriend of David Lyke.

Babcock, Haley (*Stars*) — Retired land surveyor. He has white hair and wrinkles and has just had his ninetieth birthday. He claims he was ten years old when his grandfather discovered Squunk water.

Bamba, Dominic (*Brahms*) — Engineer at the prison in Moose County. Married to Lori, Nick's a "young man with curly black hair." (*Wasn't*) — Nick shares Qwilleran's interest in crime and helps Qwilleran track down the Boulevard Prowler. (*Breakfast*) — Nick and Lori renovate an old fishing lodge on Breakfast Island and open it as a bed-and-breakfast. (*Cheese*) — Nick manages the new Cold Turkey Farm, with an option to buy. He quits his unrewarding job at the state prison.

Bamba, Jason (*Breakfast*) — Nick and Lori's older son, a "lively six year old with his mother's blond hair." He's in charge of "wastebaskets and litter boxes" at the Domino Inn.

Bamba, Lori (*Brahms*) — Mooseville postmistress, married to Nick. She wears her long, golden hair in two braids tied with ribbons, and has a dazzling smile and soothing voice. The cats like her. (*Post Office*) — Qwilleran hires her to answer his mail. She makes "each reply a little different." (*Shakespeare*) —Koko and Lori have a conversation over the phone. (*Cardinal*) — The Siamese greet her with "enthusiastic prowling and ankle rubbing." (*Breakfast*) — Lori and Nick open a bed-and-breakfast on Pear Island. (*Cheese*) — Lori opens a small restaurant in Stables Row called the Spoonery.

Bamba, Lovey (*Breakfast*) — Lori and Nick's very smart, three-year-old daughter. She's "a beautiful little girl, with a winning smile."

Bamba, Mitchell (*Breakfast*) — Lori and Nick's younger son. Mitchell is four and "in charge of deliveries and communications" at the Domino Inn.

Barbara (*Thief*) — Young waitress at the Boulder House Inn in Trawnto.

Barter, George (*Mountain*) — Attorney with Hasselrich, Bennett & Barter, who flies to Spudsboro to assist Forest Beechum. (*Cheese*) — Bart represents Qwilleran at the meetings of the Klingenschoen Foundation in Chicago. (*Thief*) — The youngest partner in the firm, he's fortyish, quiet, and effective. He changed his letterhead from "George A. Barter" to "G. Allen Barter" because the name was confused once too often with George A. Breze.

Bassett, Lenore (*Cheese*) — Trawnto Beach resident who wins first place for turnipless entries in the Pasty Bake-off.

Bates, Harold (*Backwards*) — The young managing editor of the *Daily Fluxion,* also known as Percy because of his constant use of the phrase "per se." He approaches the newspaper business "as a science rather than a holy cause." (*Shakespeare*) — Percy promises Junior Goodwinter a job any time he wants to leave Pickax, but he doesn't follow through when Junior is unemployed.

Beadle, Harriet (*Breakfast*) — Native of Breakfast Island who attended high school and worked in restaurants on the mainland before returning to the island. She operates Harriet's Family Café, serving lunch and dinner to tourists. She has the "lean face and stony expression typical of island women."

Beadle, Mr. (*Breakfast*) — Grandfather of Harriet and a resident of Breakfast Island. He's "grumpy but willing to work" and fixes the steps at the Domino Inn.

Beechum, Chrysalis (*Mountain*) — Weaver on Little Potato Mountain and the daughter of Dewey. She's a "tall young woman with hollow cheeks and long, straight hair hanging to her waist." She has "good bones and the lean, strong look of a mountaineer and the lean, strong hands of a weaver."

Beechum, Dewey (*Mountain*) — Li'l Tater resident who builds Qwilleran an octagonal, screened gazebo for the cats. His beard is "untamed," and he wears "old-fashioned striped railroad overalls and a wide-brimmed felt fedora" that's "green with age."

Beechum, Mrs. Dewey (*Mountain*) — Weaver in Potato Cove. Her gray hair is "pulled severely into a bun at the back of her head." She hasn't spoken in almost a year because of a "psychological disorder."

Beechum, Forest (*Mountain*) — Son of Dewey and artist from the Potatoes. He's in the state prison for the murder of

J. J. Hawkinfield, which his family says he didn't commit. He's a "lean, unsmiling young man with long, black hair."

Benno — See *James Henry Ducker*.

Bent, Torry (*Cardinal*) — Lawyer of Summers, Bent & Frickle in Lockmaster. He is liquidating Hilary VanBrook's estate.

Bernice (*Sang*) — A "fast-talkin' babe" who answers the phone for Northern Land Improvement in Lockmaster. She's "friendly like a snake."

Berry, Inga (*Red*) — Head of the pottery department at Penniman School of Fine Art. At seventy-five, she has a hearty voice, "gray hair and bangs and a bit of a limp." (*High*) — She's the city's "dean of potters." Inga retired last year. After arthritis hit her, she began making clay "floppy discs."

Bert (*Breakfast*) — Bartender at the Pear Island Hotel.

Bessinger, Dianne (*High*) — a.k.a., Lady Di. Part owner of the Bessinger-Todd art gallery. The forty-five year old was a vivacious woman with dark shoulder-length hair. Dianne was murdered in her Casablanca apartment. She was married for years to Jerome Todd.

Betty (*Closet*) — Manager of the Park of Pink Sunsets in Florida. She's glamorous and sells expensive cosmetics on the side.

Big George (*Brahms*) — Dirty tank truck used by Sam and Dave when they pump septic tanks.

Blythe, Gregory (*Post Office*) — Mayor of Pickax City and investment counselor. He's articulate and conducts a meeting "exceptionally well." He was principal of the high school until the scandal a few years ago when he was involved with some female students. (*Closet*) — He has Goodwinter blood. (*Cheese*) — He's a "middle-aged, well-dressed stockbroker, handsome in a dissipated way and insufferably conceited."

Bolton, Butchy (*Backwards*) — A sculptor. She teaches sculpture — welded metal — at the Penniman School of Fine Art. She has a pudgy face set in a stern expression, and tight, wavy hair.

Boswell, Baby (*Ghosts*) — Daughter of Verona, recently moved to Moose County. She's small, two-and-a-half, and "pathetically puny," but has "clear, precise speech."

Boswell, Verona (*Ghosts*) — She and Baby live with Vince in Moose County. Her voice is a soft Southern drawl, each "lilting statement ending with emphasis on the last word and an implied question mark." Her "gentle voice was a welcome contrast to her husband's shrillness." Actually, she isn't Vince's wife but, rather, she is Verona Whitmoor.

Boswell, Vince (*Ghosts*) — Man with a "loud, piercing voice with a nasal twang," a "noisy oaf." He, Verona, and Baby live in the cottage at the corner of Hummock Road and Black Creek Lane. Vince claims to be "cataloging the antique printing presses in the barn and writing a book on the history of printing." He is the great-grandson of Luther and Lucy Bosworth, which makes him a second cousin to Susan Exbridge and Larry Lanspeak.

Bosworth, Luther and Lucy (*Ghosts*) — Lucy and Luther married when Lucy was seventeen. They had four children. Luther died in 1904, the year of the mine explosion. He had been "sort of a handyman" on the Goodwinter farm. Lucy purchased the Pickax General Store in 1904. In 1905, she married Karl Lunspik. They legally changed their name to Lanspeak. In 1911, the Pickax General Store was renamed

Lanspeak's Dry Goods. Lucy was the great-grandmother of Susan Exbridge, Larry Lanspeak, and Vince Bosworth.

Bosworth, Vince — See *Vince Boswell.*

Botts, Avery (*Stars*) — Farmer who's letting the Pickax Theatre Club use his barn near Mooseville for summer productions. He was a dairy farmer until the state built the prison and bought his "back forty" acres. Avery switched to poultry.

Boulanger, Jacques (*Danish*) — a.k.a., Jack Baker. Owner of the Sorbonne Studio. A "handsome Negro with a goatee," he does work for the old families in Muggy Swamp. He's a local boy who was "born on the wrong side of the wrong side of the tracks." He studied in Paris, then became a decorator with a French accent.

Bowen, Ernestine (*Stars*) — a.k.a. Ernie. Wife of Owen and chef at Owen's Place. She's a "creative artist" who studied at a great school for chefs. She's nice, but at twenty-seven she's much younger than Owen. She works long hours in the restaurant, then studies recipes in a big recreation vehicle behind the restaurant.

Bowen, Owen (*Stars*) — Resident of Florida who comes to Mooseville to run Owen's Place restaurant during the tourist season. He's disagreeable and "a horse's tail." Phreddie has better manners than Owen. Owen, age forty-eight, is a boozer who tends to start drinking in the morning. Owen drowns while he and Ernie are on their boat out on the lake.

Breze, George (*Closet*) — An "airhead" who runs for mayor of Pickax. He's "a one-man conglomerate" whose empire is in a shack on Sandpit Road, surrounded by "rental trucks, mini-storage buildings, a do-it-yourself car wash, and junk cars." His campaign platform is to keep the streets clean. (*Thief*) — The locals call him "Old Gallbladder" because he had the gall to run for mayor, garnering only two votes. He can't read.

Broadnax, Mr. (*Closet*) — Principal of Mooseland High School.

Brodie, Chief Andrew (*Post Office*) — Police chief and Francesca's father, a "pleasant guy, very cooperative." (*Shakespeare*) — The police chief can be depended upon for "friendly conversation and off-the-record information." (*Glue*) — Brodie is a "popular lawman not yet fifty, an amiable Scot with a towering figure, a beefy chest, and sturdy legs that looked appropriate with the kilt, tam-o'-shanter, and bagpipe." Brodie knows everything about what's going on and will usually reveal a few facts off the record. (*Wasn't*) — A seventh-generation piper, he plays his bagpipes at funerals and weddings. (*Thief*) — Brodie earnestly hates computers, which he's forced to use for police business. His grandmother in Scotland could "tail a thief with scissors, a piece of string, and a witch's chant." (*Sang*) — Andy plays his bagpipes at Mrs. Coggin's funeral. (*Stars*) — Andy, in full Scottish regalia, is grand marshal for the Fourth of July parade. He plays patriotic tunes on his bagpipe. He looks like a giant in his "lofty feather bonnet" and an armful of bagpipes. The police chief sometimes leaks official information if it aids Qwill's unofficial investigations.

Brodie, Francesca (*Post Office*) — Assistant in Amanda Goodwinter's studio. She's a friendly young lady whose father is the police chief. (*Glue*) — She's "tall like her father, with the same gray eyes and strawberry-blond hair." She directs the Theatre Club's production of *Arsenic and Old Lace.* (*Ghosts*) — She's talented, but "was a brat in school and she's still a brat." (*Cardinal*) — Fran is cast as Anne Boleyn in *Henry VIII* at the Theatre Club. Fran's a "good designer, easy to like, half Qwill's age, and refreshingly impudent." She wears three-inch heels and skirts shorter than most Pickax hemlines. (*Wasn't*) — She designs costumes for *Macbeth* and is codirector. (*Whistle*) — Fran directs the Theatre Club's production of *A Midsummer Night's Dream*. She does a complete facelift on Qwill's old apartment to suit Celia Robinson. (*Thief*) — Fran furnishes Qwilleran's condo at Indian Village. She regains the lead in *Hedda Gabler*. (*Stars*) — Fran is an attractive and talented young woman, the second-in-command at Amanda's Studio of Interior Design. She now has "the added glamor that seems to come with foreign travel," having recently returned from Italy. Fran is redesigning the interior of the Pickax Hotel. Her greatest passion is the Pickax Theatre Club. She and Dr. Prelligate have been seeing a lot of each other, but she's had a good job offer in Chicago. Fran is always "coolly dynamic."

Bruno (*Backwards*) — Bartender at the Press Club. He "gives his drinks a lot of personal expression." Bruno calls himself an artist who makes collages by soaking labels off whiskey bottles, cutting the labels up, and then gluing them into presidential portraits. (*Danish*) — Bruno wants to be featured in *Gracious Abodes* for his monochromatic chartreuse decorating scheme. (*On/Off*) — Bruno has a collection of about ten thousand swizzle sticks from bars all over the country.

Buchwalter, Franz and Sadie (*Backwards*) — A short, fleshy couple who goes to the Valentine Ball in peasant costumes. He teaches art at Penniman School of Fine Art. He is referred to as a "vegetable who does lovely watercolors." Sadie is a social worker who speaks for her husband.

Bunker, Captain (*Stars*) — Captain of the sailing vessel *Princess*, the great-grandfather of Tess and Joe. When pirates attacked his ship, Capt. Bunker told his crew to go down below.

When the pirates stormed the hold, the crew took the lids off kegs of horseradish and the pirates were overcome.

Bunker, Dr. Teresa (*Sang*)—Cousin of Wetherby Goode. (*Stars*) — a.k.a., Tess. A corvidologist at a Southern university. She's looking for a collaborator for an animated feature about crows, and Qwill has said he might be interested. She's a little younger than Wetherby Goode, her cousin. She was married once, but she's an "incorrigible optimist" and he was a "card-carrying pessimist," so they divorced. She has dark hair that she wears in a bun, thin lips, and high cheekbones. She drives a yellow minibus named "Republic of Crowmania."

Bulmer, Mike (*Danish*) — Worker in the Circulation Department of the *Morning Rampage*. He's a creep with a loud laugh.

Bunsen, Odd (*Backwards*) — Photographer for the *Daily Fluxion* who likes a martini "without the garbage in it." He's a loud, cocky photographer who smokes huge cigars, which are greatly out of proportion to his thin body. (*Danish*) — He's the *Daily Fluxion*'s specialist in train wrecks and five-alarm fires. He recently climbed a skyscraper's flagpole. He's the "most daring of the photographers," has the loudest voice, and smokes "the longest and most objectionable cigars."

Bushland, John (*Underground*) — He is a photographer and the husband of Vicki. He has a photo studio in Lockmaster County and is also an avid fisherman. He's outgoing, likable, and self-assured. (*Cardinal*) — Bushy "jokes about losing his hair early." (*Wasn't*) — Bushy joins the Bonnie Scots Tour and takes multitudes of pictures. He decides to move to Pickax and open a studio—his wife is divorcing him and he has to move out of her family home. Arch Riker also hires Bushy to do some photography for the *Moose County Something*. (*Sang*) — Bushy is responsible for opening the Click Club, a space in the

Art Center dedicated to photography. (*Stars*) — Bushy takes a professional group picture of the Ogilvies at their annual reunion. For the picture of the oldest and the youngest, he used a hundred-year-old woman and a two-day-old lamb. Bushy was born and reared near the lake and has a passion for fishing and boating. His family was in commercial fishing for three generations before his grandfather sold out to the Scottens. His grandfather lost his father and two older brothers in an unexplained incident on the lake: Their boat, the *Jenny Lee*, vanished suddenly and was never found.

Bushland, Vicki (*Underground*) — Wife of John. They have a photo studio in Lockmaster. (*Cardinal*) — Vicki's grandmother "Grummy" lives with the Bushlands in the Inglehart family home in Lockmaster. (*Wasn't*) — Vicki divorces Bushy and opens a catering business with an officer of the riding club.

Butra, Sorg (*High*) — Photographer in a Midwest city.

Button, Mrs. (*High*) — White-haired woman with a cane. She lives in the Casablanca. She has a high, cracked voice and takes her prescribed exercise in the hallways. Mrs. Button dies of natural causes.

Cage, Elizabeth (*Whistle*) — The new Moose County resident is helping with costumes for the production of *A Midsummer Night's Dream*, and is going out with Derek Cuttlebrink. She's changing her dress and appearance and now "looks less like a character in a horror movie." Elizabeth has a high I.Q., an "interest in esoteric subjects," and a "sizable trust fund." She decides to call herself Elizabeth Hart. See *Elizabeth Appelhardt*.

Campbell, Duffield (*Sang*) — a.k.a., Duff. Moose County artist who does watercolors of shaft houses. He worked forty years at Pickax Feed and Seed before becoming successful at painting.

Carmichael, Colin (*Mountain*) — Editor of the *Spudsboro Gazette.* He and Kip MacDiarmid, editor of the *Lockmaster Logger,* were roommates in journalism school.

Carmichael, Danielle (*Cheese*) — New wife of Willard. She's much younger than her husband, and a "trifle flashy." She has a tinny voice reminiscent of the early talkies. Everything about her is "studiously seductive." She's from Baltimore, where she had "stage experience" in a nightclub under the name Danielle Devoe. (*Thief*) — Danielle "isn't adjusting well to small-town life." Her skirts are too short, her heels too high, and everything too tight.

Carmichael, J. Willard (*Cheese*) — New president of the Pickax People's Bank. He's a "distinguished-looking man and a real live wire." (*Thief*) — He has a "suave manner, expensive suit, and styled hair of a newcomer." His first wife died three years ago, then he married Danielle. He's mugged and fatally shot on a trip Down Below.

Cavendish, Jenny (*Thief*) — Little birdlike woman, the sister of Ruth. The retired schoolteachers once lived in Southern California, where they developed a fondness for margaritas. (*Sang*) — Jenny and Ruth move to a retirement village at Ittibittiwassee Estates. (*Stars*) — She and Ruth are living in Ittibittiwassee Estates.

Cavendish, Ruth (*Thief*) — Taller and equally thin sister of Jenny, both of whom are natives of Moose County. (*Stars*) — She and Jenny visit Elizabeth's Magic in Mooseville.

Chisholm, Zella (*Wasn't*) — Unmarried sister of Grace Chisholm Utley. They live on Goodwinter Boulevard and collect teddy bears. She's "taller and thinner and plainer" than her sister. After their teddy bears are stolen, they move to Minneapolis.

Claude (*Closet*) — Owner of the Park of Pink Sunsets in Florida. He's a middle-aged man who is nice "if you played by the rules."

Claudine (*Sang*) — Owner of a florist shop in Pickax. She has "long, silky hair and a dreamy expression in her large blue eyes." (*Stars*) — She's "a gentle young person with innocent blue eyes." It's hard for her to tell when Qwilleran is kidding and when he's serious.

Cluthra (*On/Off*) — One of the sisters who run the Three Weird Sisters antique shop. She's a "voluptuous orange-redhead with green eyes, and a dazzling smile." She has a husky voice. (*High*) — Cluthra married money and moved to Texas.

Cobb, C. C. (*On/Off*) — a.k.a., Cornball. Antique dealer in Junktown and the husband of Iris. He's "tall and nice-looking," needs a shave and wears red flannel shirts. His wife says he's the "most obnoxious dealer in Junktown," a "dirty old man," and a "great kidder." His tone toward Iris is belligerent, but there's "a glint in his eye that is surprisingly affectionate." He is killed while scrounging for salvageable materials in an old house.

Cobb, Iris (*On/Off*) — Antique dealer in Junktown and wife of C. C. She's a very pleasant woman, with "large, round pupils in round eyes in a round face." She has "ash-colored hair that used to be a lovely blond, but it turned ashen overnight" when she lost her first husband, who died of food poisoning. Her twenty-two-year-old son, Dennis Hough, lives in St. Louis. His father, Iris's first husband, was a schoolteacher—she was an English major herself. Her husband, C. C., is killed while scrounging. (*Post Office*) — Mrs. Cobb sells her antique shop to Rosie Riker. Iris becomes Qwill's housekeeper and the caretaker of the antiques in the K Mansion. She begins dating Herb Hackpole. One of her favorite phrases is, "Oh, Mr. Qwilleran, you must be joking." (*Shakespeare*) — Mrs. Cobb is functioning as "house manager, registrar of the collection, and curator of an architectural masterpiece destined to become a museum." She's also an "obsessive cook" who bakes "endless cookies and pies." She and Herb Hackpole get married at the K Mansion. The morning after the wedding, she leaves Herb and checks into the hospital. (*Glue*) — Iris becomes the director of the Goodwinter Farmhouse Museum. (*Ghosts*) — Iris calls Qwilleran about strange noises in the house. When he arrives at the farmhouse, he finds Iris lifeless on the floor, her round face "painfully contorted." She and Susan Exbridge were partners in a new enterprise, Exbridge & Cobb, Fine Antiques, which was scheduled to open soon.

Coggin, Mrs. Maude (*Sang*) — She's an old woman in her nineties who lives on Trevelyan Road and is "kind of odd," but "smart and spunky"—the "last traditional farmwife in Moose County." Her face is "furrowed and leathery," her white hair is untamed. She grew up in Little Hope, on the farm next to Homer Tibbitt. Her husband, Bert, lived to be seventy-eight. She dies when her house burns.

Compton, Lisa (*Underground*) — Wife of Lyle. She's a "jogger who regularly pounded the shoreline in a green warm-up suit." (*Wasn't*) — She goes with her husband on the Bonnie Scots Tour. She has "dancing eyes" and a sense of humor that contrasts with her husband's "dour demeanor." (*Closet*) — She's a "cheerful, middle-aged woman" in charge of patient activities at the Senior Care Facility.

Compton, Lyle (*Underground*) — Superintendent of Pickax schools and the husband of Lisa. Lyle is a "tall, thin, saturnine man with a perverse sense of humor and blunt speech." (*Cardinal*) — Lyle's a painfully thin man who smokes "too many cigars" and never eats vegetables or salads. (*Wasn't*) — Lyle goes on the Bonnie Scots Tour, where he corrects and contradicts Irma Hasselrich's tour commentary. (*Breakfast*) — Lyle tells "hair-raising tales about Scottish history." (*Stars*) — Their house at Top o' the Dunes Club is called "Bah Humbug." He's a "grouch with a sense of humor" who looks "underfed and overworked" after thirty years as school superintendent.

Cook, Amos (*Shakespeare*) — One of the Old Timers in Moose County. He's "eighty-eight and still cooking." He worked at the *Picayune* as a printer's devil when he was ten. He was head pressman when Titus Goodwinter was alive.

Cooper, Mr. (*Post Office*) — Accountant for the Klingenschoen estate in Pickax. He's "ghastly pale" and has a "perpetually worried expression."

Corcoran, Shirley (*Cardinal*) — Chief librarian in Pickax. Her husband, Alan, is in real estate. She gives Bootsie to Polly.

Cottle, Clem (*Underground*) — Son of Doug. He works on his father's Moose County farm. He's a "very good, very reliable" young man who is getting married soon. Clem's voice has the "chesty resonance of a man who had spent his life on a farm and on a softball field." Qwilleran discovers that Clem has been murdered.

Crispen-Schmitt, Sasha (*High*) — Reporter Down Below who replaces Jack Murphy as writer of the gossip column for the *Morning Rampage*.

Crocus, Gerard F. (*Closet*) — Nice old gentleman with a "magnificent head of white hair" who lives in the Park of Pink Sunsets in Florida. He plays the violin and has a crush on Mrs. Gage.

Croy, Isabelle (*Cheese*) — Manager of the New Pickax Hotel, from Lockmaster.

Cuttlebrink, Derek (*Shakespeare*) — New employee at the Old Stone Mill restaurant. (*Glue*) — He delivers gourmet food to the Siamese. Derek is a member of the Theatre Club, rehearsing for his first role. He's thinking about getting into law enforcement. (*Ghosts*) — Derek was going away to college, but he gets a good role in the next play and he meets a girl from Lockmaster, so he decides to work another year. (*Cardinal*) — Derek has five minor roles in the production of *Henry VIII*. He's "six-foot-seven and still growing." He decides to be an actor instead of a cop. (*Wasn't*) — Derek decides to stay in the food business. He's being promoted to the kitchen at the end of the month. (*Breakfast*) — Derek goes back to waiting tables because he can make more money as a waiter with tips. He's dating a girl who is "into ecology pretty heavy," so he plans to study ecology at the new community college. Derek becomes captain at the reservation desk of the new hotel on Pear Island. Qwilleran recruits him to do some undercover work. (*Whistle*) — Derek plays Nick Bottom in *A Midsummer Night's Dream*. Derek and Elizabeth Cage are seeing each other. His "turnover in female companions was of more interest than the Dow Jones averages in Pickax." (*Thief*) — Derek is enrolled in Restaurant Management at MCCC. (*Sang*) — Derek says he's been offered the job of manager at Chet's Bar and Barbecue in Kennebeck. Derek is spelling for the Hams, sponsored by the Pickax Theatre Club. (*Stars*) — Derek is playing the Visitor in the summer theater production *Visit to a Small Planet*. He steals the show! Derek is assistant manager at Owen's

Place, the new restaurant in Mooseville, and is enrolled in Moose County Community College to study restaurant management. Derek's personality appeals to "young girls, bosses, grandmothers, and cats and dogs." He treats CEOs and bishops "with the same offhand bonhomie that captivated the young girls who adored him."

Cuttlebrink, Mr. (*Cardinal*) — Owner of the Cuttlebrink's Hdwe. & Genl. Mdse. store in Wildcat. He has a "high-pitched, reedy voice" and "yellowish-white whiskers and strands of matching hair."

Daphne (*Sang*) — Moose County artist who does life studies and teaches a class in figure drawing.

Darlene (*Brahms*) — Friendly blond waitress at the Northern Lights Hotel in Mooseville.

Dave (*Brahms*) — Worker for the Mooseville company that pumps septic tanks.

David (*Stars*) — Young backpacker found dead on the beach. He had a strong interest in UFO's. The manner of his death is very mysterious.

Dear Heart (*Cardinal*) — Resident of Moose County. She calls the *Something* to accuse Lyle Compton of murdering Hilary VanBrook. Her second choice is Larry Lanspeak. See Grace Utley.

Dingleberry, Adam (*Ghosts*) — Oldest mortician in three counties, including Moose. He's a "frail, stooped figure dependent upon a walker." The ninety-eight year old was a holy terror when in school, getting expelled for playing practical jokes.

Dingleberry, Joshua (*Ghosts*) — Adam's father. He participated in Ephraim Goodwinter's plot to stage his own death. He also made an agreement with Titus Goodwinter to cover up the interment of Luther Bosworth.

Dingwall, Silas (*Thief*) — Innkeeper of the Boulder House Inn in Trawnto. He's "short, rotund, leather-aproned, and jolly."

Dolman, Ona — See *Onoosh Dolmathakia.*

Dolmathakia, Onoosh (*Cheese*) — Mystery woman from Columbus, Ohio, registered at the New Pickax Hotel. She's not exactly young, she avoids people, and she always wears black. She has an olive complexion, "sultry brown eyes," and a "lush mop of dark hair" covering the left side of her face, which has a long scar. (*Thief*) — She opens a Mediterranean café in Pickax. (*Sang*) — Onoosh is the "olive-skinned, dark-haired, sultry-eyed" owner of Onoosh's Café.

Doone, Kevin (*Post Office*) — Qwill's gardener in Pickax. He "goes to Princeton now and does gardening during summer vacation." (*Glue*) — Kevin writes a garden column for the *Moose County Something.* He runs a landscape service, whose motto is "Call Doone to Prune!" (*Sang*) — Kevin develops an avian garden behind the barn-house for the Siamese.

Dublay, Shirley (*Whistle*) — Barmaid at the Trackside Tavern in Sawdust City.

Ducker, James Henry (*Whistle*) — a.k.a., Benno. Friend and construction helper to Eddie Trevelyan. He's a "short, stocky fellow with a ponytail" from Chipmunk. He's killed in a knifing at the Trackside Tavern in Sawdust City.

Duckworth, Mary (*On/Off*) — a.k.a., The Dragon. Owner of the Blue Dragon antique store in Junktown. Her face seems "made of porcelain — blue-white porcelain." She has "wide cheekbones, hollow cheeks, flawless complexion, blue-black hair worn Oriental style, haunting eyes, earrings of jade." Her father is a banker who doesn't approve of her living on Zwinger Street and "peddling junk." Her real name is Mary Duxbury, daughter of Percival. (*High*) — Mary is an officer in SOCK. She has "gone back to being preppy, pearls and everything."

duLac, George (*Breakfast*) — Man who drowns in the pool at the hotel on Pear Island.

duLac, Noisette (*Breakfast*) — Owner of the Antiques by Noisette store on Pear Island and wife of George. She sells only antiques, reads French magazines, and speaks with an accent. Noisette doesn't want publicity.

Duncan, Lynette (*Wasn't*) — Polly's sister-in-law. Lynette works in the office at the Goodwinter Clinic in Pickax. She's "modest and efficient and serene." (*Whistle*) — She invites Polly and Bootsie to share the old Duncan homestead with her. (*Cheese*) — She's "pleasant, helpful, generous, and well-meaning," but she doesn't understand that Qwilleran and Polly would like a little privacy. (*Thief*) — She has a fortune's worth of antiques in her family home and is the last of the Duncans-by-blood. Lynette is active in volunteer work. She surprises everyone by marrying Carter Lee James, in a Scottish wedding. She dies on her honeymoon in New Orleans, of "gastrointestinal complications."

Duncan, Polly (*Shakespeare*) — Head librarian in Pickax. She and Qwilleran share an interest in literature. She's a "charming though enigmatic woman," and she has a "speaking voice that he finds both soothing and stimulating." Her father, a Shakespearean scholar, named her Hippolyta, after a Shakespearean character from *A Midsummer Night's Dream*. Polly has lived in Pickax for twenty-five years. Her volunteer-fireman husband, William Wallace Duncan, was killed in a fire years ago. (*Glue*) — Polly's reserved personality and gentle manner don't suggest that she possesses a handgun. (*Underground*) — Polly spends the summer in England on an exchange program, but has to cut her visit short because of bronchitis and asthma. (*Ghosts*) — Polly is "intelligent, cultivated, stimulating, loving . . . and jealous." (*Cardinal*) — Polly and Qwilleran's relationship seems to be cooling off, particularly since Polly met an interesting red-haired man at a wedding. But Qwill and Polly are reunited, realizing they belong together. (*Wasn't*) — She's "jealous of women younger and thinner," but has absolute integrity. Polly is well-versed in classical music and can name whatever music is being played. She receives an award for public service at the Distinguished Women's Awards program. (*Breakfast*) — Polly's old college roommate invites her to visit Oregon for two weeks, and they spend most of the time designing a house for Polly. (*Whistle*) — Polly plans to build her house on a couple of acres at the east end of Qwilleran's old apple orchard. She suffers a heart attack and undergoes coronary bypass surgery in Minneapolis. (*Thief*) — Polly has a "soft and musical voice," but an "iron hand in the velvet glove" that runs the library. (*Sang*) — If she could be any artist who ever lived, she'd be Mary Cassatt. (*Stars*) — Polly is gone for a month, on a trip to Canada with her sister Mona, whom she hasn't seen in years. Desdemona is from Cincinnati. Polly also has a sister Ophelia. One of Polly's favorite colors is Alice blue. Her favorite "pick-me-up" is a cup of tea and a Lorna Doone.

Dunfield, Buford (*Brahms*) — a.k.a., Buck. Former chief of police. He's a "well-built man with plentiful gray hair and an authoritative manner." Buck spent twenty-five years in law enforcement Down Below and is a former Pickax chief of police. Buck is privately investigating suspicious happenings in

Mooseville. His wife, Sarah, and sister, Betty, find him brutally murdered in his shop.

Dunwoody, Raymond (*High*) — Charlotte Roop's friend, who moves in with her in the Casablanca. He wears suits off the rack and shirts that are too loose around the neck. He has a white bandage where his right ear should be, having lost his ear in a dynamite explosion. It's assumed he loses his life in an explosion in the Casablanca.

Duxbury, Mary — See *Mary Duckworth.*

Duxbury, Mr. and Mrs. Percival (*Backwards*) — An important art collector and president of the fund-raising group. She was a Penniman before her marriage. (*On/Off*) — Percival, an Englishman, is a banker at Midwest National Bank and Mary Duckworth's father.

Elpidia (*High*) — Miss Plumb's personal maid, who dies of food poisoning.

Elsie (*Danish*) — Housemother for Mrs. Allison's establishment.

Emerson, Dr. (*Stars*) — Surgeon in Moose County.

Exbridge, Don (*Shakespeare*) — Co-owner of XYZ Enterprises, Inc. He's a "string bean of a man, six-feet-five, with a smile that made him popular and successful." (*Glue*) — Don tried to have the historic courthouse demolished. Recently divorced, he's "one of the most eligible catches in town." (*Breakfast*) — His "cheerful face always looked scrubbed and polished," and he has a "fringe of brown hair over his ears" but none on the top of his head. He's "a hard guy to reason with," who "never lets reality and common sense get in the way of a fanciful idea."

Exbridge, Susan (*Shakespeare*) — Former wife of Don Exbridge. She wants to open an antique shop. (*Glue*) — Susan plays one of the "wacky old sisters" in *Arsenic and Old Lace* and writes social news for the *Moose County Something*. (*Ghosts*) — Susan and Iris Cobb plan to go into business together as partners in Exbridge & Cobb, Fine Antiques. After Iris's death, Susan is sole owner. Susan's great-grandmother was Lucy Bosworth. (*Cardinal*) — Susan is cast as the Old Lady in *Henry VIII*.

Farhar, Noel (*Backwards*) — Director of the art museum. He leaves because of the "muckraker down at the newspaper," art critic George Mountclemens. Noel is a young man with a thinness that gives him a "ghostly look of old age."

Feathering, Trudy (*Breakfast*) — One of the two widows who run the Island Experience bed-and-breakfast. She has a "designer-style appearance and personality."

Ferdinand (*High*) — Houseman, butler, and bodyguard for Miss Plumb. He has the "build of a linebacker, with hamlike hands, beefy shoulders, a bull neck, and a bald head." He used to wrestle on TV as "Ferdie Le Bull."

Fetter, Donald (*Cheese*) — Son of Elaine. He's confined to a wheelchair, having been incapacitated when the car he was driving crashed. His father was killed in the accident.

Fetter, Elaine (*Cheese*) — Snobbish Pickax woman who lives in West Middle Hummock. She volunteers at the hospital, the museum, and the library. She's a gourmet cook and grows shiitake mushrooms. She's always taking credit for what others do.

Fincher, Dan (*Closet*) — Deputy who was once married to Nancy Inchpot Fincher.

Fincher, Nancy Inchpot (*Closet*) — Young woman in Moose County with a "cascade of dark, wavy hair." She's slightly built and has large brown eyes. She breeds Siberian huskies as sled dogs and works part-time at an animal clinic in Brrr. The "shy, inarticulate, almost pathetic young woman became self-possessed and authoritative" when talking about her dogs. She's discovered to be a cousin of Junior Goodwinter.

Finney, Rhoda (*Ghosts*) — Eighty-five-year-old woman with "thirty-year-old hair." She's been chasing Homer Tibbitt for years. She taught English at the school where he was principal. She won't get her hearing aid fixed and can't hear a thing without it. She and Homer get married on a trip to Lockmaster. See *Rhoda Tibbitt.*

Fish-eye, Mrs. (*Ghosts*) — Down Below high school English teacher of Qwilleran and Arch Riker. She regularly assigned the class to write "a thousand words on such subjects as the weather, breakfast, or the color green." (*Sang*) — After Qwilleran writes his column about Mrs. Fish-eye, he receives a letter from Martha V. Snyder—Mrs. Fish-eye.

Fitch, Belle Urkle (*Glue*) — Wife of Harley, from Chipmunk. Belle has a pretty little-girl face, with eyes that are set close together. She was one of Mrs. Fitch's maids before she married Harley in Las Vegas. The twenty-one-year-old pregnant woman is found shot to death in her home.

Fitch, David (*Post Office*) — Twin brother of Harley, from Pickax. They are students at Yale home for the summer. (*Glue*) — David is now a vice president at the Pickax bank. The twenty-four-year-old David and his wife, Jill, have a new house. He's playing the "slimy doctor" in the Theatre Club's production. He's murdered by his brother.

Fitch, Harley (*Post Office*) — Twin brother of David, from Pickax. They play footmen and waiters at Qwilleran's dinner party. (*Glue*) — He's now a vice president at the Pickax bank. Harley spent a year in prison before coming back to Pickax. The charge was criminal negligence in a car accident in which a girl was killed. Harley and his new bride, Belle, live in the old Fitch mansion. They are expecting their first child. Harley's an avid sailor, who builds "model ships with exquisite detail."

Fitch, Jill (*Glue*) — David's wife, from Pickax. Jill is very clever and designs the sets and costumes for the Theatre Club.

Fitch, Margaret Doone (*Glue*) — Wife of Nigel, from Pickax. She's a "wonderful person—so generous with her time," including serving on the library board. After her son and Belle are murdered, Margaret suffers a massive stroke and dies.

Fitch, Nigel (*Post Office*) — Trust officer at the Pickax People's Bank. (*Shakespeare*) — He's president of the Historical Society and presides on the evening the K Mansion becomes the Klingenschoen Museum. (*Glue*) — Nigel is now president of the bank. He's "distinguished looking: tall, straight, perpetually tanned, with polished manners and affable personality." After his wife, Margaret, dies, Nigel goes out to the parking lot and shoots himself.

Fleudd, Rexwell (*High*) — One of principals of Penniman, Greystone & Fleudd. The developer has a "long, narrow face with high cheekbones and blow-dried hair." He wears custom-tailored suits and "ostentatious gold jewelry."

Forfar, Beverly (*Sang*) — Businesslike young woman who is the manager of the Art Center. Her straight dark hair fits her head "like a helmet." She's attractive, "buxom, but slim-hipped." She's a native of Moose County who went Down Below and worked in art galleries, returning to Pickax after a divorce. She's on the Daubers spelling team.

Fred (*Stars*) — Bartender at the Shipwreck Tavern in Mooseville. He plays the guitar and sings about the fate of the *Jenny Lee.*

Fred, Foxy (*Shakespeare*) — Auctioneer for the Goodwinter auction who wears a western hat and red down jacket. (*Wasn't*) — He manages the tag sale for Dr. Melinda. (*Cheese*) — He's the auctioneer at the celebrity auction.

Frobnitz, Ronald (*Sang*) — False name used by Qwilleran when he wants to remain anonymous. He uses an "adenoidal twang" to disguise his voice. Ronald pretends to have a wife and three children and teach psychology at a California university. His hobby is racing cars. (*Stars*) — Dr. Frobnitz teaches at Branchwater University.

Fugtree, Captain (*Shakespeare*) — Former resident of Pickax City. His funeral procession had seventy-five cars. (*Ghosts*) — He was Kristi Fugtree Waffle's great-grandfather.

Fugtree, Emmaline (*Ghosts*) — Kristi's grandmother, from Moose County. She and Samson Goodwinter had a son, whom the Captain brought up and who was Kristi's father.

Fulgrove, Mrs. (*Post Office*) — Pickax resident and applicant for the position of housekeeper for Qwill. She's a "scrawny woman who virtually vibrated with energy or nervousness." She used to work for Aunt Fanny. Qwill hires her. (*Shakespeare*) — Mrs. Fulgrove cleans and polishes six days a week at the K Mansion, with "almost religious fervor." (*Closet*) — One day she accidentally shuts Koko in the cleaning closet, where he activates a can of foam carpet cleaner.

Gafner, Sam (*Post Office*) — Real-estate broker. He's a "smooth-looking sandy-haired man."

Gage, Euphonia Roff (*Shakespeare*) — Junior Goodwinter's grandmother, his mother's mother. She "drives a Mercedes and honks the horn at every intersection." Grandma is eighty-two and "still stands on her head every day." Grandma goes to Florida and leaves Junior to house-sit. (*Closet*) — Euphonia sells all her antiques and paintings and relocates to Florida. The eighty-eight-year-old woman plays shuffleboard, goes to the dog races, and wears elaborate makeup. She always wears a violet scent. She is found dead in bed at the retirement village in Florida. Police say it's suicide, but Qwilleran uncovers a murder plot.

Geb, Otto (*Post Office*) — Owner of Otto's Tasty Eats.

Ghirotto (*Backwards*) — An artist whose work is very valuable. He painted ballerinas or monkeys during his "celebrated Vibrato Period."

Gippel, Scott (*Post Office*) — Overweight city councilman. He's "scared to death of Hackpole" and they're next-door neighbors. (*Cardinal*) — Scott's girth is so enormous that he requires two chairs when sitting. (*Wasn't*) — He's a used-car dealer in Pickax. (*Closet*) — He drop-ships a bright yellow sports car to Euphonia Gage in Florida. (*Whistle*) — He's "notorious for his pessimism," and is the only businessman who refuses to join the Pickax Boosters Club. (*Sang*) — He's on the Oilers spelling team, sponsored by his garage. (*Stars*) — Scott is playing the overbearing general in *Visit to a Small Planet.*

Glanz, Andrew (*On/Off*) — Antique dealer who died when he fell from a ladder onto a sharp finial in his store. He was "a highly respected authority on antiques" who knew too much.

Glinko, Mr. and Mrs. (*Underground*) — Glinko and his wife run a "service network" for people on his list. People "go to his shop, sign up, pay a fee, and give him a key" to the house. He sends out repairmen. Mr. Glinko has a "face almost obscured by a wild set of whiskers, a rat's nest of hair under a greasy beret, and a pair of bright, merry eyes." The ample Mrs. Glinko is "all smiles and affability" and a "living computer."

Goode, Wetherby (*Closet*) — Meteorologist at WPKX radio station in Pickax. He has a "hearty, jovial manner that could make floods and tornadoes sound like fun." (*Thief*) — He always has a parody of a song or literary work to fit the weather. Wetherby plays cocktail music on the piano. His real name is Joe Bunker. (*Stars*) — The WPKX meteorologist is an "unstoppable extrovert." He plays cocktail piano at parties and brags about being a native of Horseradish. His cousin, Dr. Teresa Bunker, is a corvidologist at a Southern university.

Goodwinter, Alexander (*Brahms*) — Aunt Fanny's attorney. He wears a tailor-made business suit with a white shirt and "proper striped tie." He and his sister, Penelope, are sole partners in their family's law firm. (*Post Office*) — He's probably in his mid-thirties, but his "cool magisterial manner" makes him appear older. He makes a lot of trips to Washington. There's a rumor he has a woman down there. Alex dies when his plane crashes as he's leaving town.

Goodwinter, Amanda (*Post Office*) — Interior decorator in Pickax. She's a "gray-haired woman with a perpetual scowl" who wears baggy clothes and thick-soled shoes and looks frumpy. (*Glue*) — Amanda's never been married, but Arch Riker asks her to marry him and she accepts. (*Underground*) — Amanda and Arch break up. He calls her "the most cantankerous, opinionated, obstinate, unpredictable woman" he's ever met. (*Ghosts*) — Amanda is of the "Drinking Goodwinters," the branch of the family tree that's crazy. On Amanda, "every new garment looked secondhand and every hair looked purposely out of place." (*Wasn't*) — As a city council member, she "minced no words, spared no feelings, played no politics." (*Thief*) — She's a perennial member of the Pickax City Council, reelected because she's a Goodwinter. (*Sang*) — Moose County citizens say she "would go anywhere and do anything to get votes and/or publicity for her studio." (*Stars*) — She's quitting the city council and running for mayor.

Goodwinter, Emory (*Wasn't*) — Melinda's brother, who was reported to have died in a car accident when Melinda was in medical school. Only a year apart, they "grew up like twins." He's in Pickax under the name Charles Edward Martin.

Goodwinter, Ephraim (*Shakespeare*) — Founder of the *Pickax Picayune* and grandfather of Senior. He was a "rich mine owner and lumber baron who would do anything for money." He hanged himself, or so some say, "on a big oak tree near the old plank bridge." Others say he was lynched by angry townspeople. (*Ghosts*) — Ephraim's branch of the family tree has always been rich and mean, although Junior is neither. Ephraim's ghost is said to walk around once in a while. Ephraim staged his own death and burial, then moved to Europe.

Goodwinter, Gertrude (Gritty) Gage (*Shakespeare*) — Senior Goodwinter's forty-eight-year-old wife who likes "the country club life." After Senior dies, Gritty plans to sell the *Pickax Picayune* to XYZ Enterprises. She also sells the old farmhouse and moves into Indian Village with Don Exbridge. She dies with Harry Noyton in a car crash as they are leaving on a trip together.

Goodwinter, Dr. Halifax (*Post Office*) — Local doctor in Pickax. He's a "white-haired country doctor with two claims to fame: He is Melinda's father" and he has taken care of half of Moose County. (*Mountain*) — Dr. Hal is going on eighty, "dearly loved" and the "last of the old-fashioned country doctors." Dr. Hal takes his own life after his wife dies. The rumor circulates that "his wife's death was a mercy killing."

Goodwinter, Mrs. Hal (*Mountain*) — Invalid wife of Dr. Hal in Pickax. She dies after fifteen years of illness.

Goodwinter, Jack (*Closet*) — Junior Goodwinter's brother in Los Angeles who has two kids.

Goodwinter, Jody (*Shakespeare*) — Junior Goodwinter's girlfriend in Pickax. A dental hygienist at Dr. Zoller's dental clinic, Jody is tiny, with "straight blond hair and big blue eyes." She and Juney fly Down Below to get married. (*Ghosts*) — She has their first child, a son. (*Closet*) — Their second child, Leslie Ann, is born right before the Big Snow hits.

Goodwinter, Junior (*Brahms*) — Managing editor of the *Pickax Picayune.* He also sells advertising. He has worked at the paper since he was twelve. Junior graduated from journalism school at the state university last year. (*Post Office*) — He looks "like a high school sophomore," wearing running shoes and a "Pickax varsity letter." (*Shakespeare*) — Junior exhibits an "innocent enthusiasm that was rare in a journalist with a cum laude degree from a state university." After his father is killed and the *Picayune* building burns down, Junior interviews for a job at the *Daily Fluxion,* but he isn't hired. He tries at the *Morning Rampage,* but isn't hired there, either. Jody and Junior fly Down Below to get married. (*Glue*) — Junior becomes managing editor of the new *Moose County Something.* (*Ghosts*) — He's maintaining his "boyish look and boyish build" and is growing a beard "in an attempt to look older than fifteen."

(*Whistle*) — Junior played Puck in a college production of *A Midsummer Night's Dream*, and he's repeating the performance for the Pickax Theatre Club. (*Stars*) — Junior is past thirty, but "slight stature and boyish features" give him the "look of a perennial schoolboy."

Goodwinter, Dr. Melinda (*Brahms*) — Doctor in Mooseville. She has "attractive green eyes and the longest eyelashes" Qwilleran has ever seen. She is the daughter of a general practitioner in Pickax and the cousin of Alex and Penelope. (*Post Office*) — Melinda takes care of Qwill in the hospital and they continue to date. (*Shakespeare*) — Melinda has left for a hospital in Boston, where she'll be able to specialize. She "never really wanted to be a country doctor," but she was "hot to marry Qwilleran." (*Mountain*) — Melinda returns to Pickax for her mother's funeral, then her father's. She plans to stay and take over her father's practice. (*Wasn't*) — Melinda asks Qwilleran to marry her for three years, after which he can have his freedom, and their children would revert to the name Goodwinter. After her complicity in several plots is uncovered, she dies when she crashes her car at high speed into the monument at the end of Goodwinter Boulevard.

Goodwinter, Penelope (*Brahms*) — Aunt Fanny's attorney. She handles Fanny's tax work, lawsuits, and real-estate transactions. Penny reads Qwill's column "religiously" and quotes him as if he were Shakespeare. (*Post Office*) — She's in her mid-thirties, but appears older. She's "conspicuously well dressed for a town like Pickax" and drives a tan BMW. She commits suicide after the crimes she and her partners committed are revealed.

Goodwinter, Pug (*Shakespeare*) — Daughter of Senior and Gritty, and sister of Junior. She lives in Montana. (*Closet*) — She has three kids.

Goodwinter, Samson (*Shakespeare*) — Oldest son of Ephraim. There's a story that his horse was frightened by a flock of blackbirds, and that's how he was killed. Others say there was "something fishy" about his death. He's Kristi Fugtree Waffle's grandfather, making her Junior's cousin.

Goodwinter, Senior (*Brahms*) — Owner of the *Pickax Picayune* and father of Junior. He sells ads and sets the type. (*Post Office*). He wears a leather apron and a square paper cap made of folded newsprint. Senior has been setting type since the age of eight. (*Shakespeare*) — Senior can "set more than thirty-five letters a minute without looking at the typecase." He's killed when his car strikes the Old Stone Bridge. There are ninety-three cars for his funeral.

Goodwinter, Titus (*Shakespeare*) — Former owner of the *Pickax Picayune* in Pickax. He was Senior's father. Many years ago Titus seduced Ellie, Zack Whittlestaff's daughter. After Ellie threw herself in the river, Zack killed Titus with a knife. (*Ghosts*) — In 1904 Titus gave Lucy Bosworth $3,000 in compensation for her husband's death. He made an agreement for $2,000 and $500 a month with Joshua Dingleberry for burying Luther Bosworth.

Gow, Bruce (*Wasn't*) — Driver of the minibus on the Bonnie Scots Tour. He's a "sullen, red-haired man" of about forty who speaks Gaelic and argues with Irma Hasselrich. He disappears from the tour at the same time as Grace Utley's jewelry.

Graham, Dan (*Red*) — Joy's husband, also a potter. He has "faded carrot hair, a prominent Adam's apple, and freckled skin" covering prominent bones in his face and hands. His worn corduroy jacket and barefoot sandals make him look "seedy and forlorn."

Graham, Joy Wheatley (*Red*) — A potter and Qwill's old flame from Down Below. She has a "tiny figure, heavy chestnut hair, and a provocative one-sided smile." She is now married to Dan. Joy disappears one evening, and Qwill soon discovers that she's been murdered.

Greenleaf, Deputy (*Stars*) — Moose County's first woman deputy, needed to escort women prisoners to the Bixby County detention facility. She responds to the 911 call that said there was a body buried on the beach. She's nice looking, but "stony-faced," which seems to be part of a deputy's official expression.

Greer, Victor (*Cheese*) — White male about forty who plants a bomb in the New Pickax Motel. The motel is severely damaged by the explosion that kills Anna Marie Toms. Victor was wearing a blue nylon jacket and a black baseball cap with a fancy letter *D* for Detroit. He's found dead of bee stings in a cabin owned by Scotten Fisheries.

Gumboldt, Roy (*Sang*) — New fire chief of Pickax. He's Chet Ramsbottom's brother-in-law.

Gus (*Glue*) — Founder of Tipsy's Restaurant. He used to be a "cook in a lumbercamp and then a saloonkeeper." During Prohibition he went Down Below and ran a blind pig. After Repeal, he came back to Moose County with a black-and-white cat named Tipsy and opened a steakhouse. (Read about Tipsy and Gus in "Tipsy and the Board of Health" in *The Cat Who Had 14 Tales.*)

Gus (*High*) — Doorman at the Casablanca. He liked to put on his old uniform and open car doors and collect a few tips. One night someone drove by and shot Poor Old Gus dead.

Hackpole, Herb (*Post Office*) — Used-car salesman. He's a "belligerent-looking middle-aged man with an outdated crew cut." He physically attacks township supervisor Clem Wharton during a public annexation hearing. (*Shakespeare*) — Hackpole has a "reputation for being obnoxious," but Mrs. Cobb finds him attractive. He has "red devils tattooed on his arms" and wears "his thinning hair in a crew cut." He was in the army, and has a couple of kids who are grown. He buys the old Goodwinter farmhouse and he and Iris are married in the Klingenschoen Mansion. The next morning, Iris leaves her new husband. When Herb sets fire to the Klingenschoen Mansion in revenge, he dies in the conflagration. His real name was Basil Whittlestaff.

Haggis, Thornton (*Sang*) — Winner of a prize raffled off at the Art Center. He's the white-haired former owner of H & H Monument Works and H & H Sand and Gravel— his two sons, Eric and Shane, own the businesses now. His great-grandfather, Eero Haakon, came from Finland to work in quarries but was put on the payroll as Earl Haggis. He's on the Daubers spelling team.

Halapay, Cal (*Backwards*) — Very rich commercial artist who owns a successful agency. He paints pictures of kids with curly hair and rosy cheeks.

Halapay, Sandra (*Backwards*) — a.k.a., Sandy. Wife of Cal. She's "lyrically tall and lovely," with almond eyes, which are "roguish as well as exotic," and straight, dark hair. She and Cal have an eight-year-old daughter, Cindy, and a six-year-old daughter, Susan. The girls have the Oriental look of their mother.

Halliburton, June Kale (*Closet*) — New music director in Pickax, from Lockmaster. Her "red hair was cut shorter and curlier than the accepted style in Moose County." (*Breakfast*) — She's the one person that Qwilleran actively dislikes. June is the head of music for the Moose County schools. She has "lots of degrees and lots of talent, as well as sexy good looks." June directs the music and entertainment for the Pear Island Resort. She dies in a fire at her cottage, a victim of murder.

Hames (*Backwards*) — Detective from the homicide division Down Below. He's relaxed and amiable, with a mind like a computer or a cement mixer. (*Danish*) — He's a heavy-set, smart police detective with "an off-duty personality." (*Glue*) — He's a brilliant detective, although he likes to play dumb. (*High*) — Now a lieutenant in the Homicide Squad, the "portly and easygoing" Lieutenant Hames introduces Qwilleran to the *Fluxion*'s police reporter, Matt Thiggamon. He and his wife have a Siamese, who is "more interested in breaking the law than enforcing it." (*Whistle*) — He and his family vacation in Moose County.

Hampton, Courtney (*High*) — Resident of the Casablanca. He's a young man with "square shoulders, slim hips, and suits of the latest cut." He works at Kipper & Fine, a fashionable men's store.

Handley, Jill (*Cheese*) — New feature editor of the *Something*. She's pretty and eager, and she loves Qwill's column. She moved from the *Lockmaster Ledger* because her husband opened the new Scottish Bakery in Pickax. (*Stars*) — Jill writes in folk-style about the missing hiker.

Hanstable, Mildred (*Brahms*) — Resident of Mooseville. She's the wife of Stanley, the mother of Sharon Hanstable, and the mother-in-law of Roger MacGillivray. She's scatterbrained, but nice, and she likes to laugh. Mildred teaches in Pickax. (*Post Office*) — Mildred's new project is getting Dimsdale women to make crafts by hand and sell them in Sharon Hanstable's shop, "sort of a cottage industry." (*Glue*) — Mildred handles the food page for the *Moose County Something*. She teaches home economics and art at Pickax High School, where she also directs the senior play and coaches girls' volleyball. (*Underground*) — Mildred writes the food page for the *Something*, and is a "superlative cook." (*Ghosts*) — She's "up to her eyebrows in good causes," still trying to lose weight, and "still carrying the torch for that husband of hers." A lifelong resident of Moose County, Mildred has taught school for almost thirty years, and she knows everybody. (*Closet*) — Her latest project is collecting loose change for spaying stray cats. Mildred and Arch Riker are married on Christmas Eve. See *Mildred Riker*.

Hanstable, Sharon (*Brahms*) — Wife of Roger MacGillivray in Mooseville. She owns a little candle and gift shop, Night's Candles, in the Cannery Mall. (*Glue*) — Sharon's not working, but staying home with the new baby. (*Ghosts*) — She has gone back to teaching. (*Cheese*) — She's now managing the Kitchen Boutique in Stables Row. (*Stars*) — Sharon is "plump, good-natured, and wholesomely pretty," a younger version of her mother. She and Roger share homeschooling duties for their children. She works part-time at the Great Dune Motel and Roger works weekends at the paper so he can have two weekdays off.

Hanstable, Stanley (*Brahms*) — Resident of Mooseville and husband of Mildred. He runs the turkey farm on Pickax Road. He has an "idiopathic stink" that makes it impossible to be around him. (*Cardinal*) — Stanley has died in prison.

Harding, Arledge and Dorothy (*Breakfast*) — Arledge was the vicar of a small church in Indiana before he retired. He falls on a step of the Domino Inn on Pear Island and cracks a rib.

Harold — See *Harold Bates*.

Harry (*Mountain*) — Owner of furniture store in Spudsboro.

Hart, Elizabeth (*Sang*) — Elizabeth opens a gift boutique in Mooseville. (*Stars*) — Elizabeth's new gift boutique in Mooseville is named Elizabeth's Magic. Elizabeth and Derek Cuttlebrink are still dating. He tones down her "citified pretensions" and she convinces him to enroll at Moose County Community College to study restaurant management. Elizabeth has changed from a "shy bewildered young woman" to a "forceful and successful businesswoman." See *Elizabeth Cage*.

Harvey (*Underground*) — Waiter at the Fish Tank in Moose County, once a student in Mildred's art class.

Hasselrich, Irma (*Shakespeare*) — Volunteer at the Pickax Hospital Senior Care Facility. Her father is the attorney for the Klingenschoen Fund. (*Underground*) — She's the chief canary at the Senior Care Facility. Her voice is "cultivated, well-modulated, and melodic." Irma never married, and she "dedicated her life to helping others." When she was eighteen, she killed her boyfriend, and Judge Goodwinter sentenced her to twenty years. She received probation in the custody of her parents, plus orders to do ten years of community service. (*Wasn't*) — The "well-groomed, well-dressed Irma is influencing Polly to wear brighter colors and touch up her graying hair." The trouble Irma had been in when she was younger was actually precipitated by date rape. The jury recommended leniency. Irma plans and leads the Bonnie Scots Tour, during which she dies in her hotel room, a victim of what Dr. Melinda calls cardiac arrest.

Hasselrich, Osmond (*Shakespeare*) — Attorney for the Klingenschoen Fund in Pickax. He prosecuted Zack Whittlestaff who was convicted of killing Titus Goodwinter. (*Glue*) — He represents Chad Lanspeak when he's picked up on suspicion of murder. (*Ghosts*) — He's the kind of attorney who "made it a pleasure to be sued, or divorced, or found guilty." (*High*) — The senior partner of Hasselrich Bennett & Barter, he's "an elderly man with stooped shoulders and quivering jowls, but he has the buoyant optimism and indomitability of a young man." He likes to pour coffee "from his paternal grandmother's silver teapot into his maternal grandmother's Wedgwood cups." (*Closet*) — His "fleshy eyelids frequently flickered and his sagging jowls quivered" during meetings with Qwilleran.

Hawkinfield, J. J. (*Mountain*) — Former owner of Tiptop in Spudsboro. He refurbished the inn for a family home. He had plans to develop the inside of Big Potato Mountain. He grew up in Spudsboro and went to law school, but dropped out and went back to Spudsboro to run the paper. He was "psychologically abusive to his wife and daughter." He was murdered at Tiptop.

Hawkinfield, Mrs. J. J. (*Mountain*) — Patient in a mental hospital for a few years. Three of their sons were reported killed within a year, in two accidents a few months apart. Mrs. Hawkinfield "couldn't cope and had a nervous breakdown" and was hospitalized somewhere in Pennsylvania.

Hawkinfield, Sherry (*Mountain*) — Daughter of J. J. She owns a shop in Maryland called "Not New But Nice." She was once married to Hugh Lumpton.

Hawkins, Mrs. (*Danish*) — The Taits' housekeeper, Down Below. She's a "sassy, flirtatious woman" with a musical voice. Qwill likes "sassy, flirtatious females" if they are "young and attractive," but Mrs. Hawkins is neither.

Hawley, Doris (*Stars*) — Wife of Magnus. She's famous for baking, especially homemade ginger snaps and cinnamon rolls.

Doris has gray hair and a "gardener's slight stoop" but the energy level of a younger woman.

Hawley, Magnus (_Stars_) — Seventy-year-old veteran of commercial fishing boats.

Hawley, Rebecca (_Stars_) — Ninety-year-old widow of Primus, the mother of Magnus who makes a sampler for Qwilleran.

Hedrog, Keestra (_High_) — Qwill's neighbor in the Casablanca. She has a dance group named the Gut Dancers.

Helmuth, Carla (_Breakfast_) — One of two widows who own the "Island Experience" bed-and-breakfast on Pear Island. She's a "handsome, well-dressed, mature woman with a sparkling smile."

Henry (_Breakfast_) — Gaunt young islander who drives a carriage on Pear Island.

Herbert, Dr. (_Closet_) — Doctor present at the Brrr Community Church when Hixie Rice falls and breaks her foot. He's adorable, caring, and unmarried.

Herbert, Mrs. (_Closet_) — Mother of Dr. Herbert. Hixie Rice moves in with her temporarily after Hixie breaks her foot. They speak French.

Hettie (_Breakfast_) — One of the workers at Vacation Helpers on Pear Island.

Highspight, "Dr." (_Danish_) — A psycatatrist who speaks with "a folksy English accent." She's not a real doctor, but just "a cat fancier with a bit of common sense." She has a "pudgy, middle-aged face with a sweet smile." Her house is filled with cats.

Hooper, Lionella (*Whistle*) — a.k.a., Nella. Floyd Trevel-yan's secretary at the Lumbertown Credit Union. She's an "eye-catching beauty" from Texas. Her apartment in Indian Village is decorated in a southwestern theme. She disappears after the Lumbertown Credit Union is closed by the banking commission. Her real name is Lionel.

Hopkins (*High*) — Server at Courtney Hampton's party. He's "an emaciated gray-haired man in a white duck coat."

Hornbuckle, Mr. (*Wasn't*) — Elderly man in the Senior Care Facility who is part of the Pets for Patients program. He's a "small, weak figure" on oxygen, but he has "bright eyes and a toothy grin." He was Dr. Hal's caretaker and "drove 'im all over, makin' calls."

Hough, Cheryl (*Ghosts*) — Wife of Dennis and mother of Dennis Junior, a.k.a. Denny. (*Cardinal*) — Cheryl and their two-year-old son are still in St. Louis. She calls Dennis and tells him not to come home, that she's found someone else and is getting a divorce.

Hough, Dennis (*On/Off*) — Twenty-two-year-old son of Iris Cobb in St. Louis, a clean-cut young man who is "sort of an architect." His father, Iris's first husband, had been a school-teacher. (*Ghosts*) — Since Qwilleran had met him Down Below, Dennis has married Cheryl, fathered a son, and become a building contractor. He has a "lean and melancholy face, in comparison with his mother's plump and cheery counte-nance." He plans to open a construction business in Moose County. (*Cardinal*) — Dennis designs and engineers the ren-ovation of Qwilleran's apple barn into his new home. He plays the Duke of Buckingham in *Henry VIII*. After a divorce message from his wife, Dennis hangs himself from a beam in Qwilleran's barn.

Huggins, Abner (*Underground*) — Oldest person at the Wimsey reunion. He lives at the Senior Care Facility in Pickax.

Huggins, Mr. and Mrs. Cecil (*Underground*) — Owners of Huggins Hardware Store in Moose County. He's president of the Chamber of Commerce.

Huggins, Unc (*Stars*) — White-bearded great-uncle of Cecil. He has worked in the store since he was twelve.

Iggy — See *Ignatius K. Small.*

Inchpot, Gilbert (*Closet*) — Moose County potato farmer and father of Nancy Fincher. He has "hardly been out of Moose County except for Vietnam." The fifty-seven-year-old man can "fix anything mechanical and was proud of it." He disappears one day, and Qwilleran later discovers his body on Klingenschoen property.

Inchpot, Lena Foote (*Closet*) — Wife of Gil and mother of Nancy Fincher. Born Lethe Gage, she was Euphonia's real daughter, but then became Euphonia's housekeeper. She died of cancer a few years ago.

Inchpot, Lenny (*Cheese*) — Desk clerk at the New Pickax Hotel and son of Lois. His ambition is to be manager of the hotel. He and Anna Marie Toms are planning to be married, but she is killed in an explosion. (*Thief*) — Lenny is working as part-time manager of the clubhouse at Indian Village and taking morning classes at the college. He's "clean-cut and good with people." (*Sang*) — Lenny is spelling for the Nailheads, sponsored by XYZ Enterprises.

Inchpot, Lois (*Closet*) — Owner of Lois's Luncheonette in downtown Pickax. She has been "feeding downtown Pickax for thirty years," and her customers often take up collections to finance building repairs. (*Cheese*) — She's a "buxom, bossy woman" whose customers are devoted to her. (*Sang*) — She's the "loud, bossy, hardworking proprietor" who's also known as a "civic treasure." (*Sang*) — The Pickax mayor recently proclaimed a Lois Inchpot Day because of her thirty years of feeding Pickaxians.

Inglehart, Mrs. "Grummy" (*Cardinal*) — Eighty-eight-year-old grandmother of Vicki Bushland in Lockmaster. She's "a sweet old lady," distinguished-looking, with white hair. She speaks in a "cultivated voice" that has become "tremulous with age." She dies of natural causes while everyone is at the steeplechase.

Ivrene (*On/Off*) — a.k.a., Ivy. One of three sisters who runs The Three Weird Sisters antique shop in Junktown. A tiny blonde, not yet eighteen, with "upturned nose and pretty legs." She's still in art school.

James, Carter Lee (*Thief*) — So-called cousin of Danielle Carmichael. He supervises restorations of old houses, for a fee, and would like to restore the houses on Pleasant Street in Pickax. His voice is "ingratiatingly pleasant," and he has "blond hair, medium good looks, and a relaxed way with strangers."

Jasper, Mrs. (*High*) — Resident at the Casablanca, Down Below. The seventy-five-year-old woman cleans apartments, including Qwilleran's. Mrs. Jasper did housework in the Casablanca "way back when." She was born in Chipmunk in Moose County where her father had a potato farm.

Jaunti, Jack (*On/Off*) — The *Fluxion*'s "young smart aleck in the Sunday Department." He took a job as undercover valet for Percival Duxbury to write an inside story on the town's richest man.

Jennifer (*Brahms*) — Teller at the Mooseville bank. She's a sunburned blonde who is "almost unbearably friendly."

Jimmie (*Mountain*) — Young Spudsboro man who assists Sabrina Peel by delivering and placing her design accessories.

Jupiter, Randy (*High*) — Young jogger with a large reddish moustache who lives at the Casablanca. He's a bartender at Penniman Plaza and a jazzhound with a "fantastic stereo system."

Kale, Elijah (*Breakfast*) — Gatekeeper at The Pines on Grand Island and June Kale Halliburton's father.

Katzenhide, Sylvia (*On/Off*) — Antique dealer in Junktown. Her shop is called Sorta Camp. She's a "handsome, well-groomed, self-assured woman who looked forty and was undoubtedly fifty-five." She lives in Skyline Towers, where she has a lovely apartment, not furnished in camp.

Kemple, Ernie and Vivian (*Thief*) — Ernie is the Boosters Club's official "back-slapper and glad-hander." The couple collects antique dolls. Ernie retired in January after selling Kemple Life and Accident to the Brady brothers. He plays Judge Brack in *Hedda Gabler*.

Kemple, Tracy (*Thief*) — Pretty, young blond daughter of Ernie and Vivian of Pickax. Tracy works lunches at the Old Stone Mill and dinners at the Boulder House Inn. Lenny Inchpot was her boyfriend in high school, but she eloped with a football player from Sawdust City. She's divorced and has a son, Bobbie. She's seeing Carter Lee James. When he marries Danielle, Tracy tries to overdose.

Kendall, Lodge (*Backwards*) — Police reporter for the *Fluxion*. He's "young, earnest, and happy in his work," literal, and unsmiling. (*Danish*) — He's the *Fluxion*'s regular man at police headquarters. Though happy in his work, he's careful to exhibit a "professional air of boredom."

Kenneth (*Stars*) — Big, blond, husky male assistant for Elizabeth Hart at her boutique, Elizabeth's Magic. A rising senior at Mooseland High School, he's stockboy, delivery man, and salesman.

Kirk (*Breakfast*) — Barhop at the Corsair Room of the hotel on Pear Island.

Klaus, Karl Oskar (*Wasn't*) — New chef at the New Pickax Hotel, from Fall River, Massachusetts. He has a shaggy beard, which he wears in a hair net while he's cooking. (*Cheese*) — He was mixing a cake when the bomb exploded, and "both he and the batter ended up on the floor."

Klingenschoen, Francesca (*Brahms*) — Resident of Pickax and a friend of Qwilleran's mother. Qwill called her Aunt Fanny when he was a kid, but he hasn't seen her in forty years. Fanny and Qwill's mother were "doughnut girls in World War I." When Fanny retired to Pickax City at sixty-five, she could "buy and sell anyone in the county." After she dies in a fall down some stairs, Qwilleran learns she was once an exotic dancer in a club in New Jersey. She was never married, but had a son who was killed in "a mysterious accident on the New York waterfront."

Kowbel, Amber — See *Amberina*.

LaBlanc, Tom (*Backwards*) — Houseboy for the Halapays Down Below. He dresses in "dirty chinos and a half-buttoned shirt," carrying trays with the "charm of a gorilla."

Lambreth, Earl (*Backwards*) — Formal proprietor of the Lambreth Gallery. Earl is older than his wife Zoe, "painfully dapper," and supercilious. Earl is found murdered in his gallery.

Lambreth, Zoe (*Backwards*) — An artist. Zoe shows her work at her husband Earl's gallery. (*High*) — Zoe has sold the gallery and moved to California.

Landrum, Dave (*Cardinal*) — Ashen-haired photographer for the *Moose County Something*. He is playing Suffolk in *Henry VIII* until he walks out. Dave's daughter and her boyfriend committed suicide by running their car into a bridge.

Lanspeak, Carol (*Glue*) — Resident of Moose County and wife of Larry. Chad is their youngest son. Their older son is studying for the ministry, and their daughter, Diane, is pre-med. Carol is full of energy and enthusiasm, and she laughs a lot. She's playing one of the "wacky sisters" in *Arsenic and Old Lace*. (*Ghosts*) — Carol is the spokesperson for the Goodwinter Farmhouse Museum's reopening, which features major disasters in Moose County. (*Cardinal*) — Carol is president of the Theatre Club, assistant director of the production of *Henry VIII*, and understudy for the queen. (*Wasn't*) — She's half of the "most likable couple in Pickax." Carol plays Lady Macduff. (*Whistle*) — She's playing the duke's bride and Titania in *A Midsummer Night's Dream*, roles she has played before. (*Thief*) — She's directing *Hedda Gabler* for the Theatre Club.

Lanspeak, Chad (*Glue*) — Native of Pickax and nineteen-year-old son of Carol and Larry. He "runs with a pack from Chipmunk, the slummiest town in the county." Chad works in his parent's store as a bored salesclerk. He has a "pigtail and Fu Manchu moustache." Chad and two other teenagers are killed in a car-train collision.

Lanspeak, Dr. Diane (*Whistle*) — Native of Pickax, daughter of Carol and Larry. Diane decides to return to Moose County to go into a medical practice with Dr. Herbert. She's a "fresh-faced young woman" who looks "inordinately happy." (*Sang*) — Dr. Diane is on the spelling team for the Pills, sponsored by Sloan's Drug Store.

Lanspeak, Larry (*Post Office*) — Owner of Lanspeak Department Store in Pickax, with his wife, Carol. He plays the butler at Qwilleran's dinner party. (*Glue*) — He does impersonations of his more eccentric customers at Qwill's birthday party. He and Carol are the "lifeblood of the Theatre Club." (*Ghosts*) — Larry is of "ordinary height, ordinary coloring, and ordinary features." His appearance gives him "an anonymity that enabled him to slip into many different roles for the Theatre Club." Larry's great-grandmother was Lucy Bosworth, who was also the great-grandmother of Susan Exbridge and Vince Boswell/Bosworth. (*Cardinal*) — Larry plays King Henry in the Theatre Club's production. His "slight build requires fifteen pounds of padding to play the well-fed monarch." (*Wasn't*) — Larry is "a mild-mannered man, difficult to imagine as the murderous Macbeth." (*Whistle*) — He plays the duke and Oberon in the Theatre Club's production of *A Midsummer Night's Dream*, roles he has played before. (*Thief*) — He plays Tesman in *Hedda Gabler*. (*Stars*) — Larry is playing the commentator in *Visit to a Small Planet*.

Lessmore, Dolly (*Mountain*) — Owner of Lessmore Realty in Spudsboro with her husband, Robert. Dolly is "on the young side of middle age, short and rather pudgy, dressed in bright green, and coiffed with an abundance of fluffy hair."

Lessmore, Robert (*Mountain*) — Owner of Lessmore Realty with his wife, Dolly, although Robert tends to play golf more than he sells real estate. "He's *less* and she's *more*."

Limburger, Gustav (*Cheese*) — Resident of Black Creek in Moose County. He's a "short, bent-over, mean-spirited, eighty-year-old Scrooge" who owns the New Pickax Hotel. His clothes are dingy gray, and his face is gray with untamed whiskers. He falls down the steps and is hospitalized. He dies and leaves his entire estate to a daughter in Germany.

Linguini, Mr. and Mrs. (*Glue*) — Mama-and-papa operation in Moose County. He cooks fabulous food, and she waits on tables.

Little Henry (*Brahms, Underground*) — a.k.a., Harry. Chimney sweep in Moose County. A young man "of slight build," he wears a tall silk top hat.

Lois — See *Lois Inchpot.*

Lombardo, Mr. (*On/Off*) — Owner of Lombardo's Market in Junktown.

Lowell, Jefferson (*High*) — Employee of Grinchman & Hills, architecture and engineering firm Down Below.

Lumpton, Grammaw (*Mountain*) — Apple peeler on Little Potato Mountain. The Lumptons have been on the mountain for more than a hundred years.

Lumpton, Hugh (*Mountain*) — Top gun in the country club in Spudsboro. He has a "gauntly handsome face," a golfer's suntan, and ash-blond hair. He was appointed to represent Forest Beechum at his murder trial, but he didn't go to Forest's arraignment and didn't offer a single defense witness.

Lumpton, Josh (*Mountain*) — Former sheriff of Spudsboro — for twenty-four years — whom everyone calls Uncle Josh. He owns the Lumpton Transport. He's a "jolly mountain of flesh in khaki chinos" who always plays Santa at Christmas, but isn't so innocent with what he transports.

Lumpton, Reverend Perry (*Mountain*) — Minister who has the oldest church in Spudsboro, in a historic building. He is supportive of the environmentalists.

Lyke, David (*Danish*) — Co-owner with Starkweather of Junktown's largest decorating firm. He's a "good-looking man in his thirties," with "brooding eyes with heavy lids and long lashes." His snow-white hair surrounds his suntanned face, and he has a sexy voice. Koko finds him murdered in his apartment.

MacDiarmid, Kipling and Moira (*Cardinal*) — Editor of the *Lockmaster Logger*. They vacationed in the Potato Mountains and recommended them to Qwilleran.

MacGillivray, Roger (*Brahms*) — History teacher who works at the Tourist Development Association in Mooseville in the summer. His wife is Sharon Hanstable. He's "a pale young man with a very black beard and a healthy head of black hair." The MacGillivrays and the Mackintoshes are from the same clan. (*Post Office*) — He's "not comfortable with cats," but Koko wins him over. (*Glue*) — Roger quits his teaching job to cover "city hall, police, and general assignment" for the new *Moose County Something*. He has a "history teacher's nose for accurate facts, and he writes well." (*Wasn't*) — Roger covers an important story in Kennebeck: The Tuesday Afternoon Women's Club plants a tree in the village park. (*Whistle*) — Roger is assigned to cover the Lumbertown Credit Union scandal, but runs into difficulty getting people to talk to him. He says he's finally "learned how to make no news sound like news." (*Cheese*) — He's assigned an interview with Gustav Limburger about the bombing, but the old man throws a bedpan at him. (*Stars*) — Roger helps his wife, Sharon Hanstable, homeschool their children. The students receive their lessons by e-mail and take achievement tests.

MacGregor, Mr. (*Shakespeare*) — Polly's landlord in Moose County. He's a "nice old widower" who sits up waiting for Polly to drive in so he'll know she's safe. Years ago when Polly's husband was killed on his farm while fighting a barn fire, the MacGregors offered Polly the cottage rent-free.

MacMurchie, Gil (*Thief*) — A Pickax dowser. He's retired from the plumbing and hardware business, but is an active water witch. He's a "leathery-faced Scot" with red hair that is turning sandy with age.

MacWhannell, Whannell "Big Mac" and Glenda (*Wasn't*) — Couple from Pickax who go on the Bonnie Scots Tour. They are a "quiet couple, stiffly formal." He's a "tall, portly man" and she's a "tiny birdlike woman." He's a CPA, and he constantly rattles off statistics about people and places while on the Scotland tour. (*Whistle*) — He wears a "pleated all-wool kilt and full Scottish regalia" when riding on the Lumbertown Party Train's first run. He and Gordie Shaw own the MacWhannell & Shaw accounting firm. (*Sang*) — He is on the spell team for the Moneybags, sponsored by Pickax People's National Bank.

Madley, Doc and Dottie (*Underground*) — Dentist from Pickax. They go to the dunes at Mooseville on weekends.

Mad Mack (*Underground*) — Glinko's electrician in Mooseville. He's a "hulking individual with bulging biceps and no neck."

Marron, Mrs. (*Red*) — Robert Maus's housekeeper who assists him in the kitchen. She's a "sad-faced woman with dull eyes and a sallow complexion."

Martin, Charles Edward (*Wasn't*) — Bearded stranger who drives a maroon car with a Massachusetts license plate. See *Emory Goodwinter.*

Mary (*Breakfast*) — One of the owners of Vacation Helpers on Breakfast Island.

Mason, Mrs. (*On/Off*) — Old lady in the hotel room next to Qwilleran at the Medford Manor who complains when the cats yowl.

Matthew (*Post Office*) — Young waitperson at Stephanie's, the Lanspeaks' restaurant.

Maus, Robert (*On/Off*) — Attorney in the firm of Teahandle, Burris, Hansblow, Maus and Castle. He's a superb cook, especially fruitcake, and an avid collector. (*Red*) — Robert's home is the Maus Haus, meeting place of the Gourmet Club. He can tell the "right wing from the left wing of the chicken by its taste." He's a "towering, well-built man of middle age," with the "dignity of a Supreme Court justice," plus a slight stoop. (*Brahms*) — Robert sells Maus Haus and gives up his law practice to open a restaurant. (*High*) — Robert opens his classy restaurant, Roberto's, with Charlotte Roop as manager. He's an officer in SOCK, and he knows exactly how to restore the Casablanca.

McBean, Kathryn Gow (*Wasn't*) — a.k.a., Katie. Bruce Gow's sister, who lives in Edinburgh. She and Irma Hasselrich were in art school at the same time.

McBee, Boyd (*Sang*) — Farmer and brother of Rollo. His wife is a substitute teacher who writes frequent letters to the editor.

McBee, Culvert (*Sang*) — Chubby, rosy-cheeked nine-year-old son of Rollo McBee. He takes good pictures and is an excellent speller. He's decided to be a veterinarian. Culvert substitutes on the Muckers spelling team, sponsored by the Farmers' Collective.

McBee, Rollo and Dawn (*Sang*) — Moose County farmer who lives on Base Line. He's a fortyish, rugged figure. Dawn does accounting for other farmers.

McGuffey, Mrs. (*On/Off*) — Retired schoolteacher who owns a Junktown antique shop, the Piggin, Noggin and Firkin. She seems to be a "sensible sort." She taught Andrew Glanz to read, up north in Boyerville.

McIldoony, Mr. (*On/Off*) — Elderly clerk in the Medford Manor hotel Down Below where Qwilleran has a room.

Merle and wife (*Brahms*) — Owners of the FOO in Moose County. The cashier is a "heavy woman" more than a hundred pounds overweight in "snugly fitting pants." He's "tall, obese, forbidding, with one eye half-shut and the other askew," a big guy who can't talk after an industrial accident Down Below.

Merrio (*Breakfast*) — Young girl who lives at the Vacation Helpers and is a waitress in the Corsair Room at the Pear Island Hotel. She provides Derek with clues about the food poisoning incident.

Mert (*Underground*) — Moose County underground builder. He was working on a garage for the Comptons when he disappeared.

Mervyn (*Closet*) — Star linebacker of Mooseland High School, who carries in Qwilleran's equipment for "The Big Burning of 1869."

Middy, Mrs. (*Danish*) — A decorator Down Below who loves Early American interiors. She's a "dumpling of a woman" who tends to wear shapeless hats and frilly lace collars. Qwilleran learns she can change from a dumpling to a "granite boulder."

Midge (*Breakfast*) — One of the owners of Vacation Helpers on Pear Island.

Mighty Lou (*Underground*) — Underground builder in Mooseville. He has "a fortune in tools, but doesn't know which end of the nail to hit." He wears silk designer shirts and alligator loafers. When Nick and Lori are out of town, Mighty Lou takes care of the Bambas' cats, who really like him.

Mike (*On/Off*) — The grocer's son in Junktown. He helps C. C. move antiques around. He's a "nice boy," but he thinks "antique dealers are batty."

Missy (*Mountain*) — Candle-dipper in Potato Cove.

Mona (*Stars*) — Polly's sister, Desdemona, called Mona for short. She lives in Cincinnati. She is touring Ontario with Polly, whom she hasn't seen in years.

Moseley, Edith (*Breakfast*) — White-haired, retired Boston dramatic arts teacher on vacation on Pear Island with her sister. She "always projects from the diaphragm."

Moseley, Edna (*Breakfast*) — White-haired, retired science teacher from Boston, who is on vacation on Pear Island with her sister. The prettier of the two sisters, Edna wears corrective shoes and speaks with a soft voice.

Mountclemens, George Bonifield the Third (*Backwards*) — Art critic for the *Fluxion* and gourmet cook. He never goes to the office, but puts his column on tape and sends it down. He's "aloof, opinionated, and hard to get along with," living alone with a cat. There's a rumor that the cat writes the column. He has a talent for "being obnoxious when it suits his whim." Qwill finds him murdered on his own patio.

Mull, Daisy (*Post Office*) — Former housemaid at the K Mansion who painted her apartment with wild daisies and hearts. She was from Dimsdale and had a reputation for gallivanting around, staying up late, and not working. She's buried during a cave-in at the Three Pines Mine.

Mull, Della (*Post Office*) — Moose County resident and Daisy's mother. She's a forty-four-year-old woman who has a drinking problem and isn't sober very often. Della is found dead, a victim of alcohol and drugs.

Narx, Oscar (*Backwards*) — Artist of robots in Junktown. He has "square shoulders, square jaw, and high square brow." O. Narx and Scrano are one and the same.

Newton-Ffiske, Martta (*High*) — Replacement for Fran Unger on the *Daily Fluxion*.

Nibble, Jack (*Cheese*) — Cheese expert of the Sip 'n' Nibble shop in Stables Row in Pickax, along with Jerry Sip.

Nicholas, Benjamin X. (*On/Off*) — Antique dealer in Junktown who runs Bit o' Junk. He wears a Santa Claus cap or Napoleonic bicorne or silk top hat. A former actor, he likes to play Santa for the children's hospital wards. Ben buys an audience for his Shakespeare with a round of drinks at the Lion's Tale.

Nino (*Backwards*) — a.k.a., Joseph Hibber. He is an artist in Junktown. Nino is a *Thingist*, a sculptor "who makes meaningful constructions out of junk and calls them Things." His full name is Nine Oh Two Four Six Eight Three Five, because "he doesn't subscribe to the conventions of ordinary society." He plunges to his death from a scaffolding during The Happening.

Noyton, Harry (*Danish*) — The "most vocal silent partner in town" in the Midwest city. The promoter owns "the ballpark, a couple of hotels, and probably City Hall." He's aggressive, rich, and lonely. (*Shakespeare*) — Harry's a "self-made man with a talent for attracting women as well as money." He's a "reckless entrepreneur who is always searching for a new challenge or a financial gamble." While in Pickax to buy the *Picayune,* he dies in an accident with Gritty Goodwinter when their car collides with a large buck.

Noyton, Natalie (*Danish*) — Resident of the Midwest city and Harry's artistic wife, who is becoming a "middle-aged artistic sot." She's divorcing Harry because she wants to "weave rugs and things." She's "plump in all areas except for an incongruously small waist and tiny ankles." She takes her own life.

O'Dell, Mr. Pat (*Shakespeare*) — Qwilleran's houseman at the K Mansion in Pickax. He was a "school janitor for forty years and has shepherded thousands of students through adolescence." He has "silver hair, ruddy complexion, and benign expression." (*Whistle*) — Mr. O'Dell makes a good impression on Celia Robinson. (*Cheese*) — He does the floors and vacuums the furniture before the cheese-tasting at the apple barn. He and Celia Robinson seem to be hitting it off. (*Thief*) — He has Christmas dinner with Celia and her grandson. (*Sang*) — He and Celia Robinson are going into business together in Robin O'Dell Catering. They're talking about getting married. He's a pinch-speller.

Ogilvie, Alice (*Stars*) — Handspinner whose husband owns the sheep ranch on Sandpit Road. She sells her yarn to weavers and knitters. She's a "demure pioneer woman" on the parade float, but actually has a "vigorous voice and outgoing personality." Barb is her daughter.

Ogilvie, Barbara (*Stars*) — Handspinner and teacher of knitting who runs a knitting day camp for kids. She prefers to be called Barb. She, Derek and Deputy Greenleaf were in high school together. Derek says she prefers older men. She has long, straight blond hair and sultry "sheep's eyes" and is very talented. While living in Florida, she worked on a crew that chased hot air balloons. When she found out the older man she was dating was married, she came home to Moose County.

Ogilvie, Mitch (*Ghosts*) — Night desk clerk at the New Pickax Motel and a member of the Historical Society. He's a big good-looking, blond, young man who lives over the Pickax drugstore. Mitch applies for the job of manager at the Good-winter Farmhouse Museum. (*Cheese*) — Mitch is now a goat farmer with a beard and grubby denims. Kristi Waffle hired him to make improvements in the house and farm. He's the cheese-maker, having taken a course in Wisconsin. (*Thief*) — He and Kristi are thinking about getting married. Once fastidiously groomed, he now looks bucolic in a rough beard and clothing suitable for goat farming.

O'Hare, Steve W. (*Cardinal*) — Trainer at Amberton's horse farm in Lockmaster. He has a red beard and wears a green plaid coat. He attaches himself to Polly at the Corcoran wedding. He's known as a womanizer, and he likes his liquor. Steve got into trouble Down Below for doping racehorses.

Olson, Grandma (*Wasn't*) — Jennifer's grandmother, who waves her program and tells everyone her granddaughter is in the play.

Olson, Jennifer (*Wasn't*) — Actress who is playing Lady Macduff in *Macbeth,* but is also understudy for Melinda Good-winter as Lady Macbeth, "just in case." (*Whistle*) — Jennifer Olson plays Hermia in *A Midsummer Night's Dream.* (*Cheese*) — She treats her celebrity auction "buyer" (her father) to a feast and rock concert at the Hot Spot.

Onoosh — See *Onoosh Dolmathakia.*

Ooterhans, Fred (*Whistle*) — Resident of Moose County. A retired fireman who worked with Ozzie Penn, he lives in the Railroad Retirement Center.

Ophelia (*Stars*) — One of Polly Duncan's sisters.

Orax, Bob (*Danish*) — A decorator with "an oval aristocratic face with elevated eyebrows." He has a little shop on River Street, specializing in PLanned UGliness (PLUG).

Otto (*Mountain*) — Potter in Potato Cove. He's a soft-spoken man who speaks in a monotone.

Pam (*Shakespeare*) — Receptionist at Dr. Zoller's dental clinic in Pickax. She has "dazzlingly capped teeth."

Paolo (*Danish*) — Mexican houseboy for the Taits in the Midwest city. He's "a nice kid—quiet and shy—and anxious to help."

Parrott, Pete (*Glue*) — Paperhanger from Brrr, the "best in the county." He's a "burly young man in white coveralls and white visored cap, with thick blond hair bushing out beneath it." After Belle Fitch is murdered, Pete says she was pregnant with his kid.

Patch, Russell (*On/Off*) — Refinisher in Junktown. He wears only white clothes. A blond fellow on crutches, he once worked for Andy Glanz, but they parted company and he opened his own shop.

Peabody, Ann (*On/Off*) — Ninety-year-old woman who still runs an antique shop, Ann's 'Tiques, in Junktown. She's a "little old white-haired woman" who resembles "a dandelion gone to seed." She's also virtually deaf.

Peel, Sabrina (*Mountain*) — Co-owner of Peel & Poole De-sign Studio in Spudsboro. She dresses in smart suits and has the "same suave buoyancy and the same reddish blond hair" as Fran Brodie. Sabrina is married to Spencer Poole.

Penn, Letitia — See *Letitia Trevelyan.*

Penn, Ozzie (*Whistle*) — Moose County resident and re-tired SC & L hoghead (engineer) after fifty years. Ozzie lives in the Railroad Retirement Center in Sawdust City. He's the engineer for the Lumbertown Party Train's first run. Ozzie hasn't seen his daughter, Florrie, since she married Floyd Tre-velyan, but is reunited with Florrie and meets his granddaugh-ter, Letitia. He buys the Party Train from Florrie, then goes out whittlin'.

Penney, Yates and Kate (*Mountain*) — Owners of the Half-Baked Bakery at Potato Cove.

Pennimans (*Danish*) — Wealthy residents of Muggy Swamp who own the *Morning Rampage.* (*High*) — The Penni-mans are big in newspapers, radio, and television. Penniman is spelled P-O-W-E-R.

Penniman, Basil and Bayley (*Red*) — Brothers and mem-bers of the Civic Arts Commission in the Midwest city. The paunchy brothers are called "Tweedledum and Tweedledee" by "irreverent citizens." Their money founded the *Morning Rampage,* endowed the art school, and financed the city park system.

Percy — See *Harold Bates.*

Pete (*Closet*) — Assistant to Betty and Claude at the Park of Pink Sunsets in Florida. He takes over whenever Betty and Claude go out of town. He's "handy with tools and electricity and all that."

Peters, Tony (*Shakespeare*) — Chef at Old Stone Mill restaurant in Pickax. "Tall, blond, and very good looking," he's dating Hixie Rice. He invents a line of frozen gourmet dinners for pets, "Fabulous Frozen Foods for Fussy Felines." He's also writing a cookbook. His real name is Antoine Delapierre, a French Canadian who is living in the states illegally. He dies when his car is stuck in a snowdrift.

Phlogg, Captain (*Brahms*) — Owner of the Captain's Mess antique and junk shop in Moose County. He's an "old man with a stubby beard and well-worn captain's cap" who smokes a carved pipe. (*Glue*) — He's a "crooked little man" who runs a "crooked little shop" in Mooseville. (*Underground*) — He's "inattentive, evasive, and rude," and he sells junk and fakes. He dies in his shop.

Pickett, Franklin (*Cheese*) — Owner of Franklin's Flowers in downtown Pickax. He's killed because he was a witness to the man who set off the bomb in the New Pickax Hotel.

Plensdorf, Sarah (*Cheese*) — Office manager of the *Moose County Something.* She's a small woman with "steel-gray hair and thick glasses, who had never married." A tasteful dresser who speaks in a cultivated voice, she crochets catnip toys for the Siamese. Sarah volunteers at the animal shelter every Saturday, where she washes dogs. Sarah "buys" Qwilleran at the celebrity auction. (*Thief*) — Sarah gives Qwilleran a leather-bound copy of *The Old Wives' Tale* by Arnold Bennett. She sends an anonymous check to replace the money that was stolen from the clubhouse. (*Sang*) — Sarah is "well-educated but rather prim." She's a fan of Phoebe Sloan.

Plumb, Adelaide St. John (*High*) — Seventy-five-year-old owner of the Casablanca. Her father was Harrison Wills Plumb, who built the Casablanca in 1901. She never leaves her apartment on the twelfth floor. She carries her head "cocked gra-

ciously to one side" and speaks in "a breathy little-girl voice."
Brown hair is "plastered flat against her head in uniform
waves." She has penciled eyebrows and a red Cupid's-bow
mouth. Her father's pet name for her was Zizou.

Poole, Billy (*Whistle*) — Moose County resident, an old retired brakeman who worked with Ozzie Penn. He now lives in
the Railroad Retirement Center.

Poole, Spencer (*Mountain*) — Partner with Sabrina Peel
in Peel & Poole Design Studio in Spudsboro. He's "an older
man and a wonderful person" who is married to Sabrina.

Popopopoulos, Papa (*On/Off*) — Owner of the Fruit, Cigars, Work Gloves and Sundries, a small neighborhood store
in Junktown. He's a lonely old fellow who chews on his tobacco-
stained moustache of great flamboyance.

Prantz, Hollis (*On/Off*) — Antique dealer in Junktown,
whose shop is Tech-Tiques. He's a thin, "ordinary-looking man
in an ordinary-looking gray car coat." He has a theory about
"artificially accelerated antiquity."

Pratt, Gary (*Glue*) — Owner of the bar at the Hotel Booze.
Gary's a "hefty man with a sailor's tan, an unruly head of black
hair, and a bushy black beard." He has a surprisingly high-
pitched voice. He says he is descended from Pratt the Pirate
who operated in the Great Lakes in the 1800s until he was
hanged. (*Wasn't*) — The proprietor with his "shaggy hair and
beard" resembles the mounted black bear at the entrance.
He's into dog sledding. (*Closet*) — His "muscular hulk and
lumbering gait and shaggy black hairiness explain the name of
his restaurant," the Black Bear Café. (*Sang*) — Gary's shaggy
beard has been clipped and his uncut hair has been tamed.
He's getting married to a lady who owns the Harborside Marina. (*Stars*) — His "shaggy hairiness and shambling gait"

make you wonder if the Black Bear Café were named for him or the mounted black bear.

Prelligate, Dr. (*Whistle*) — New president of the new Moose County Community College. He has a solid academic background, a "congenial personality," and "ingratiating Southern charm." (*Stars*) — Dr. Prelligate and Fran Brodie have been seeing a lot of each other.

Ramsbottom, Chester (*Sang*) — Moose County commissioner and owner of Chet's Bar and Barbecue restaurant in Kennebeck. He's a "chesty man with thinning hair and an air of authority." His father was a bootlegger during Prohibition. The ownership of Northern Land Improvement is in the name of his wife, Margaret.

Randy (*Sang*) — Young man who works for Rollo McBee.

Rasmus, Ross (*High*) — Young artist who did the mushroom paintings in Qwilleran's apartment at the Casablanca. He was a nice, quiet, serious twenty-five-year-old man. Police believe he murdered Dianne Bessinger. They found a confession, then his own body on the parking lot, evidently a suicide.

Rice, Hixie (*Red*) — Copywriter at an agency that handles food accounts. She writes menus for third-rate restaurants. She's "young, plump, loud, and has long eyelashes." She's "rabid for chocolate." She's a husband hunter who likes to throw around French phrases. (*Shakespeare*) — A "member of a select gourmet group," Hixie loves to eat. She's dating a chef and taking courses in restaurant management. She and the chef move to Pickax to work at the Old Stone Mill. Hixie is "deliriously happy" since she's found a wonderful man. (*Glue*) — She becomes the advertising manager of the new Moose County newspaper. Hixie has given up "married men, cigarettes, and high heels," but she hasn't given up men, and goes out with Don Exbridge, Gary Pratt, and Qwilleran. (*Cardinal*) — Hixie is the volunteer publicist for the Theatre Club. She has "a long history of getting locked in restrooms, setting her hair on fire, picking the wrong men, and more." (*Closet*) — She produces and directs *The Big Burning of 1869*. Arch promotes her to vice president in charge of advertising and promotion. (*Thief*) — Hixie writes for Indian Village's monthly newsletter, *The Other Village Voice*. Hixie's brilliant idea is the Moose County Ice Festival, that melted into disaster. (*Sang*) — Hixie's latest brilliant idea is to have an adult spelling bee to benefit Moose County's literacy program. (*Stars*) —Hixie is always "recklessly vivacious." She enthusiastically approves of Qwilleran's plan to hold an annual Mark Twain celebration in Pickax.

Riggs, Mr. and Mrs. Ben H. (*Backwards*) — An art couple Down Below. Riggs is a sculptor who does "stringy, emaciated things that are shown at the Lambreth Gallery." He works in clay and bronze and teaches art at Penniman School of Fine Art.

Riker, Arch (*Backwards*) — Feature editor of the *Flux*. Arch and Qwill worked together in Chicago, years ago, but Arch is plumper and balder now. (*On/Off*) — When Qwilleran suggests a feature on Christmas in Junktown, Riker's face has "the composure of a seasoned deskman, registering no surprise, no enthusiasm, no rejection." (*Red*) — Arch has the "comfortably upholstered contours" of a newspaper deskman. He and Rosie used to double-date with Qwilleran and Joy while the two men were both cub reporters in Chicago. (*Post Office*) — Arch is a "paunchy man with thinning hair and a ruddy face" who has been "unduly morose" because Rosie is divorcing him. Arch tells Qwill to buy the *Picayune* newspaper so he can run it for him. (*Shakespeare*) — Arch retires from the *Daily*

Fluxion, and Qwill hosts a dinner at the Press Club to which he invites the entire staff of the newspaper. (*Glue*) — Arch comes up from Down Below to run Moose County's newest newspaper, the *Moose County Something.* Arch asks Amanda Goodwinter to marry him, and she says yes. (*Underground*) — Arch and Amanda break off their engagement. He says that she's "the most cantankerous, opinionated, obstinate, unpredictable woman he's ever met." (*High*) — Arch goes Down Below to feed the cats and claim Qwilleran's body at the morgue, after Moose County hears that Qwilleran has died in a car accident. (*Cardinal*) — As publisher of the *Moose County Something,* Arch has "a large carpeted office with a desk the size of a Ping-Pong table" and draperies on the windows. (*Wasn't*) — Arch decides that Mildred Hanstable is more his type. (*Closet*) — He and Mildred marry on Christmas Eve. (*Whistle*) — Since he and Mildred married, he says, "Every day in my life is Christmas since we took the plunge." (*Sang*) — If Arch could be any artist who ever lived, he'd be Charles Schulz. (*Stars*) — Arch and Mildred have moved to their beach house, called Sunny Daze, in Mooseville. His well-fed silhouette indicates that he's happy and relaxed. In his younger days, his nickname was Tubby. Once he became sick after eating erasers. Arch and Qwill have a "lifetime license to be rude to each other." He's learning to knit socks.

Riker, Mildred (*Breakfast*) — Mildred and Arch invite Qwill and Polly to their remodeled beach house for chocolate cake and coffee. The handmade quilts have been removed from the walls, and the interior is light and airy. (*Cheese*) — She recently retired from teaching fine and domestic arts in the public schools. (*Sang*) — Mildred is a "paragon of pleasing plumpness." (*Stars*) — Mildred "single-handedly dragged the Fourth of July parade from the pits and launched it to the stars!" She has "a heart of gold and the patience of a saint."

Mildred reads palms, handwriting, and tarot cards. See *Mildred Hanstable.*

Riker, Pop (*Stars*) — Arch's father, "as good a father as [Qwilleran] had ever known."

Riker, Rosie (*On/Off*) — Arch Riker's matronly first wife. Rosie is a junker who enjoys looking for antiques in Junktown. (*Post Office*) — She divorces Arch and buys Iris Cobb's antique shop, the Junkery, where she lives over the store. Rosie "took a few college courses and got in with a young crowd," including a young lover. (*Underground*) — Rosie has remarried, to a man she has to support.

Robinson, Celia (*Closet*) — Friend and next-door neighbor of Euphonia Gage at the Park of Pink Sunsets retirement center in Florida, originally from Illinois. She likes to laugh merrily and has a nice singing voice. Qwill enlists her as an "undercover agent" to discover what's really happening at the Park of Pink Sunsets. She decides to leave Florida because there are too many old people, and go back to Illinois where she can be closer to her grandson. (*Whistle*) — Celia sends Kabibbles, a snack food, to Qwilleran, and the cats love it. She also sends brownies. Qwilleran invites her to occupy the carriage-house apartment that he has vacated. She calls Qwilleran "Chief" because she was an "undercover agent" for him in Florida. Her next assignment is as a part-time worker and companion for Mrs. Trevelyan. (*Cheese*) — Celia supplies Qwilleran (and the cats) with home-cooked dishes for his freezer. She's probably the only person in Moose County who can keep a secret. Celia and Pat O'Dell seem to be hitting it off. (*Thief*) — Celia takes a temporary position at the Indian Village clubhouse so she can investigate on behalf of Qwilleran. (*Sang*) — At seventy, Celia has the "gray hair of age," but "the laughter of youth." She and Pat O'Dell are partners in a new business, Robin O'Dell Catering. They are talking about getting married.

Robinson, Clayton (*Closet*) — Grandson of Celia Robinson, just turned thirteen. He's "a very bright boy with a crazy sense of humor" who reads a lot. In Florida, he interviews Mr. Crocus and obtains information that helps solve the mystery of Mrs. Gage's death. (*Thief*) — Celia's fourteen-year-old nephew comes to visit her for Christmas and ends up taking pictures for Qwilleran during an interview with a dowser. He's a "healthy farm-bred youth with an intelligent face, freshly cut hair," and a deep voice.

Roop, Charlotte (*Red*) — Manager of a Heavenly Hash House in the Midwest city. She's a "small sprightly woman" with white hair "like spun sugar" and "an abundance of nondescript costume jewelry." She loves crossword puzzles and "disapproves of *everything*." (*High*) — Charlotte is now manager of Robert Maus's classy restaurant. Gone is the "straitlaced, spinsterish woman with the scowl and tightly pursed lips." Charlotte lives at the Casablanca and is serious about Raymond Dunwoody.

Rupert (*High*) — Custodian of the Casablanca in the Midwest city. He wears a red golf hat on his sandy hair. He's "a thin, wiry man of middle age, all elbows and knees and bony shoulders," with a prisonlike pallor.

Sam, Old (*Brahms*) — Gravedigger in Moose County. He's "over eighty and puts away a pint of whiskey every day except Sunday." (*Underground*) — He's been "digging graves with a shovel for sixty years."

Sarah (*Breakfast*) — Polly's college roommate, a residential architect who invites Polly to visit her in Oregon.

Scott, Bruce (*Shakespeare*) — a.k.a., Scottie. Owner of Scottie's Men's Store. He speaks with a brogue when he needs to. A big, ungainly man with a craggy face, he's the chief of the volunteer fire department. (*Cardinal*) — Scottie tells Qwilleran he "canna remember any dead bodies before you moved to town."

Scotten, Aubrey (*Cheese*) — Large Moose County man who takes care of Gustav Limburger. He has four brothers who run Scotten Fisheries. Aubrey sells honey from his honeybees. He's also maintenance engineer at the new Cold Turkey Farm, hired because he's a genius at fixing things.

Scotten, Mrs. (*Cheese*) — Aubrey's mother. She lives on the Scotten farm on Sandpit Road and grows flowers to sell. She's a tall woman with a gaunt, weathered face.

Scotten, Phil (*Stars*) — One of the owners of Scotten Fisheries. His dog is a black Labrador named Einstein.

Scrano (*Backwards*) — An artist Down Below. He's one of the "foremost contemporary artists," an Italian recluse who is "hooked on triangles." Scrano is actually nonexistent, part of an art fraud scheme.

Shaw, Gordie (*Whistle*) — Partner in MacWhannell & Shaw accounting firm. The Shaws have Mackintosh connections.

Shawn (*Cardinal*) — Moose County resident and installer for Fran Brodie. He has "more brains than brawn," but is "good at what he does."

Shelley (*Breakfast*) — One of the owners of Vacation Helpers on Breakfast Island.

Sigmund (*Cheese*) — Chef at the Old Stone Mill restaurant in Pickax.

Simms, Russell (*Underground*) — "Painfully thin young woman" who's spending the summer in the Dunfield house in Mooseville. She likes to read and walk on the beach. She "acts like a sleepwalker" and never really looks at anyone who's speaking to her. She dresses like she is in 1935.

Sims, Donna (*Closet*) — Pastor of Brrr Community Church who officiates at Arch and Mildred's wedding.

Sip, Jerry (*Cheese*) — Owner of Sip 'n' Nibble shop in Stables Row in Pickax, along with Jack Nibble. He knows everything about wine.

Sisler, Mae (*Backwards*) — Art reporter for the other newspaper Down Below (*Morning Rampage*). She avoids controversy by gushing about everything.

Skumble, Paul (*Sang*) — Lockmaster artist. He has a "bifurcated beard" and twinkling eyes in a face "that crinkled easily." Qwilleran commissions him to paint a portrait of Polly.

Sloan, Phoebe (*Sang*) — Moose County artist who paints butterflies. She's a diminutive young woman with innocent large brown eyes. Her boyfriend, Jake Westrup, calls her Monkey. She attended Lockmaster Academy. Her parents, Mary and Orville, own the drugstore and live in West Middle Hummock. She's on the spelling team for the Daubers, sponsored by the Art Center.

Small, Ignatius K. (*Underground*) — a.k.a., Iggy and Old Horse-face. A carpenter. He's a skilled craftsman, but he's inclined to be lazy. He's a very skinny guy with "a nicotine habit that won't stop," and he "does his share of boozing." He has a "peculiar speech pattern, starting almost inaudibly and ending" IN A SHOUT. Koko finds his body buried under Qwilleran's cabin.

Smfska, Ilya (*Post Office*) — Lawyer in Washington, rumored to be Alexander Goodwinter's fiancée.

Smith, Eddington (*Glue*) — Owner of Edd's Editions, a bookstore in Pickax. He's a "small, thin man with gray hair and gray complexion and nondescript gray clothing." He's never been to a birthday party before, not even his own. His great-grandfather founded Smith's Folly in 1856. (*High*) — He amazes his customers by having a quotation for every occasion. (*Cardinal*) — Edd is playing Cardinal Campeius in *Henry VIII*. He doesn't project, so no one can hear him. He helps the cats catch a crook.

Smith, John (*Backwards*) — Chief curator of the museum Down Below. He's a "handsome dark-haired man with a sallow skin" and eyes that are "green like jade." (*Red*) — Jack is now the *Fluxion*'s art critic.

Snyder, Martha V. (*Sang*) — See *Mrs. Fish-eye*.

Somers, Dwight (*Wasn't*) — New employee with XYZ Enterprises and director of the Theatre Club, recently arrived from Iowa. (*Breakfast*) — Dwight is director of community services for XYZ Enterprises until he leaves because of problems with the Pear Island Resort. (*Whistle*) — Dwight has a new job and a clean-shaven face. He's opening a Pickax branch for a public relations firm in Lockmaster and dating Hixie Rice. After the credit union closes, he lines up Moose County Community College as a client, along with a project with the K Foundation. (*Stars*) — Dwight recommends a "less somber color and a livelier logo" for Bushy's photography business.

Sorrel, Max (*Red*) — Owner of The Golden Lamb Chop. He's a "bald brute with a facile smile," a confirmed bachelor. He has a brooding expression that changes to a "dazzling smile" whenever a woman glances his way. (*Brahms*) — Max buys out Rosemary Whiting's interest in her health-food store and opens a natural food restaurant in Toronto.

Spence, Hettie (*Shakespeare*) — One of the Old Timers in Pickax, eighty-six next month. She's a "frail woman dependent upon a walker." She speaks "with a fluttering of eyelids, hands, and shoulders." She wrote obituaries for the *Picayune* before her arthritis got too bad.

Spencer, Marv (*Cardinal*) — Soft-drink distributor in Moose County. He was a witness to Dave Landrum's threats against Hilary VanBrook.

Spencer, Mathilda (*On/Off*) — Ghost in the Cobbs' house in Junktown, a blind woman who died when she fell down the stairs. She walks through doors and moves Mrs. Cobb's eyeglasses and other small items.

Spencer, William Towne (*On/Off*) — A famous abolitionist who built the Cobb mansion in 1855. His sister was Mathilda.

Spooner, Tiny (*On/Off*) — Photographer for the *Fluxion* with a Ph.D. in mathematics. He's a "clumsy oaf," six-feet-three and weighs close to four hundred pounds.

Sprott, Claude — See *Claude*.

Stacy, Mr. and Mrs. Wayne (*Stars*) — Co-owners of the Northern Lights Hotel in Mooseville. Her job is to keep the guests happy; his is to solve problems. She's so compassionate that she would rather lose customers than fire her old cook before his retirement. Wayne is president of the Chamber of Commerce.

Stanley (*On/Off*) — Russell Patch's roommate in Junktown. He's a hairdresser at Skyline Towers where all those "rich widows and kept women live." He wears a "diamond of spectacular brilliance."

Starkweather, George (*Danish*) — Co-owner with Lyke of the Midwest city's largest decorating firm. He has gray hair, "a bland appearance and a bland manner," tending toward laconic.

Starkweather, Mrs. (*Danish*) — Wife of Stark, as she calls him. She's a lovely wife who's getting to be "a middle-aged sot." There is a "frantic gaiety in her aging face," and her costume is a "desperate shade of pink."

Stebbins, Sally (*Glue*) — New server at the Old Stone Mill restaurant in Moose County. She's "pretty nervous, and she's kinda slow," and she stutters. Sally plans to go to art school somewhere Down Below.

Stendhup, George (*Cheese*) — Resident of Sawdust City. He wins first prize in the turnip category of the Pasty Bake-off.

Stucker, Fiona (*Cardinal*) — Lady from Lockmaster who plays Katharine in *Henry VIII*. She plays Queen Katharine "with regal poise and forceful emotion." Off-stage, she's "small and mousy," and has a limp handshake and a shy smile. She grew up with an alcoholic mother and an absent father, and her husband deserted her right after her son, Robin, was born. She makes a living by housekeeping. Before VanBrook moved to Pickax, she was his live-in housekeeper.

Stucker, Robin (*Cardinal*) — Seventeen-year-old son of Fiona. He dropped out of school, and his only interest is horses. He wins a race while riding Son of Cardinal in an event that permits amateurs. Later he's seriously injured in a riding accident.

Sugbury, Wilfred (*Cheese*) — Secretary to Arch Riker. He's a "thin, wiry, sober-faced young man, intensely serious about his job." He wins the seventy-mile Labor Day Bike Race and signs up for the Wheels for Meals bike-a-thon. (*Thief*) — Wilfred is a "quiet, hardworking young man" who takes origami at the community college.

Susie (*Mountain*) — Secretary for Lumpton Transport in Spudsboro.

Tait, George Verning (*Danish*) — Wealthy man living quietly in a "pseudocastle" in the exclusive Muggy Swamp area and owner of an exquisite jade collection. A man of about fifty, his face has a "scrubbed pink gleam." He has a "heavy growth of hair on his arms, yet a complete absence of hair on his head." He speaks with "religious fervor" about his jade collection.

Tait, Signe (*Danish*) — a.k.a., Siggy. George's wife. She's "unwell," a "thin, sharp-featured woman" in a wheelchair. Her husband finds her dead of a heart attack in her bedroom.

Targ, Ylana (*High*) — Art reporter for the *Fluxion* who writes about Dianne Bessinger's murder.

Terry (*Post Office*) — Dimsdale dairy farmer. He's in a wheelchair because of a tractor rollover a few years ago. The Dimsdale Diner's customers put up a ramp for him when he comes for coffee.

Thelma (*Post Office*) — Waitress at the Black Bear Café at Hotel Booze in Brrr. She's a "homey-looking woman in a faded housedress." She's known as "Thumbprint Thelma" because the hamburger is so big that she serves it "with her thumb on top of the bun to hold it all together." (*Glue*) — Thelma has retired.

Thiggamon, Matt (*High*) — New police reporter for the *Fluxion* in the Midwest city. He wants to do a story on Koko and his sleuthing.

Thorvaldson, Mr. and Mrs. Victor (*Danish*) — Signe Tait's parents of Aarhus, Denmark.

Tibbitt, Homer (*Shakespeare*) — Retired school principal. Homer is ninety-three and a "dear old man." A mousehole plugger, he offers his services to Qwilleran for the K Mansion. He started teaching seventy years ago and was principal of Pickax Upper School when he retired. He walks "vigorously with arms and legs flailing in awkward coordination." Homer moved back to Pickax because he was born there and because a retired Lockmaster English teacher was after him. (*Glue*) — Homer is the "official historian for the *Something*." (*Ghosts*) — Homer rides herd on the maintenance staff at the Goodwinter Farmhouse Museum. He's dating Rhoda Finney, who's been chasing him for years. He and Rhoda get married while on a trip to Lockmaster. (*Closet*) — He's the official historian for the county. He pushes the even more elderly Adam Dingleberry's wheelchair. Because of his career as a teacher and principal, he knows everyone in two counties. (*Whistle*) — Homer is always in the library, "pursuing some esoteric research project." His current topic is a paper on Moose County mines, 1850 to 1915. His thermos of decaf always has a shot of brandy in it. He grew up outside of Little Hope, near the tracks. (*Cheese*) — Homer is researching the Goodwinter clan. (*Thief*) — Homer contributes the first story for Qwilleran's tape-recorded book, the story of the Dimsdale Jinx. (Read about Homer and Rhoda in "The Mad Museum Mouser" in *The Cat Who Had 14 Tales*.)

Tibbitt, Rhoda (*Closet*) — Rhoda is from Lockmaster. (*Thief*) — Her responsibilities to Homer are "to find his glasses, watch his diet, and drive the car." (Read about Rhoda in "The Mad Museum Mouser" in *The Cat Who Had 14 Tales*.) See *Rhoda Finney*.

Todd, Jerome (*High*) — Partner in the Bessinger-Todd Art Gallery. He's from Des Moines, a "tall, distinguished-looking man." He and Dianne were partners for eighteen years and were married for several years.

Toddwhistle, Wally (*Glue*) — Taxidermist in Pickax, the best around. He always looks "hollow-eyed and undernourished, but he was a nice kid—and talented." He builds sets for the Theatre Club out of orange crates, bailing wire, and glue.

Toddwhistle, Mrs. (*Glue*) — Mother of Wally. She's "short, chunky, and aggressively pleasant." She used to work for the Fitch family. (*Wasn't*) — She makes costumes for the Theatre Club.

Tom (*Brahms*) — Aunt Fanny's gardener. He's a "jewel," a "simple soul but dependable, a competent handyman and careful driver." His age is hard to guess. His pale blue eyes wear "an expression of serene wonder." He speaks in a "gentle, musical voice," with a "singsong inflection." He knows how to "repair everything under the sun." Qwill discovers that he's an ex-convict who had been paroled. He takes his own life.

Toms, Anna Marie (*Cheese*) — Lenny Inchpot's girlfriend who worked as a page in the library during high school. She's enrolled at the nursing program at MCCC and works part-time at the New Pickax Hotel. She is killed with a bomb meant for Onoosh. She and Lenny were childhood sweethearts who were going to be married.

Toodle, Grandma (*Cheese*) — Mrs. Toodle runs the business with the assistance of her family. (*Sang*) — She helps Qwilleran select fruit and vegetables for Polly at Toodle's Market.

Toodle, Mrs. (*Post Office*) — "Plump, white haired, smiling" woman who takes care of Qwill in the Pickax Hospital.

Treacle, Bill (*Mountain*) — Manager of the market at Five Points in Spudsboro. He's "briskly managerial—a smiling, rosy-cheeked, well-scrubbed, wholesome type." He used to work for J. J. Hawkinfield at the *Gazette*.

Trevelyan, Birch (*Post Office*) — a.k.a., Birch Tree. Carpenter and part owner of the Dimsdale Diner in Moose County. He's an "excellent workman," but he would rather go fishing than work. He bleats like a sheep. He rides a flashy black motorcycle and has a lavishly outfitted forty-foot boat. He apparently dazzles Mrs. Cobb with his "macho glamour."

Trevelyan, Edward Penn (*Whistle*) — Son of Floyd and a builder in Moose County. He's a "hairy Welshman" with "a full beard and a mop of black hair, and his grammar is atrocious." He was always in trouble in high school, alcohol being his chief problem. He dies after a tractor accident.

Trevelyan, Florrie (*Whistle*) — A frail woman in an electric wheelchair, wife of Floyd. Her voice is thin and whiny. Her wedding took place in the cab of a steam locomotive. Her face and figure are "ravaged by some kind of disease." There's a report of a doctor in Switzerland with a cure, and she and Letitia make plans to go there after receiving money from the sale of the Lumbertown Party Train.

Trevelyan, Floyd (*Whistle*) — President of the Lumbertown Credit Union in Sawdust City. Floyd's head is rimmed with hair that's black and bushy. He started out as a carpenter and developed the largest construction firm in the county, which he sold to XYZ Enterprises, then opened the Lumbertown Credit Union. He has a real steam locomotive that he has refurbished for charter excursions, the Lumbertown Party Train. Floyd disappears after the state banking commission padlocks the credit union, pending an audit. His body is found under the foundation of Polly's new house.

Trevelyan, Letitia (*Whistle*) — a.k.a., Tish. Daughter of Floyd Trevelyan. Her mother calls her Lettie, which she detests. She also calls herself Letitia Penn, which is her mother's maiden name. She's a "plain young woman of serious mien," in her early twenties. She's a would-be writer who follows Qwill's advice about writing.

Trilby (*Wasn't*) — Young waitress at the Palomino Paddock who has "the breezy self-confidence of a young woman who keeps her own horse, wins ribbons, and looks terrific in a riding habit." Vicki Bushland is her aunt.

Trotter, Steve (*Post Office*) — Painter in Pickax. He drinks diet cola and has the "wholesome look of a Moose County native." He's been hired to paint the carriage house apartment. He's extremely slow, but leaves "no laps, no sags, no drips, no pimples." His wife, Tiffany, is shot to death.

Trotter, Tiffany (*Post Office*) — Applicant for housekeeper at the K Mansion and wife of Steve. She's a "rosy-cheeked, clear-eyed young woman in jeans and T-shirt, obviously strong and healthy." The twenty-two-year-old farmer's daughter has a part-time job as a cow-sitter. It's reported that Tiffany is killed when she falls from a tractor on a farm owned by her father, Terence Kilcally, but she's killed by a gunshot wound.

Trupp, Joanna (*Underground*) — a.k.a., Little Joe. Plumber in Moose County. She drives a "rusty, unmarked vehicle."

She's a "husky young woman with mousy hair stuffed into a feed cap," and has a "large, flat face and dull gray eyes." She likes animals and rescues those who are injured or ill, keeping them in "boxlike structures built of chickenwire and scrap lumber." Qwilleran uncovers her disturbing personality.

Trupp, Joe (*Underground*) — a.k.a., Big Joe. Father of Joanna. He's a forty-three-year-old carpenter who is killed when the tailgate of a dump truck falls on him.

Tuttle, Jessica (*High*) — Manager of the Casablanca, called Madame Defarge by Qwilleran. She's a large, powerful-looking woman with a broad smile on her ebony face. She has a stern and forbidding eye, and she tolerates no nonsense from the residents or resident cats.

Uncle Waldo (*Backwards*) — A retired butcher in the Midwest city who began painting animals when he was sixty-nine. After severe criticism by an art critic, Uncle Waldo is so upset that he stops painting his "very charming primitives" until Qwill writes a feature article that rekindles people's interest.

Unger, Fran (*Danish*) — Women's editor of the *Daily Fluxion* who wears a hat of zebra fur and gives Qwill a "prolonged friendly stare" that embarrasses him. She has a "syrupy charm" that Qwill does not trust.

Urbank, Leo and Sue (*Underground*) — He's a "retired chemist and a golf nut and a bore" who flaunts "his academic degrees, professional connections, and club affiliations."

Utley, Grace Chisholm (*Wasn't*) — Rich widow who lives with her unmarried sister Zella Chisholm on Goodwinter Boulevard in Pickax. They have 1,862 teddy bears. She's a "short, stocky woman wearing a dazzling array of jewelry." They move to Minneapolis.

Valdez (*High*) — Short man who lives in the Casablanca. He often wears a yellow satin jacket with his name on the back.

VanBrook, Hilary (*Cardinal*) — Principal of Pickax High School and director of *Henry VIII*. VanBrook used to be principal of Lockmaster High School. He has "an abrasive personality and unbearable conceit," but he has a habit of "being eminently successful at everything." He casts himself as Cardinal Wolsey in *Henry VIII*. VanBrook is found in his car in Qwilleran's orchard, killed by a shot to the head. Qwilleran discovers that VanBrook's credentials were faked, and his real name was William Smurple.

Vance (*Mountain*) — Owner of Vance the Village Smith shop in Potato Cove. He's a "sinewy young man with full beard and pigtail." He wears a "leather apron and a soiled tee with the sleeves cut out."

Van Roop, Janelle (*Stars*) — Soft-spoken young lady who works at the Safe Harbor Residence. She has a sweet smile and auburn hair that reaches her shoulders. She's an MCCC student in health care and gets credits for community service at the Residence.

Van Roop, Mr. and Mrs. (*Stars*) — Owners of The Little Frame House beach house and a picture framing shop in Lockmaster. Janelle is their niece.

Vee Jay (*Mountain*) — Waiter at the country club in Spudsboro.

Verna (*Danish*) — Boulanger's niece. She's a "dark-skinned young woman of rare beauty" with a sinuous walk.

Vicki (*Post Office*) — Young hostperson at Stephanie's, the Lanspeaks' restaurant.

Vitello, William (*On/Off*) — Houseboy for Robert Maus. (*Red*) — He's a slender young man with "impudent eyes and ridiculous sideburns, long and curly" and "nosy but likable." Qwilleran thinks he has a "healthy curiosity—a virtue, from a newsman's point of view." William doesn't want to be an artist; he'd really like to be a private operator. William disappears one night and his body is discovered in the pottery.

Vitello's girlfriend (*Red*) — William's girlfriend. She's a "serious young girl" who wears "serious glasses and unflattering clothes." She and William plan to be married.

Waffle, Brent (*Ghosts*) — Kristi's ex-husband, a guy from Purple Point. He's a snob and a loafer with a large ego. He was popular with the girls and probably thought Kristi had Fugtree money. When they moved Down Below, he started doing drugs and fell apart. Brent walks away from a minimum-security camp near Lockmaster, then sabotages Kristi's farm by killing all her female goats with poison. He's found murdered in a barn.

Waffle, Kristi Fugtree (*Ghosts*) — She lives on Black Creek Lane at the Fugtree farm in Moose County. She's about thirty, with a "designer figure" but not designer coveralls or feed cap. Her eyes are "heavy with sorrow, or regret, or worry." She raises goats and produces goat cheese. She lives in a shabby house that she inherited from her mother. Kristi is "a talented girl, but flighty," who in high school "hopped from one great idea to another." (*Thief*) — She and Mitch Ogilvie are thinking about getting married. They run the Split Rail Farm and produce cheese.

Ward, Clara Wimsey (*Underground*) — Resident of Moose County. She's eighty-two and lives in the Senior Care Facility in Pickax.

Wesley (*Mountain*) — Woodcrafter at Potato Cove who sells Qwilleran a large bowl made of cherry wood.

Western, Stan (*Whistle*) — Barkeeper of the Trackside Tavern in Sawdust City.

Westrup, Jake (*Sang*) — Good-looking young man with unruly red hair. He's Phoebe Sloan's boyfriend, a bartender who says he's going to be promoted to restaurant manager of Chet's Bar and Barbecue.

Wharton, Clem (*Post Office*) — Pickax township supervisor. He's assaulted by Herb Hackpole during a public hearing on annexation.

Whatley, Mr. and Mrs. (*Brahms*) — "Cranky-looking" vacationing couple from Cleveland. The man is "fat and red-faced" and speaks with gasps. He's in wholesale hardware. The woman is "scrawny and hard-of-hearing," with a shrill voice and a frosty manner.

Whiting, Rosemary (*Red*) — A "nice-looking woman of indefinite age and quiet manner" with licorice-black hair. Her husband died about two years ago, so she sold the house and invested the money in her health-food shop. (*Brahms*) —She's in favor of "fresh air, exercise, and all that jazz." She thinks that all behavior can be attributed to a healthy (or unhealthy) diet. She spends a week at the lake with Qwilleran. She decides to sell her interest in her business and move to Toronto to go into business with Max Sorrel.

Whitmoor, Verona — See *Verona Boswell.*

Whittlestaff, Basil (*Shakespeare*) — Son of Zack. He was a bully. When he was young, he robbed Mrs. Woolsmith. See *Herb Hackpole.*

Whittlestaff, Ellie (*Shakespeare*) — Resident of Moose County some years back and daughter of Zack. She "worked at the paper for a spell" folding papers, making tea, and sweeping up. Titus Goodwinter "took a shine to her" and seduced her. She left a "suicide note addressed to her cat," then threw herself in the river.

Whittlestaff, Zack (*Shakespeare*) — Wagon-driver at the old *Picayune* before 1921. His father was a miner, "blown to bits in an underground explosion" at Ephraim Goodwinter's mine. Zack became a bitter and violent man who "drank and regularly beat his wife and two children." After Titus Goodwinter seduced his daughter Ellie, she threw herself in the river. Zack killed Titus in a fight and went to prison.

Wickes, Dr. John and Dr. Inez (*Mountain*) — Veterinarians in Spudsboro. They have a "perfectly enchanting house over a waterfall," called Hidden Falls. His "sober mien was emphasized by owl-like eyeglasses."

Wilbank, Del and Ardis (*Mountain*) — Couple who lives on Hawk's Nest Drive. Del is the sheriff of Spudsboro.

Wilburton, Isabelle (*High*) — Middle-aged woman who lives in the Casablanca. Qwill finds her in a phone booth wearing a red cocktail dress and clutching a rum pint bottle. She invites Qwilleran to her apartment for a drink, anytime.

Wilk, Rewayne (*High*) — Di Bessinger's new protégé. He's "a big blond with long hair and a cleft chin." He paints pictures of people who are eating.

Wilmot, Pender (*Closet*) — Qwilleran's next-door neighbor and Mrs. Gage's attorney. The Penders sell their home on Goodwinter Boulevard and move to West Middle Hummock. (*Sang*) — He's on the spelling team for the Ladders, sponsored by the Pickax Boosters.

Wilmot, Timmie (*Closet*) — Son of Pender, a small boy in large eyeglasses who tries to catch Yum Yum. (*Sang*) — He's in the third grade and knows a lot about ecology.

Wimsey, Emma Huggins (*Underground*) — She's "real old but still sharp" and has "the most wonderful cat story." In a wheelchair at the Senior Care Facility in Pickax, Emma is a "frail woman with thinning white hair." Several days later, Qwill learns that she has passed away.

Wimsey, Maryellen (*Underground*) — Young Moose County woman engaged to Clem Cottle. An October wedding is planned. She's a "lovely girl" who used to be in Mildred Hanstable's art classes.

Wingfoot, Winnie (*High*) — Resident of the Casablanca. She "could only be described as a vision," with "model's figure and an angel's face," enhanced by "incredibly artful makeup." She has "a model's walk and an heiress's clothing budget" and drives a BMW.

Wix, Vonda Dudley (*Mountain*) — Columnist for the *Spudsboro Gazette.* Qwill calls her Vonda Tiddledy Winks. Her column is called "Potato Peelings," written in "a cloyingly outdated style." She has "the embalmed look that comes from too many facelifts." J. J. Hawkinfield called her "Cookie" because she baked cookies for him all the time.

Wojcik, Detective (*Backwards*) — Detective from homicide Down Below. He's "brusque and impatient," all business. (*Danish*) — He has a nasal voice "well suited to sarcasm."

(*High*) — He's a "by-the-book cop" who lacks imagination and has "a lip-curling scorn for meddling journalists and psychic cats."

Woolsmith, Sarah (*Shakespeare*) — An Old Timer in Moose County. She's over ninety, but is sharp and has a "reliable memory." She's a "frail little woman with nervous hands, sitting in a wheelchair and clutching her shawl." She spent all her life on a farm. She and her late husband, John, had seven children, five of them boys. (*Underground*) — Mrs. Woolsmith has passed on. She was ninety-five and had nearly all her own teeth.

Wright, Alacoque (*Danish*) — a.k.a., Cokey. Assistant at Mrs. Middy's business in the Midwest city, a tall young woman with straight brown hair, "roguish green eyes, an appealing little nose, an intelligent mouth, a dainty chin." She's an architect by training and sneaky by nature. Qwill likes her spirit, her "provocative face, and the coltish grace of her figure." (*Glue*) — Alacoque is a "tough baby" from a Cincinnati architectural firm, a "flighty young woman who dated Qwill before she eloped with an engineer." She has a "good job and a bad marriage," although she is not divorced.

Wyckoff, W. C. (*Sang*) — Moose County artist whose intaglio Qwilleran wins.

Yarrow, Buddy (*Underground*) — A carpenter in Mooseville who's employed in the construction of the East Shore Condominiums. The twenty-nine-year-old man drowns while fishing in the Ittibittiwassee River, apparently by slipping down the riverbank into the river and hitting his head on a rock.

Yazbro, Jack (*High*) — Tenant of the Casablanca and furniture mover. He's a giant with bulging muscles and aggressive jaw. Rasmus's body landed on the roof of Jack's car.

Young, Caspar (*Shakespeare*) — Contractor and partner in XYZ Enterprises. (*Glue*) — He constructed David and Jill's contemporary house.

Yushi (*Danish*) — Japanese caterer who slips Qwill "kitty" bags. He's owner of Cuisine Internationale.

Zander, Mike (*Stars*) — a.k.a., Junior. Commercial fisherman whose hobby is metalwork. Qwilleran buys a handcrafted copper sailboat. He also makes skewers for potatoes for Owen's Place and Elizabeth's Magic. He and his wife just had a baby boy.

Zoller, Dr. (*Shakespeare*) — Dentist in Pickax. He's the financial backer of XYZ Enterprises.

THE CATS' ANIMALS

Alvis Parsley (*Thief*) — Tomcat belonging to Mildred Riker's grandkids. He likes rock and roll.

Arpeggio (*Thief*) — Kitten belonging to the MacWhannells' daughter. It runs up and down the piano keys.

Attila (*Ghosts*) — One of Kristi's male goats on her Moose County goat farm.

Billy (*Breakfast*) — Nice stray cat on Pear Island, taken care of by the Bambas.

Black Tulip (*Ghosts*) — One of Kristi's goats, a big black Nubian, with a striped face, Roman nose, and elegantly long ears.

Blackberry (*Cheese*) — One of Kristi Waffle's new goats on the Split Rail Farm in Moose County.

Blackie (*Mountain*) — One of Mrs. Lumpton's cats on Li'l Potato Mountain.

Blackie (*Sang*) — One of Mrs. Coggin's old mongrel dogs.

Bob (*Breakfast*) — Old plodding horse with a swayback, belonging to John on Pear Island.

Bootsie (*Ghosts*) — Polly's kitten, a.k.a., Bigfoot and Brutus. He's a small white kitten with large brown ears, large brown feet, a dark smudge on his nose, and the "indescribably blue eyes of a Siamese." Qwilleran agrees to keep him overnight. Bootsie creates chaos with his wild flight—he slams into furniture, breaks a piece of antique glass, and climbs Qwilleran's pant leg. He eats his "medically approved food," the Siamese's turkey loaf with olives and mushrooms, and grabs a piece of salmon off Qwill's fork. Bigfoot pounces on Qwilleran's back and clings to his sweater, firmly hooked into the yarn. This necessitates a rescue visit from Verona Boswell, who frees the cat and puts antiseptic on the scratches on Qwill's back. Qwilleran locks him in the broom closet after he tries to climb Larry's leg. When he hears a minor explosion, he yanks the door open and finds Bootsie sitting on the shelf with the remaining unbroken light bulbs. When Polly comes to pick him up, he's sound asleep in the gravel in the cats' commode. (*High*) — The kitten with the hollow leg grabs one of the lamb chops Polly brings home for dinner. (*Mountain*) —Qwilleran considers Bootsie a "frivolous name for a pedigreed Siamese with the appetite of a Great Dane." He now weighs ten pounds. (*Wasn't*) — Bootsie greets Qwill with "ears back and fangs bared," and a hiss. When Polly returns from Scotland, the "husky Siamese approaches with curiosity, appraises her coolly, then turns abruptly and walks away." Bootsie has the "brassy voice of a trumpet." (*Whistle*) —Bootsie is in the hospital for feline urological syndrome. After Polly moves in with her sister-in-law, Bootsie slims down by eating less and running up and down the stairs. (*Cheese*) —He's a fifteen-pound missile who always escorts Qwill to the door. (*Thief*) — He always gives his paw three licks before eating. He's learned to stand on his hind legs and hang on the lever-type door handle until it opens. After his name change to Brutus, the cat begins to act like a noble Roman, parading back and forth with tail erect to "demonstrate his nobility."

Brandy (*Wasn't*) — Lockmaster Buckskin horse owned by Trilby. "No papers, but beautiful points."

Brutus — See *Bootsie*.

Buttercup (*Ghosts*) — One of Kristi's goats at her Moose County farm.

Catta (*Thief*) — Anticipated cat companion for Bootsie/ Brutus. (*Sang*) — She's a tiny kitten, all ears and feet, who's learning to hold her own with Brutus. She'll end up being a "tough lady cat" who "doesn't take harassment from man or beast."

Chris (*Closet*) — One of the wheel dogs in Nancy Fincher's group of Siberian huskies on her Moose County farm. He works right in front of the sled.

Cleo (*Ghosts*) — Pregnant cat in charge of rodent control at the Goodwinter Farmhouse barn.

Cody (*Thief*) — Black schnauzer belonging to Gil Mac-Murchie. Celia finds a new home for her with Mitch Ogilvie and Kristi Waffle. She lies down flat on the floor on her belly, all four legs extended, in her "froggy-doggy" trick. Cody likes a combination of rice and lamb, popcorn, and bananas. Her bed is a horse blanket and her toys are socks knotted together. She likes "*National Geographic* TV programs and dog-food commercials."

Corky (*Closet*) — Gil Inchpot's dog, a "large, friendly, all-American, farm-type, cork-colored mongrel" on his Moose County potato farm.

Dolly (*Sang*) — One of Mrs. Coggin's old mongrel dogs.

Dumbo (*Cheese*) — Large gray cat who lives at the Boulder House Inn.

Dutch (*Stars*) — Moose County sheriff's dog, a German shepherd. Dutch was trained for search-and-rescue. He never gives up.

Einstein (*Stars*) — Retired G-dog, a black Labrador, trained to search for drugs. He's very intelligent. When he finds something, he simply sits down. He belongs to Phil Scotten.

Equanimity (*Thief*) — a.k.a., Quinky. Golden Persian cat belonging to the Cavendish sisters in Pickax.

Foggy (*Thief*) — Gray cat belonging to the MacWhannells.

Frankie (*Danish*) — Alacoque Wright's beautiful orange cat who lived to be fifteen. He drank soapsuds.

Gardenia (*Ghosts*) — One of Kristi's goats, a white Saanen, on her Moose County farm.

Geranium (*Ghosts*) — One of Kristi's goats on her Moose County farm.

Haggis MacTavish (*Thief*) — Silver tabby who sleeps in the window of Scottie's men's shop in Pickax.

Hannibal (*Breakfast*) — One of the resident stray cats on Pear Island, who frequents the Vacation Helpers for picnic scraps.

Hepplewhite (*On/Off*) — Large belligerent German police dog belonging to Mary Duckworth in Junktown.

Holy Terror (*Breakfast*) — Siamese who once lived in the vicarage with Reverend and Mrs. Harding. He would go into a "Siamese tizzy," once landing on a tray and "spraying tomato juice over the walls, furniture, carpet, ceiling, and the august person of the bishop" who was visiting.

Honeysuckle (*Ghosts*) — One of Kristi's goats, a fawn-colored one with two stripes on the face, on her Moose County farm.

Jasper (*Sang*) — Amazon hookbill, a green parrot with a touch of red on his tail, who makes rude comments.

Jeoffrey (*Stars*) — One of Tess Bunker's two cats.

Jerry (*Closet*) — One of the lead dogs of Nancy Fincher's Siberian huskies. He's a captain and "very brainy."

Jet Stream (*Thief*) — a.k.a., Jet-boy. Orange tiger cat belonging to Wetherby Goode. The "technocat" rubs his jaw against the controls on the Sousa box and turns it on. He also opens louvered bi-fold doors with his nose.

Katie (*Sang*) — One of the two cats left on Qwilleran's doorstep. She becomes a Pickax Library cat. She's a brown-and-black with tortoiseshell markings.

Kitty-Baby (*High*) — Cat that lives in the Casablanca.

Leon (*Thief*) — Orange cat formerly belonging to Wetherby Goode. He had a "head as big as a grapefruit, no neck, and a disposition like a lemon." Leon stayed with Wetherby's ex-wife.

Li'l Yaller (*Sang*) — One of Mrs. Coggin's old mongrel dogs.

Long John Silver (*Thief*) — Big gray cat belonging to Wetherby Goode's great-uncle Joe.

Lucy (*Mountain*) — Large Doberman, "grossly rotund," who rescues Qwilleran when he is lost on the mountain.

Mabel (*Sang*) — One of Mrs. Coggin's old mongrel dogs.

Mac (*Sang*) — a.k.a., Mackintosh. One of the two cats left on Qwilleran's doorstep. He becomes a Pickax Library cat. He's a big orange cat with plumed tail and large, gold, almond-shaped eyes.

Magnificat (*Thief*) — Cat who lives at the Old Stone Church in Pickax.

Marconi (*Whistle*) — Great horned owl in Qwilleran's apple orchard. (*Sang*) — He hoots in Morse code.

Mibs (*Post Office*) — Beautiful old longhair cat belonging to the Rikers Down Below. When they divorced, they had it put to sleep.

Misty (*Thief*) — Gray cat belonging to the MacWhannells.

Moonlight (*Cheese*) — One of Kristi Waffle's new goats on the Split Rail Farm in Moose County.

Mosca (*Thief*) — Housefly in Qwilleran's condo.

Napoleon (*Ghosts*) — One of Kristi's male goats on her Moose County farm.

Napoleon (*High*) — Cat belonging to Mrs. Jasper, who lives in the Casablanca.

Natasha (*Breakfast*) — One of the Bambas' cats in Moose County.

Octopuss (*Thief*) — Cat belonging to Polly Duncan's assistant.

Oedipuss (*Thief*) — Cat belonging to Polly Duncan's assistant.

Oh Jay (*Closet*) — Timmie Wilmot's great big orange cat with bad breath. He weighs twenty pounds and has fleas. (*Whistle*) — Oh Jay disappears from the Wilmots' new home in West Middle Hummock and appears back at their old house on Goodwinter Boulevard. He's going to stay on the Moose County Community College campus as a mascot.

Patches (*Mountain*) — One of Mrs. Lumpton's cats, a calico, on Li'l Potato Mountain.

Pete (*Cheese*) — Reddish-brown dog at the Limburger mansion in Moose County. He comes to the back door to be fed and to the front door to be stoned by Gustav Limburger.

Phreddie (*Stars*) — Long-haired black and white dog who stays at Arnold's Antique Store. Arnold received a dog dish with the name Phreddie on it, so he named his dog to match the dish. Phreddie has better manners than Owen Bowen.

Platypuss (*Thief*) — Cat belonging to Polly Duncan's assistant.

Princess (*Stars*) — One of Tess Bunker's two cats.

Propinquity (*Thief*) — a.k.a., Pinky. Golden Persian cat belonging to the Cavendish sisters in Pickax.

Punkin (*Underground*) — Emma Huggins Wimsey's orange cat, who saved Emma and family on several occasions.

Punky (*Post Office*) — Beautiful old longhair cat belonging to the Rikers Down Below. When they divorced, they had it put to sleep.

Pushkin (*Breakfast*) — One of the Bambas' cats.

Quantum Leap (*Cardinal*) — Four-year-old chestnut gelding that races in the steeplechase at Lockmaster.

Quinky — See *Equanimity*.

Raku (*Red*) — Joy Graham's cat who disappeared. He was a big, smoky-brown longhair.

Rasputin (*Ghosts*) — One of Kristi Waffle's male goats.

Ruby (*Cheese*) — One of Kristi Waffle's new goats at the Split Rail Farm.

Sheba (*Breakfast*) — One of the Bambas' cats.

Sherman (*Breakfast*) — One of the Bambas' cats. Sherman's pregnant.

Shoo-Shoo (*Breakfast*) — One of the Bambas' cats.

Skip (*Breakfast*) — Horse that pulls a carriage owned by Henry on Breakfast Island.

Snuffles (*Shakespeare*) — One of the cats belonging to the Bambas. She takes hormones due to some kind of dermatitis that sometimes affects spayed cats.

Son of Cardinal (*Cardinal*) — Horse ridden by Robin Stucker in the Lockmaster steeplechase.

Spot (*Sang*) — One of Mrs. Coggin's old mongrel dogs.

Spots (*Breakfast*) — Nice stray cat on Pear Island, taken care of by the Bambas.

Spunky (*Closet*) — One of the wheel dogs in Nancy Fincher's group of Siberian huskies. He works right in front of the sled.

Stephanie (*Post Office*) — The Lanspeaks' Jersey cow, who has lots of personality. The Lanspeaks name their restaurant for her.

Susie (*Breakfast*) — Nice stray cat on Pear Island, taken care of by the Bambas.

Sweetie Pie (*High*) — Kitten adopted by Isabelle Wilburton at the Casablanca. It's white with an orange head and tail.

Switch (*Underground*) — Canine assistant to electrician in Purple Point. He selects tools and carries them up a ladder.

Terry (*Closet*) — One of the lead dogs of Nancy Fincher's Siberian huskies. He's a captain and "very brainy."

Theoria Dominys du Manoir des Ombreuses (*Thief*) — a.k.a., Dodo. Siamese cat belonging to Carter Lee James's mother, who lives in Paris.

Tiger (*Mountain*) — One of Mrs. Lumpton's cats on Li'l Potato Mountain.

Tinkertom (*Mountain*) — One of Lori Bamba's cats, an elderly one who has lost his sight.

Tipsy (*Glue*) — Black-and-white cat that belonged to the founder of Tipsy's Restaurant. She was a white cat with black boots and a black patch that seemed to be slipping over one eye. She also had a deformed foot that made her stagger and added to her inebriated image. (*Cardinal*) — Her boozy antics and agreeable disposition made customers smile and attracted diners from far and wide. (Read about Tipsy's past in "Tipsy and the Board of Health" in *The Cat Who Had 14 Tales.*)

Tommy (*Danish*) — Large, smoky-blue cat who notifies Mrs. Highspight when the kettle is boiling.

Toulouse (*Breakfast*) — Black-and-white cat with rakish markings who goes to Arch and Mildred's house and just moves in. He pounces "on the kitchen counter when Mildred is cooking and steals a shrimp or a pork chop, right from under her nose." (*Thief*) — He's an alley-smart stray in a "tuxedo with white shirtfront and spats" who very intelligently chooses a food writer's house for his home. (*Stars*) — Toulouse says "a polite meow" when Mildred feeds him. "For a stray, he's very well-mannered." He often stares into space. Mildred says he's "watching for visitors."

Trish (*Breakfast*) — One of the Bambas' cats.

Vincent (*High*) — Persian cat who lives in the Bessinger-Todd Gallery. He belonged to Dianne Bessinger, who named him after Vincent Van Gogh.

Whisker-Belle (*Closet*) — Pastor Donna Sims's cat. Whenever Donna sneezes, her cat makes a sound as if she were blessing her.

William Allen (*Shakespeare*) — Large white cat, the staff mouser of the *Pickax Picayune*. He's feared lost in the big fire that destroyed the building. (*Ghosts*) — He escapes from the fire in the old building. Ten months after the fire, Junior finds him sitting in front of the State Unemployment Office. He's the "general manager" of the *Moose County Something*.

Winston (*Glue*) — Eddington Smith's cat, a smoky-gray Persian with a plume of a tail like a feather duster. (*Cardinal*) — His voluminous tail dusts the books as he walks. (*Thief*) —Qwill gives him smoked turkey pâté and gourmet sardines for Christmas. Winston resembles an elder statesman.

Wrigley (*Closet*) — A nice black and white cat Celia Robinson receives from Chicago. (*Thief*) — He receives gourmet sardines from Qwilleran for Christmas.

Zak (*Whistle*) — Beautiful chow dog belonging to Eddie Trevelyan. He's beautiful, friendly, and well-behaved.

UNNAMED ANIMALS

Siamese cat (*High*) — Cat belonging to Lieutenant Hames and his wife, who is "more interested in breaking the law than enforcing it."

cat (*Backwards*) — Pregnant cat belonging to the Halapays.

cat (*Ghosts*) — Calico cat who thinks the Bambas' baby son is a kitten and tries to mother him.

cat (*Closet*) — June Halliburton's cat when she was a little girl taking piano lessons. The cat howled every time June hit a wrong note.

cat (*Whistle*) — She attends services every Sunday at the Little Stone Church in Pickax. She "walks in, picks out a lap, and sleeps all through the sermon."

Great Dane (*Cheese*) — Dog on Kristi Waffle's Split Rail Farm.

Kerry Blue terriers (*Backwards*) — Several unnamed pets of the Halapays.

dog (*Brahms*) — Brittany spaniel hunting dog belonging to Roger MacGillivray.

dog (*Brahms*) — Scottie belonging to Sharon Hanstable.

dog (*Underground*) — Captain Phlogg's dog with a reputation as a cat-killer. He wanders around the dunes like the "hound of the Baskervilles."

dogs (*Breakfast*) — Three Jack Russells, belonging to Richard Appelhardt. They are well-behaved dogs who "mingled with the family and never barked, jumped, or sniffed."

bird (*Cardinal*) — Moose County cardinal friend of Koko's who is killed by Steve O'Hare.

In *The Cat Who Tailed a Thief*, Qwilleran collects names of cats he and his readers have known:

Agatha and Christie — Two cats abandoned in the parking lot of a library.

Allegro and Adagio — One lively cat and one quiet cat.

Beethoven — A white cat born deaf.

Metro, short for Metronome — Cat belonging to the church choir leader. She sits on the piano and swings her tail to music.

Catsanova — A tomcat.

Stir Fry — A shrimp addict.

Ping and Pong — Two Burmese cats.

Many Moose County cats are named after edibles: Pumpkin, Peaches, Sweet Potato, Butterscotch, Jelly Bean, Ginger, Huckleberry, Pepper, Marmalade, Licorice, Strudel, and Popcorn.

Some names are not complimentary: Tom Trouble, Stinky, Lazy Bum, and Hairball. Some are named for famous personalities: Babe Ruth, Socrates, Walter Mitty, Queen Juliana, Maggie and Jiggs, Eleanor Roosevelt, George Washington. Cats in the same family often have rhyming names: Mingo and Bingo, Cuddles and Puddles, Noodle and Yankee Doodle.

Qwilleran invents a few appropriate names: Beau Thai, Chairman Meow, Sir Albert Whitepaws, Lady Ik Ik, Samantha Featherbottom.

5

The Cats' Pages

Welcome to the Cats' Pages, a listing of businesses, clubs, groups, events, and buildings in the places the Siamese and Qwilleran live or visit.

Al's Fix-All Truck (*Ghosts*) — Business in Moose County.

Allison's, Mrs. (*Danish*) — Residence for "career girls" in an old mansion on Merchant Street. It used to look like "a Victorian bordello." After it's redecorated, it looks like "an Early American bordello."

Amanda's Studio of Interior Design (*Post Office*) — Business owned by Amanda Goodwinter in downtown Pickax. The building is "pure Dickens" in its architecture. (*Wasn't*) — The Old English storefront is "squeezed between imitation forts, temples, and castles" on Main Street.

Amberton Farm (*Cardinal*) — Horse farm owned by the Ambertons in Lockmaster.

Amy's Lunch Bucket (*Mountain*) — Small restaurant in Potato Cove with four old kitchen tables and "some metal folding chairs obviously from the Just Rust collection." The floorboards are grass green and the white walls have an "abstract panorama of green mountains against a blue sky."

Ann's 'Tiques (*On/Off*) — Antique store in Junktown, owned by Ann Peabody. It's a "subterranean shop smelling of moldy rugs and rotted wood."

Antique Dealers' Association (*Brahms*) — Group Down Below that gives Qwilleran an expensive watch at a testimonial dinner.

Antiques by Noisette (*Breakfast*) — Business on Pear Island, owned by Noisette duLac.

Arnold's Antique Shop (*Stars*) — Shop in Mooseville on Sandpit Road.

Art Center (*Sang*) — Local art community's place for exhibitions and related activities.

Artist and Model (*Backwards*) — French restaurant in a cellar in the Midwest city.

Athletes for Peace (*Stars*) — One of the entries in the Fourth of July parade in Mooseville. Each athlete has a large letter of the alphabet on a pole, and they were scrambling their letters "to spell *cheat, shoot, treason,* and worse!"

Aurora's Boutique (*Cheese*) — Moose County store with ladies' dresses.

Beechum Family Weavers (*Mountain*) — Craft store in Potato Cove. The building looks like an old schoolhouse.

Bessinger-Todd Art Gallery (*High*) — Gallery located in the financial district at the same address as the old Lambreth Gallery, owned by Dianne Bessinger and Jerome Todd.

Bid-a-Bit Auctions (*Shakespeare*) — Business in Pickax City owned by Foxy Fred. (*Wasn't*) — He handles Melinda Goodwinter's tag sale. (*Cheese*) — He runs the Celebrity Auction.

Big Burning of 1869 (*Closet*) — Docu-drama based on devastating Moose County fire on October 17–18, 1869.

Bit o' Junk (*On/Off*) — Antique store in Junktown, next to the Cobb Junkery, owned by Ben Nicholas. It's a town house "similar in design to the Cobb mansion, but only half as wide and twice as dilapidated."

Bixby Bugle (*Stars*) — Newspaper in Bixby that's sending reporters to review the Pickax Theatre Club's summer production in Mooseville.

Black Bear Café (*Glue*) — Café located in Hotel Booze in Brrr, run by Gary Pratt who sells "no-holds-barred hamburgers." (*Underground*) — It also features delicious homemade pies. (*Wasn't*) — There's a mounted black bear at the entrance to the bar. (*Closet*) — The bar is the site of a presentation of *The Big Burning of 1869* for the Outdoor Club. (*Stars*) — The shabbiness of the café is part of its attraction. Gary Pratt's bearburgers are the best in the county.

Blue Dragon (*On/Off*) — Junktown antique store owned by Mary Duckworth. It's an "enchanted palace in the depths of the dark forest" featuring many Oriental items.

Bob's Chop Salon (*Brahms*) — Barber shop located at the Cannery Mall in Mooseville.

Bonnie Scots Tour (*Wasn't*) — Tour of Scotland taken by sixteen Moose County residents, fifteen of whom return alive.

Books 'n' Stuff (*High*) — Bookstore Down Below that stocks more videos and greeting cards than books.

Bottom Line (*Mountain*) — Craft store owned by a chair caner in Potato Cove.

Boulder House Inn (*Cheese*) — New inn in Trawnto. It's constructed of rough boulders, piled one on another, with floors that are giant flagstones and staircases chipped out of rock. (*Thief*) — It has a cavernous fireplace that burns four-foot logs.

Brenda's Salon (*Cheese*) — Hair salon in Moose County.

Brrr Community Church (*Closet*) — Church in a "modest frame building with a cupola" and arched windows.

Brrr Eskimos (*Glue*) — Softball team from Brrr.

Buccaneer Den (*Breakfast*) — Restaurant at Pear Island Hotel, frequented by families who like hamburgers.

Bushland Fisheries (*Stars*) — Commercial fishing business owned by the Bushlands for three generations before Bushy's grandfather sold out to the Scottens. They shipped dried salted herring Down Below.

Bushland Photo Studio (*Underground*) — Business located in Lockmaster and owned by John and Vicki Bushland. (*Closet*) — Bushy transfers his commercial photography studio to Pickax after his divorce.

Buster's Collision Service (*Underground*) — Business in Moose County whose motto is "Where We Meet by Accident."

Cannery Mall (*Brahms*) — Several shops, two miles beyond Mooseville in an old fish cannery.

Captain's Mess (*Brahms*) — Shop in Pickax that's a "jumble of antiquities and fakes" in a little storefront. The building is "so loose and out-of-joint that only the solid oak door holds it upright." It smells "of mildew, whiskey, and tobacco." (*Glue*) — It's a "crooked little shop run by a crooked little sea captain," Captain Phlogg.

Carriage House Café (*High*) — Coffeehouse Down Below occupying premises of a former furniture-refinishing shop.

Casablanca (*High*) — Big, old, white apartment building in Junktown. It looks like a refrigerator, with "a dark line across the facade at the ninth floor, as if delineating the freezer compartment." It was built in 1901 as the first high-rise apartment building in the city, and the first with an elevator. After the stock market crash in 1929, "more millionaires jumped off the roof of the Casablanca than any other building in the county."

Celebrity Auction (*Cheese*) — Charity "auction" of evenings with ten Moose County celebrities, including Qwilleran.

Chet's Bar and Barbecue (*Sang*) — Business in Kennebeck, owned by Chester Ramsbottom. It's a dump, but the food is good: pork barbecue with baked beans and coleslaw.

City of Brotherly Crime (*Cardinal*) — Bestselling book written by Qwilleran some years ago.

Click Club (*Sang*) — Space on lower level of Art Center. It will be used for "photo exhibitions, slide showings, video-viewing, and talks on photography."

Cold Turkey Farm (*Cheese*) — Moose County farm managed by Nick Bamba, with an option to buy. The farm raises turkeys, fast-freezes them, and ships them Down Below.

Concerned Parents of Pickax (*Cardinal*) — Group of parents who oppose Hilary VanBrook's regime as principal of the high school in Pickax.

Corsair Room (*Breakfast*) — Upscale dining room at the Pear Island Hotel.

Cottle Roosters (*Underground*) — Mooseville softball team.

Cuisine Internationale (*Danish*) — Catering service Down Below owned by Yushi.

Cuttlebrink's Hdwe. & Genl. Mdse. (*Cardinal*) — Store in Wildcat established in 1862. It has "dirty glass windows through which a dusty horse harness, fan belts, and rusty cans of roof cement were visible."

Cybernetic Poultry Farms, Inc. (*On/Off*) — Company that donates frozen turkeys as honorable mentions for the annual newspaper writing competition Down Below.

Daffy Diggers (*Thief*) — Garden club in Pickax.

Daily Fluxion (*Backwards*) — Daily Midwest paper with a circulation figure of 427,463. The publisher's slogan is *Fiat Flux.* The young managing editor is one of the "new breed of editors who approach newspapering as a science rather than a holy cause." (*Post Office*) — It's noted for its "twenty-four-point bylines and meager wage scale." (*Shakespeare*) — The metropolitan circulation approaches a million. The *Fluxion* adopts every technological advance and journalistic trend that comes along. (*Glue*) — It has a "slick, color-coordinated, acoustically engineered, electronically equipped workstation environment."

Delicious Dishes for Dainty Entertaining (*Cheese*) — Book published in 1899 by the Pickax Ladies' Cultural Society.

Delphine's (*Glue*) — Beauty salon in Pickax.

Diamond Jim's Jewelry (*Post Office*) — Pickax business with expensive diamonds.

Dimsdale Diner (*Brahms*) — a.k.a., Dismal Diner. Diner near the old Dimsdale Mine in a "dilapidated boxcar." It has the "worst coffee in the county and the worst hamburgers in northeast central United States." (*Post Office*) — The tables and chairs "might have been castoffs from the Hotel Booze when it redecorated in 1911." (*Ghosts*) — It's famous for its "bad food and worse coffee." It's located at the corner of Pickax Road and Ittibittiwassee Road. (*Stars*) — The diner has "bad coffee, good gossip."

Dingleberry Funeral Home (*Ghosts*) — Pickax funeral home that arranges Iris Cobb's funeral. It occupies an old stone mansion on Goodwinter Boulevard. The interior has "plush carpet, grasscloth walls, and raw silk draperies in pale seafoam green, accented with eighteenth-century mahogany furniture and benign oil paintings in expensive frames."

Distinguished Women Awards (*Wasn't*) — Awards presented by the Pickax hospital auxiliary in collaboration with XYZ Enterprises. Proceeds go to the Pickax Hospital for an intensive care unit.

Domino Inn (*Breakfast*) — Nick and Lori Bamba's bed-and-breakfast on Pear Island. It was a private lodge in the Twenties, owned by a family that was "nuts about dominoes." It's a "large ungainly building with small windows, completely sided with a patchwork of white birchbark." It withstands the fierce storm that destroys new construction.

Double-Six (*Breakfast*) — Nick Bamba's small cabin cruiser, named after a domino.

East Shore Condominiums (*Underground*) — Condos being built in Brrr on the lake by XYZ Enterprises.

Edd's Editions (*Glue*) — Bookstore in Pickax owned by Eddington Smith. It crouches "on the backstreet behind Lanspeak Department Store." Rough feldspar stones are "piled up to simulate a grotto." On a sunny day, it glitters "like the front of a burlesque house." Tables are loaded with "haphazard piles of dingy books," shelves are jammed with bindings, and there's a shaky wooden stepladder. The building has a "smell of old books and sardines." It's "over a hundred years old, a blacksmith's shop originally." (*Cheese*) — There's always an odor of mildewed books, sardines, and liver and onions.

Elizabeth's Magic (*Stars*) — Store owned by Elizabeth Hart on Oak Street in Mooseville, at the foot of the Great Dune. It features "exotic wearables, crafts by local artisans," and "mystic paraphernalia." Elizabeth is opening a lending library that had belonged to her father: everything ever written about UFOs. It will be available only to serious researchers and scholars.

Ellsworth House (*On/Off*) — Home of the Midwest city's former mayor, an "Italianate sandstone" on Fifteenth Street.

Engine No. 9 (*Whistle*) — Old steam locomotive that is revitalized to pull the Lumbertown Party Train. She has six huge driving wheels, a firebox that uses coal, and black cinders from the smokestack.

Equus (*Cardinal*) — Men's store in Lockmaster.

Exbridge & Cobb, Fine Antiques (*Ghosts*) — Antique business in downtown Pickax, which Susan Exbridge and Iris Cobb plan to open. Upon Iris's death, Susan becomes sole owner.

Fabulous Frozen Foods for Fussy Felines (*Shakespeare*) — Line of gourmet cat food developed by Tony Peters of the Old Stone Mill restaurant.

Fantaisie Féline (*Post Office*) — Penelope Goodwinter's very expensive and entrancing perfume that Melinda Goodwinter smuggles in from France.

Farmers' Collective (*Sang*) — Moose County group that attends Mrs. Coggin's funeral.

Fast Mama (*Stars*) — Older speedboat spotted out on the lake at Mooseville.

FBI (*Whistle*) — Feline Bureau of Investigation, Qwilleran's name for the cats' investigations.

First National Bank of Spudsboro (*Mountain*) — a.k.a., First Potato National Bank.

Fish Tank (*Underground*) — New restaurant in Mooseville known for fabulous navy grog, clam chowder, and broiled whitefish. It's in an old warehouse on the fishing wharves.

Fishhook Festival (*Glue*) — Contest in Mooseville in June, which includes selection of a beauty queen.

Fitch Witch (*Glue*) — Twenty-seven-foot boat owned by Harley Fitch.

Five Points Café (*Mountain*) — Café in Spudsboro.

Five Points Market (*Mountain*) — Spudsboro store managed by Bill Treacle.

FOO (*Brahms*) — Lakeside eating place that lost the D. It's a "dump," but famous for pasties. It's a strictly "hats-on" restaurant in a two-story building badly in need of repair. (*Underground*) — The FOO is "close to the docks, the food is cheap and plentiful, and the unlicensed establishment serves illegal beverages in coffee cups."

Foxhunters' Club (*Cardinal*) — Social club in Lockmaster.

Foxtrottery (*Cardinal*)– Store in Lockmaster, where everything has a horse or fox motif.

Franklin's Flowers (*Cheese*) — Shop owned by Franklin Pickett in Pickax, across from the hotel and next door to Exbridge & Cobb, Fine Antiques.

Friendly Fatties (*Red*) — Club for overweight people Down Below.

Friends of the Public Library (*Thief*) — Group that supports the Pickax Public Library.

Friends of the Wool (*Stars*) — New group of "woolgrowers, spinners, knitters, and other fiber artists." They sponsor a float in the Fourth of July parade in Mooseville. Arch is one of the knitters on the float! Ogilvie Sheep Ranch provided sheep and baby lambs.

Fugtree Farmhouse (*Ghosts*) — House built in the nineteenth century by a lumber baron, a "perfect example of Affluent Victorian." (*Thief*) — The house is on the National Register.

Fryers Club Summer Stage (*Stars*) — Summer theater in Mooseville for the Pickax Theatre Club. It's being held in Avery Botts's barn. The first production is *Visit to a Small Planet*. The next is *Life with Father*.

Garrick Theatre (*On/Off*) — Old theater in the demolition area in Junktown. It stands among other abandoned buildings, "looking like a relic of fifteenth-century Venice."

Gateway Alcazar (*High*) — Proposed towers Down Below, spanning Zwinger Boulevard, connected by a bridge across the top.

Gertrude (*Stars*) — A stuffed Kalico Kitten that Yum Yum lovingly adopts.

Gippel's Garage (*Glue*) — Garage in Pickax owned by Scott Gippel.

Glanz' antique store (*On/Off*) — Store owned by Andy Glanz in a large building in Junktown, dating from the 1920s.

Glinko's (*Underground*) — Moose County repair business "network" owned by the Glinkos. The building is a "greasy, shabby garage behind the post office."

Golden Lamb Chop (*Red*) — Restaurant owned by Max Sorrel. The building is a nineteenth-century landmark, having once been the depot for interurban trolleys.

Goodwinter & Goodwinter (*Brahms*) — Law firm of Alexander and his sister, Penelope, in Pickax. (*Post Office*) — It's a "prestigious third-generation law firm" in a building with a "Heidelberg influence."

Goodwinter Farmhouse Museum (*Glue*) — Museum in West Middle Hummock in Moose County. It's a rambling farmhouse, sided with cedar shakes that long ago weathered to silvery gray. It has been restored to the way it looked one hundred years before.

Goodwinter Field (*Whistle*) — Softball field built by the K Fund and named after the founders of Pickax.

Goodwinter Medical Clinic (*Wasn't*) — Clinic in Pickax taken over by Dr. Melinda after her father dies.

Goodwinter Mine (*Ghosts*) — Mine owned by Ephraim Goodwinter. Because of inadequate safety measures, an explosion killed thirty-two miners on May 13, 1904.

Grand Island Club (*Breakfast*) — Exclusive private club on Breakfast Island, with tennis courts, stables, and marina. Summer estates have flights of wooden steps leading down to private beaches.

Great Big Baked Potato (*Mountain*) — Moderately priced steakhouse in Spudsboro.

Great Dune Motel (*Stars*) — Motel on Sandpit Road in Mooseville.

Great Food Explo (*Cheese*) — Event in Moose County that celebrates all kinds of happenings related to food. Festivities include Mildred Riker's cooking class for men, official opening of Stables Row with bands and fireworks and a street dance, Celebrity Auction, and Wheels for Meals bike-a-thon.

Greenery, The (*Stars*) — Business in Lockmaster that rents plastic foliage.

Grinchman & Hills (*High*) — Architectural and engineering firm Down Below.

Grott's Grocery (*Stars*) — Store in Mooseville, run by the whole family. Four generations run the store: Gramps, Pop, Sonny, and Kiddo.

Gun Club (*Glue*) — Business near North Kennebeck, stocked with all kinds of guns, clothes, and mounted game birds.

Gus's Timberline Bar (*Cardinal*) — Waterfront bar Down Below run by Gus before he returned to Moose County and opened Tipsy's Tavern. (Read about the bar in "Tipsy and the Board of Health," in *The Cat Who Had 14 Tales*.)

Gut Dancers (*High*) — Keestra Hedrog's group Down Below. They are "non-disciplinary, non-motivational interpreters of basic sensibilities."

H&H Monument Works (*Sang*) — Moose County stone-cutters who scribed the tombstone for the Coggins.

H&H Sand and Gravel (*Sang*) — Moose County business on Sandpit Road owned by the Haggis brothers.

Half-Baked Bakery (*Mountain*) — Whole-grain bakery at Potato Cove that occupies an abandoned church, painted orchid.

Handle on Health (*Cheese*) — Store on Stables Row offering vitamins, safe snacks, organically grown fruits and vegetables, and diet-deli sandwiches.

Handy Helpers (*Sang*) — Group of volunteers that obliterate graffiti and generally help their neighbors in time of crisis. Their motto is: "Just help; don't talk about it."

Harborside Marina (*Sang*) — Business in Brrr.

Harriet's Family Café (*Breakfast*) — Restaurant on Pear Island serving lunch and dinner.

Hasselrich, Bennett and Barter (*Ghosts*) — Pickax law firm that handles the Klingenschoen Fund and Mrs. Cobb's inheritance.

Heavenly Hash Houses (*Red*) — Fast-food chain started by Mr. Hashman and now owned by three businessmen. The eighty-nine restaurants are all "uniformly mediocre."

Helthy-Welthy (*Brahms*) — Health-food store owned by Rosemary Whiting and another woman.

Hilltop Cemetery (*Closet*) — Cemetery where Euphonia Gage is buried. It dates back to pioneer days. (*Thief*) — The Duncans are buried in this cemetery.

Home Visitors Circle (*Sang*) — Moose County church group that attends Mrs. Coggin's funeral.

Hot Spot (*Underground*) — Restaurant in Brrr that occupies a former fire hall, with "thirty tables jammed into space that once housed two fire trucks." It offers Mexican, Cajun, and East Indian food.

Hotel Booze (*Post Office*) — The "oldest flophouse in the county," with a "twelve-ounce bacon cheeseburger with fries that's the greatest." The building is a stolid, ugly stone building three stories high, with plain shoebox architecture. The dim lighting in the dining room "camouflages the dreary walls, ancient linoleum floor, and worn plastic tables." (*Glue*) — Gary Pratt runs the bar and café at the Brrr hotel where he sells "no-holds-barred hamburgers," called boozeburgers, and homemade pies. The hotel is distinguished by six-foot-high letters on its rooftop: BOOZE ROOMS FOOD. (*Closet*) — The building is on a hill overlooking the harbor. The Klingenschoen Foundation provides a low-interest economic development loan so Gary can add elevators, indoor plumbing, and beds in the sleeping rooms. The hotel is becoming the "flagship of Brrr's burgeoning tourist trade." (*Stars*) — The hotel on the summit of Brrr is a "historic landmark for boaters and fishermen."

Huff & Puff Construction Associates (*Cardinal*) — Construction firm owned by Dennis Hough in Moose County. The renovation of Qwilleran's apple barn is Dennis's first (and last) project.

Huggins Hardware Store (*Underground*) — Hardware store near Mooseville. (*Stars*) — The store has an "old-time country-store atmosphere" that appeals to vacationers.

Ice Festival (*Thief*) — Winter festival scheduled for Mooseville. There will be dogsled, snowmobile, motorcycle, cross-country ski, snowshoe, and ice skate races. Plans include a fishing tournament, snow sculpture competition, and a torchlight parade. The expo is rained out—a warming trend melts all the plans.

Inchpot Centennial Farm (*Ghosts*) — Old Moose County farm that raises chickens and other animals.

Indian Village (*Shakespeare*) — Complex of apartments and condominiums on the Ittibittiwassee River. (*Cardinal*) — It's a popular apartment complex for singles in Pickax. There are eight apartments in each two-story building, with a central hall serving them all. (*Thief*) — It's well outside the Pickax city limits, in the Suffix Township. The buildings are board-and-batten, with apartments clustered randomly on Woodland Trail and condominiums in strips along River Lane. The main hall of the clubhouse has a lofty wood-paneled ceiling, exposed beams, and a huge, stone fireplace.

Intergalactic System of Managed Weather (*Stars*) — One of Wetherby Goode's practical jokes. The system would control temperature, precipitation, winds, and natural disasters.

Interiors by Middy (*Danish*) — Business Down Below owned by Mrs. Middy, with a sign lettered in Spencerian script. It has "all the ingredients of charm": yellow mums, bay windows, carriage lanterns, and a brass door knocker.

Island Experience, The (*Breakfast*) — "Posh bed-and-breakfast on the west beach" of Pear Island, run by two widows, Carla Helmuth and Trudy Feathering, former members of the Grand Island Club.

Ittibittiwassee Country Club (*Post Office*) — Social club in Pickax.

Ittibittiwassee Estates (*Sang*) — New retirement village near Kennebeck, actually on Bloody Creek.

Jenny Lee (*Stars*) — Fishing boat that suddenly disappeared with Bushy's great-grandfather and two great-uncles on board. It was never found.

Joe Pike's Seafood Hut (*Red*) — Restaurant Down Below with acres of parking, on River Road.

John Stuart Flour Mills (*Red*) — Sponsors of annual cake-baking contest at Rattlesnake Inn Down Below.

Jump-Off (*Whistle*) — Bar and grill in Sawdust City. It serves "railroad fries: thick, with skins on." It was started ten years ago by women who weren't allowed to use pool tables in the Trackside Tavern.

Junior Pal Brigade (*Cheese*) — Project of the Senior Care Facility in Pickax. College students earn money by cheering up housebound patients.

Junkery (*On/Off*) — Antique shop in Junktown owned by C. C. and Iris Cobb. It had been a "splendid Victorian mansion in its day — a stately red brick with white columns" and ornamental ironwork.

Junque Trunque (*On/Off*) — Antique store in Junktown, run by a young man in sideburns and dark glasses.

Just Rust (*Mountain*) — Shop at Potato Cove with rusty artifacts of all kinds.

Kabibbles (*Whistle*) — Snack food made by Celia Robinson in Florida and sent to Qwilleran. The cats love it.

Kalico Kittens (*Stars*) — Small stuffed kittens made of rosebud-patterned cotton. Each has its own name. They are "primitive but appealing" folk art made by the elderly ladies at Safe Harbor.

Kemple Life and Accident (*Thief*) — Firm owned by Ernie Kemple until he retires, selling it to the Brady brothers.

Kennebeck Building Industries (*Underground*) — Contracting business in Moose County.

Kennebeck Chamber of Commerce (*Cardinal*) — Civic organization that defends the image of Tipsy with black boots.

Kilcally Dairy Farm (*Glue*) — Farm in Moose County.

Kipper and Fine (*Red*) — Clothing store Down Below where Qwill buys some new clothes.

Kitchen Boutique (*Cheese*) — Store in Stables Row owned by Sharon Hanstable, with displays of "salad-spinners, wine racks, espresso-makers, cookbooks, woks, exotic mustards, and chef's aprons."

Klingenschoen Foundation (*Post Office*) — Foundation established by Qwilleran to share his inheritance with the residents of Moose County. (*Ghosts*) — Fund that disburses money "in ways that will benefit the community — grants, scholarships, low-interest business loans."

Klingenschoen Headquarters (*Cheese*) — Four floors of an office building in the Loop in Chicago. It has a think tank of specialists in real estate, economic development, philanthropy, and investments.

Klingenschoen Professional Building (*Wasn't*) — New building that will enable Pickax to "lure some specialists up here from Down Below." (*Closet*) — It's the location of Pender Wilmot's law office.

Kumquat Court (*Closet*) — Section of Park of Pink Sunsets where Mrs. Robinson lives in Florida.

Labor Day Bike Race (*Cheese*) — Moose County race won by Wilfred Sugbury.

Ladies' Tuesday Afternoon Bird Club (*Cardinal*) — Lockmaster club started by Grummy Inglehart to study birds instead of shooting them.

Lambreth Gallery (*Backwards*) — Art gallery near the financial district Down Below, in an old loft building. It's long and narrow, furnished "like a living room" in a bold modern design.

Landmarks Preservation Committee (*On/Off*) — New committee established to preserve and revitalize Junktown.

Lanspeak Department Store (*Post Office*) — Pickax store owned by the Lanspeaks. (*Glue*) — It's the largest commercial building on Main Street, a "Byzantine palace with banners flying from the battlements." (*Ghosts*) — Originally known as Pickax General Store, the business was bought by Larry Lanspeak's great-grandmother.

Lessmore and Lessmore (*Mountain*) — Spudsboro realty office owned by Robert and Dolly Lessmore. He's less and she's more.

Limburger Mansion (*Cheese*) — Run-down mansion with exterior brickwork—"horizontal, vertical, diagonal and herringbone"—and tall, stately windows with "stained-glass transoms or inserts of etched and beveled glass."

Linguini's (*Glue*) — Mama-and-papa restaurant in Moose County. "He cooks, and she waits on tables." It has fabulous food. (*Wasn't*) — The small establishment is in a storefront with a homemade sign. Mr. Linguini made the tables from driftwood, but the napkins are cloth. (*Stars*) — The restaurant is located outside the town of Brrr. It's believed that Poppa Linguini makes his own wine in the basement.

Lion's Tale (*On/Off*) — Junktown neighborhood bar. It was a neighborhood bank in the 1920s, a "miniature Roman temple now desecrated by a neon sign and panels of glass blocks" in the windows.

Lockmaster Academy (*Sang*) — Boarding school that stresses ballet and equestrian arts.

Lockmaster Art Center (*Sang*) — Center that sends spies to the new Pickax Art Center.

Lockmaster Business Academy (*Thief*) — School attended by Lynette Duncan.

Lockmaster Hounds (*Cardinal*) — Kennels in Lockmaster.

Lockmaster Indemnity Corporation (*Whistle*) — Private insurers of depositors' funds in the Lumbertown Credit Union.

Lockmaster Ledger (*Closet*) — Lockmaster newspaper in competition with the *Something*. (*Breakfast*) — Arch Riker meets with the editor of the *Ledger*. (*Cheese*) — Jill Handley used to work for the *Ledger*. Arch and the editor are meeting to discuss sharing sources and the "hostility and prejudice that exist between the two counties." (*Stars*) — The *Ledger* is sending reporters to review the Pickax Theatre Club's summer production in Mooseville.

Lockmaster Library (*Cardinal*) — Building made from the "same set of Greek temple blueprints that produced the Pickax Public Library."

Lockmaster Lilliputians (*Sang*) — Little League soccer team.

Lockmaster Logger (*Cardinal*) — Newspaper established during lumbering days, more than a century before. The circulation is 11,500; editor is Kipling MacDiarmid. The paper is more conservative than the *Something* in makeup, but it has a "friendly slant."

Lockmaster Museum (*Shakespeare*) — Museum in the county below Moose County. (See "The Mad Museum Mouser" in *The Cat Who Had 14 Tales*.)

Lockmaster Safecrackers (*Whistle*) — Local baseball team.

Lodge Hall (*Glue*) — Building that's a "small-scale Bastille." (*Wasn't*) — Qwilleran attends Scottish Night at the invitation of Andrew Brodie. (*Thief*) — Qwill wears his new kilt to Scottish Night.

Lois Inchpot Day (*Cheese*) — Day to honor Lois and try to get her to reopen her Luncheonette, which her customers are painting and repairing.

Lois's Luncheonette (*Brahms*) — Small restaurant in Pickax with the "second worst coffee in Moose County." (*Post Office*) — The downtown restaurant stays open during the noon hour. (*Closet*) — The atmosphere is bleak and the food ordinary, but it's the "only restaurant in downtown Pickax, and the old, friendly, decrepit ambience" makes the locals feel welcome. (*Cheese*) — The Luncheonette is located on Pine Street not far from Stables Row. Lois decides to close, after thirty years. The K Fund sponsored the development of Stables Row, but her customers have to pitch in and fix up her place. Customers donate labor on weekends to work on her lunchroom, an act that's the "Pickax equivalent of knighthood in the court of King Arthur." (*Thief*) — The new vinyl floor, donated and installed by devoted customers, has a "hideous pattern of flowers and geometrics." (*Sang*) — The "shabby eatery" has been feeding its super-supporters for thirty years.

Lombardo's Grocery (*On/Off*) — An old-fashioned market in Junktown with $4.95 Christmas trees piled outside and a "smell of pickles, sausage, and strong cheese" inside.

Lucky Electronics (*Thief*) — Business in Pickax run by Lucky. You're lucky if he ever shows up.

Lumbertown Credit Union (*Whistle*) — Financial institution started by Floyd Trevelyan in Sawdust City. The building looks like an old-fashioned depot, with highly varnished narrow boards and hard waiting-room benches. Model trains run in the lobby. Depositors call it the Choo-Choo Credit Union.

Lumbertown Party Train (*Whistle*) — Train in Moose County with historic Engine No. 9, a restored dining car, an Art Deco club car, and a private rail car. The private car is splendid: "richly upholstered wing chairs in the lounge, the dining table inlaid with exotic woods, the bedrooms with brass beds and marble lavatories." The woodwork is carved walnut and the light fixtures are Tiffany glass.

Lumpton Furniture Factory (*Mountain*) — Manufacturing business in Spudsboro.

Lumpton Transport (*Mountain*) — Spudsboro business, owned by former Sheriff Josh Lumpton. The motto is "You got it? We move it." Josh's office is a plain room "with a large girly type wall calendar as the sole decoration."

Lumpton's Hardware (*Mountain*) — Spudsboro business.

Lumpton's Pizza (*Mountain*) — Restaurant in Spudsboro.

Lyle and Starkweather (*Danish*) — Largest decorating firm Down Below. It's located in an exclusive shopping area, with an entrance that consists of huge double doors of "exotically grained wood" with silver door handles "as big as baseball bats."

MacWhannell & Shaw (*Whistle*) — Moose County accounting firm owned by Whannell "Big Mac" MacWhannell and Gordie Shaw.

Maus Haus (*Red*) — Home of Robert Maus on River Road. It used to be an art center, but now it's a "weird boardinghouse." (*High*) — The house has been replaced by a condo complex and marina.

Mayfus Orchard (*Cardinal*) — Business in Moose County that donates seven bushels of apples for visitors during the tour of Qwilleran's barn-home.

Medford Manor (*On/Off*) — a.k.a., Medicare Manor. Third-rate hotel Down Below where Qwilleran has a room.

Medium Rare Room (*Red*) — Restaurant in the Stilton Hotel, Down Below.

Meritorious Society of Gastronomes (*Red*) — MSG club, a "bunch of food snobs" Down Below.

Midwest National Bank (*On/Off*) — Percival Duxbury's bank Down Below.

Minnie K (*Brahms*) — Boat near Mooseville. It's an "old gray tub, rough with scabs of peeling paint" that moves with reluctance.

Moose County Airport (*Post Office*) — Small airport in Moose County. No jets land here. The landing field looks like a softball field and the terminal looks like a dugout. (*Shakespeare*) — An open field serves as a long-term parking lot. The airport manager is also "ticket agent, mechanic, and part-time pilot." (*Ghosts*) — The Klingenschoen Fund upgrades the airstrip and terminal, builds hangars, and paves a parking lot, while local garden clubs landscape the entrance and plant rust and gold mums. (*Wasn't*) — The K Foundation gives a grant to build a long-term parking structure.

Moose County Community College (*Whistle*) — New college to be located in the old vacant stone houses on Goodwinter Boulevard. The curriculum will be "English, accounting, data processing, office systems, and business management." (*Stars*) — The college will soon have a chef's school.

Moose County Courthouse (*Post Office*) — Public building located on the perimeter of Park Circle.

Moose County Electric Cooperative (*Whistle*) — Power company in Moose County, unable to explain the mysterious blackout that coincides exactly with the time Koko spends inside the pyramid.

Moose County Genealogical Society (*Ghosts*) — One of the two most important organizations in a county that takes pride in its heritage.

Moose County Gourmets (*Post Office*) — Social club in Pickax.

Moose County Historical Society (*Shakespeare*) — The Society is helping to operate the Klingenschoen Museum. (*Glue*) — The Society turns the Goodwinter farm into the Goodwinter Farmhouse Museum. (*Ghosts*) — Iris Cobb leaves her antique collection, her car, and her personal belongings to the Society to liquidate for the benefit of the museum.

Moose County Something (*Glue*) — New newspaper of "professional caliber" for Moose County. Until a printing plant and office complex are built, it's housed in a rented warehouse, a former meat-packing facility that still smells of bacon. The staff receives eighteen thousand subscriptions and orders thirty thousand copies of their initial newspaper. The first issue goes out with the name *Something* and a ballot for readers to pick the name. They pick the *Something*. (*Underground*) — It reaches the reading public twice a week. Its new building houses editorial and business offices as well as a modern printing plant, made possible by an interest-free loan from the Klingenschoen Fund. (*Wasn't*) — There are "no security guards or hidden cameras" such as there are in big-city newspapers. (*Whistle*) — The paper claims to be the "north-country newspaper of record." Its slogan is "Read all about it." (*Cheese*) — The paper has expanded to publish five days a week and is now operating in the black. The staff always seems to be having a good time. The paper's first computer-composite of a suspect is published with the article on the bombing of the New Pickax Hotel. (*Sang*) — All residents over ninety receive a free subscription.

Moose County Youth Center (*Thief*) — Center in Pickax, supported in part by the winnings from the Indian Village bridge players.

Mooseland High School (*Closet*) — Consolidated school on Sandpit Road that serves the agricultural townships in Moose County.

Mooseville Chamber of Commerce (*Underground*) — Champion of The Captain's Mess, although the junk store has been "condemned by the county department of building and safety." (*Stars*) — Wayne Stacy is president of the Chamber.

Mooseville Madness (*Stars*) — Qwilleran's description of Mooseville residents' tendencies to talk about interplanetary visitors, the Sand Giant, the disappearance of the *Jenny Lee*, the mysterious death of the backpacker, the petroglyphs, and the disappearance of Owen Bowen.

Mooseville Magic (*Underground*) — Invigorating buoyancy in the atmosphere of the resort town. (*Ghosts*) — It's an "indescribable element that elevated one's spirit and made Mooseville a vacation paradise."

Mooseville Mosquitoes (*Post Office*) — Mooseville sports team.

Mooseville Museum (*Brahms*) — Former opera house from the nineteenth century, now filled with memorabilia of the old lumber and shipping industries.

Morning Rampage (*Backwards*) — Daily newspaper Down Below owned by the Pennimans, in competition with the *Daily Fluxion*.

Mountain Charm Motel (*Mountain*) — Motel on the way to the Potato Mountains. It could be improved by "better plumbing and mattresses and fewer ruffles and knickknacks."

Nasty Pasty (*Brahms*) — Little bistro at the Cannery Mall in Mooseville, a "hats-off place," which tourists seem to like. It features nasty pasties, which are like turnovers "filled with meat and potatoes and turnips." (*Cheese*) — They cater a picnic dinner on John Bushland's cabin cruiser. (*Sang*) — The café now offers Dijon mustard and horseradish, to please tourists.

New Pickax Hotel (*Shakespeare*) — Hotel in Pickax City, built in 1935 after the original hotel burned. It has a "part-time bellhop, color TV in the lobby, indoor plumbing, and locks on the doors." The bridal suite has a round bed with pink satin sheets. (*Ghosts*) — The presidential suite is the only one with a telephone and color TV. (*Wasn't*) — The hotel is furnished in "early Modern — not comfortable, not attractive, but sturdy." A runaway snowplow that hit the front of the building demolished the lobby, but did not destroy the sturdy oak furniture. (*Cheese*) — The hotel is severely damaged by a bomb, and a staff member is killed. (*Thief*) — The K Fund plans to buy and restore the hotel.

Night's Candles (*Brahms*) — Candle and gift shop in the Cannery Mall owned by Roger MacGillivray's wife, Sharon Hanstable.

Noble Sons of the Noose (*Ghosts*) — A secret society, whose members are supposed to be direct descendants of a lynch mob that hanged Ephraim Goodwinter.

North Pole Café (*Shakespeare*) — Café in Brrr with fabulous food, but only one rest room that was "not to be believed." (*Glue*) — This ethnic restaurant, a "super little eatery," serves delicious Polish *zupa grzybowa* and *nerki duszone.*

Northern Land Improvement (*Sang*) — Lockmaster company that buys Mrs. Coggin's land.

Northern Lights Hotel (*Brahms*) — Hotel in Mooseville, a "relic from the 1860s." It's "a shoebox with windows, but a porch had been added at the rear, overlooking the wharves." It has "high-backed booths constructed from the salvaged cabins of retired fishing boats." (*Underground*) — The tourists are served "gray pork chops, gray baked potatoes, and gray broccoli." (*Ghosts*) — The hotel is a barrackslike building with "three floors of plain windows in dreary rows." (*Thief*) — The hotel is headquarters for the Ice Festival. It has twenty guest rooms and public areas, including a ballroom. In the dining room is one waiter with one choice on the menu: fried fish sandwich with lumber-camp fries and cole slaw. (*Stars*) — Mr. and Mrs. Wayne Stacy are co-owners of the hotel. It's open twenty-four hours a day, seven days a week.

Nouvelle Dining Club (*Thief*) — New gourmet club in Pickax. It's "committed to quality rather than quantity." The group plans a monthly dinner, with members taking turns as hosts.

Nuttin' But Chairs (*On/Off*) — Antique shop in Junktown run by a woman who says that "everyone resembled some kind of chair."

Obituary Club (*Brahms*) — Social club in Pickax. Members collect obituaries and produce a monthly newsletter.

Off-Links Lounge (*Mountain*) — Bar at the country club in Spudsboro.

Ogilvie Sheep Ranch (*Stars*) — Moose County ranch on Sandpit Road, two miles south of the shore.

Old Log Church (*Brahms*) — Church in Mooseville.

Old Stone Church (*Shakespeare*) — Church on Park Circle. (*Cardinal*) — It has the largest, oldest, and wealthiest congregation in Pickax. (*Closet*) — It's the site of a presentation of "The Big Burning of 1869" in the basement and a wedding upstairs, simultaneously.

Old Stone Mill (*Brahms*) — Restaurant in Mooseville, an "authentic old mill with a water wheel." The atmosphere is "picturesque, but the menu is ordinary." (*Post Office*) — The atmosphere is "conducive to intimate conversation." (*Shakespeare*) — Every table has a view of the mill, which creaks incessantly, although the millstream dried up seventy years before. The Old Stone Mill has been renovated and has a new chef. Hixie Rice is managing the restaurant. They "replaced the dreary menu with more sophisticated dishes and fresh ingredients." (*Wasn't*) — The Mill pays its chefs handsomely and offers an international menu. (*Thief*) — The giant waterwheel, weakened after years of disuse, is wrecked when an old dry riverbed floods. (*Sang*) — The waterwheel is replaced by a reproduction, but it just isn't the same.

Old Timers Club (*Shakespeare*) — Pickax club for the elderly. (*Ghosts*) — The club admits only lifelong residents of advanced age.

Olde Tyme Soda Fountain (*Cheese*) — Business on Stables Row offering ices, phosphates, and banana splits at an antique marble soda bar. (*Thief*) — Its walls and floor are "vanilla white" and its fountain bar "chocolate-colored marble." The "ice cream" chairs have strawberry-red seats.

Onoosh's Mediterranean Café (*Thief*) — New restaurant in Pickax opened by Onoosh Dolmathakia and her partner, a native of Kansas. It has small oil-burning lamps, brass-topped tables, murals, and hanging lights. (*Sang*) — The café, in Stables Row, is the first ethnic restaurant in Pickax.

Other Village Voice (*Thief*) — Monthly newsletter for Indian Village.

Otto the Potter (*Mountain*) — Craft shop in Potato Cove.

Otto's Tasty Eats (*Post Office*) — Pickax family restaurant owned by Otto Geb, with a "smoking section" and a "screaming section" for families with kids. The food is ghastly, but there's lots of it. It's in an old warehouse in the industrial area of Pickax. (*Shakespeare*) — Otto offers one price for all you can eat.

Outdoor Club (*Closet*) — Social club in Moose County that meets monthly for programs on conservation or the environment.

Owen's Place (*Stars*) — New restaurant across from the Great Dune Motel in Mooseville. Owen and Ernestine Bowen come up from Florida to run it during the tourist season. The building is on the west side of Sandpit Road, at the foot of the Great Dune. Formerly a coin-operated laundry and then a Chinese restaurant, it has stained cedar siding. The interior is mostly white, with plastic plants and indoor trees.

Palomino Paddock (*Underground*) — Expensive restaurant in Lockmaster. The hostess wears a long dress and a wine steward wears heavy chains. (*Cardinal*) — A four-star restaurant, the building resembles an old horse stable. (*Wasn't*) — The interior is "artfully cluttered with saddles, bales of hay, and portraits of thoroughbreds." (*Whistle*) — It's a "five-thousand-calorie" restaurant, a "mix of sophistication and hayseed informality." Diners sit in horse stalls. (*Sang*) — It's located near Whinny Hills.

Pals for Patients (*Whistle*) — New outreach program of the Senior Care Facility in Pickax that supplies pals to homebound patients.

PALS, Prisoner Aid Ladies' Society (*Brahms*) — Group that writes letters to inmates at the prison in Moose County and sends them little presents.

Parade of Bikers (*Stars*) — Group of bikers in the Fourth of July parade. Qwilleran brings up the rear in his reclining bike.

Parade of Moms (*Stars*) — One of the entries in the Fourth of July parade in Mooseville.

Parade of Pets (*Stars*) — One of the entries in the Fourth of July parade in Mooseville.

Park of Pink Sunsets (*Closet*) — Retirement complex in Florida where Euphonia Gage and Celia Robinson live.

Pasta Perfect (*Mountain*) — Italian restaurant in Spudsboro, a "rustic roadhouse" that appears ready to collapse.

Pasty Parlor (*Cheese*) — Restaurant in Stables Row in Pickax, whose owners from Down Below plan an exclusive "designer pasty" with a choice of four crusts, four fillings, and four veggies.

Patch's refinishing shop (*On/Off*) — Junktown business owned by Russell Patch, once a "two-carriage carriage house."

Pear Island Hotel (*Breakfast*) — New Pear Island hotel that celebrates piracy. The facade has been "artfully stained to look fifty years old." The two dining areas are the Corsair Room and Smugglers' Cove.

Pear Island Resort (*Breakfast*) — New resort that develops suddenly due to the efforts of XYZ Enterprises and the Klingenschoen Foundation. Security officers on the island are "uniformed like Canadian Mounties and look pretty impressive when they ride up on horses." The hotel is "three stories high and a city block long, with a porch running the entire length." It's "flanked by rows of rustic storefronts, each with a hitching post." The smell of fudge is everywhere. The resort is destroyed in a fierce storm.

Pedal Club (*Cheese*) — Group in Moose County that sponsors a bike-a-thon called Wheels for Meals, to benefit the hot-meal program for shut-ins.

Peel & Poole Design Studio (*Mountain*) — Studio in Spudsboro with good taste, run by Sabrina Peel and Spencer Poole.

Pennant Race (*Sang*) — Qwill's name for the great spelling bee, in the format of a spelling world series.

Penniman Art Museum (*Backwards*) — Gleaming white-marble building Down Below, copied from a "Greek temple, an Italian villa, and a French chateau."

Penniman Foundation (*Backwards*) — Foundation that owns the *Morning Rampage* and contributes heavily to various causes and charities.

Penniman Greystone & Fleudd (*High*) — Rest-estate development firm that wants to tear down the Press Club. Their newest project is a two-tower office building connected with a bridge across Zwinger Boulevard.

Penniman Plaza (*High*) — New hotel Down Below that looks like an amusement park.

Penniman Pottery (*Red*) — Original name for the pottery at the Maus Haus, Down Below.

Penniman School of Fine Art (*Backwards*) — Art school Down Below funded by the Pennimans.

Petrified Bagel (*Red*) — New Junktown restaurant, furnished with junk.

Pets for Patients (*Wasn't*) — Project at the Pickax Senior Care Facility in which volunteers bring cats and dogs on certain days to boost the morale of patients.

Pickax Arts Council (*Whistle*) — Council that campaigns to obtain the Klingenschoen carriage house to use as an art center. The K Foundation completes Polly's abandoned house as the new center.

Pickax Auto Repair and Radiator Shop (*Underground*) — Pickax business whose motto is "A Good Place to Take a Leak."

Pickax Barbershop Quartet (*Sang*) — Moose County group in "striped blazers and straw boaters" that sings for the Pennant Race.

Pickax Boosters Club (*Post Office*) — Civic club that invites Qwilleran to join. (*Glue*) — Local club in Pickax where Qwilleran gives an address at a luncheon. (*Closet*) — The Boosters deliver Christmas baskets. (*Cheese*) — The club sponsors the Celebrity Auction to benefit the community's Christmas fund.

Pickax Bridge Club (*Thief*) — Social club in Pickax.

Pickax Chamber of Commerce (*Shakespeare*) — Official organization in Pickax City. (*Cheese*) — The group sponsors the Food Fair and Pasty Bake-off during the Great Food Explo.

Pickax City Hall (*Post Office*) — "Turreted stone edifice of medieval inspiration, lacking only a drawbridge and moat," with a "parking lot, fire hall, police station, and ambulance garage," just off Main Street.

Pickax Feed and Seed (*Sang*) — Business in Pickax.

Pickax Funeral Band (*Shakespeare*) — Local band that plays for Senior Goodwinter's funeral. (*Ghosts*) — The band plays for Iris Cobb's funeral, leading the procession of cars to the cemetery.

Pickax General Store (*Ghosts*) — Original store that became Lanspeak's in Pickax City.

Pickax Hospital (*Brahms*) — Medical facility in Pickax. (*Post Office*) — The walls are supposed to be antique pink, but they look like raw veal. (*Shakespeare*) — The hospital and its adjoining Senior Care Facility are two modern buildings that look out of place in a city of imitation castles and fortresses.

Pickax Miners (*Post Office*) — Local softball team.

Pickax People's Bank (*Cheese*) — Bank managed by J. Willard Carmichael.

Pickax Picayune (*Brahms*) — A "chicken-dinner newspaper" owned by the Goodwinters, founded in 1859. It has "never acknowledged the invention of the camera." (*Post Office*) — The building is "early monastery." The paper covers all the ice cream socials and chicken dinners. The *Picayune* has "successfully resisted twentieth-century technology and new trends in journalism." Senior Goodwinter, the owner, hand-sets most of the type. (*Shakespeare*) — The building is "squeezed between the imitation Viennese lodge hall and the imitation Roman post office." There's a satisfying smell of ink, but the building looks like a museum. There are old copies of the *Picayune,* "yellow and brittle, plastered on walls that had not been painted since the Great Depression." Its antiquated presses clank out thirty-two hundred copies each issue. An arsonist destroys the building.

Pickax Power Problems (*Ghosts*) — Electric company in Pickax.

Pickax Public Library (*Shakespeare*) — Public facility run by Polly Duncan. A portrait of its founder, Ephraim Goodwinter, hangs in the lobby. (*Cardinal*) — It looks like a Greek museum except for the bicycle racks. (*Wasn't*) — After the Klingenschoen Foundation installs an elevator, the library becomes "a day care center for grandparents." (*Sang*) — It's the "central intelligence agency" of the community. The card catalogue has been computerized, and the townspeople stage a protest. The demonstrators burn their library cards.

Pickax Pygmies (*Sang*) — City Little League soccer team, coached by Roger MacGillivray.

Pickax Singing Society (*Post Office*) — Social group in Pickax that needs a few more male voices. (*Shakespeare*) — The group presents Handel's *Messiah* at the Old Stone Church in November.

Pickax Thespians (*Post Office*) — Local amateur group. See *Theatre Club.*

Picturesque Pickax (*Shakespeare*) — Book published by the Pickax Boosters Club before World War One.

Piggin, Noggin and Firkin (*On/Off*) — Antique store in Junktown owned by Mrs. McGuffey, a retired schoolteacher.

Pines, The (*Breakfast*) — Summer estate of Chicago family on Pear Island, protected by a "high iron fence similar to that in front of Buckingham Palace."

Pirate Gold (*Breakfast*) — Special drink made by Bert the bartender at the Pear Island Hotel. It's "all fresh, all natural," made of "fruit juice with two kinds of rum and a secret ingredient."

PLUG PLanned UGliness (*Danish*) — Decorating shop on River Street, Down Below. It's filled with "tawdry merchandise."

Popopopoulos' Fruit, Cigars, Work Gloves and Sundries (*On/Off*) — Small Junktown neighborhood store owned by Papa Popopopoulos. It smells of "overripe banana and overheated oil stove."

"Prandial Musings" (*Red*) — Qwilleran's column on gourmet dining for the *Daily Fluxion*.

Press Club (*Backwards*) — A restaurant and more, located in a "sooty limestone fortress with bars on the windows" (formerly the county jail). The noisy bar downstairs serves drinks and food—great corned beef sandwiches—and the dining room upstairs has tablecloths. (*Danish*) — The wall color is "Sirloin, Medium Rare." The club is soot-covered and barred, with "mangy pigeons roosted among the blackened turrets." (*Brahms*) — It's been ruined! The "murky atmosphere had been renovated by the new housekeeping committee: wallpaper, chandelier, hanging baskets, and mirrors."

Princess (*Stars*)—Sailing vessel whose captain was Tess Bunker's and Joe Bunker's great-grandfather. Captain Bunker had an unusual way of overpowering lake pirates.

Purple Point Boat Club (*Cheese*) — Club on the lake near Mooseville, whose specialty is Cajun Supreme.

"Qwill Pen, Straight from the" (*Underground*) — Column Qwilleran writes for the *Moose County Something*.

Railroad Retirement Center (*Whistle*) — Home for Ozzie Penn and other retired railroadmen. Located on Main Street in Sawdust City, it's directly across the street from the Trackside Tavern. Formerly a railroad hotel, it's a "three-story brick building without such unnecessary details as porches, shutters, or ornamental roof brackets." It has brown walls, brown floors, and brown wood furniture.

Rattlesnake Inn (*Red*) — Inn on the lake of the same name, the site of a cake-baking contest. The inn is famous for its bad food. It's a "rickety frame structure that should have burned down half a century before."

Republic of Crowmania (*Stars*) — Concept created by Tess Bunker, corvidologist who wants to do an animated feature on crows. She drives a bus with "Republic of Crowmania" painted on it. She uses the bus for educational purposes for children.

Riding and Hunt Club (*Cardinal*) — Social club in Lockmaster.

River Road Pottery (*Red*) — Forerunner of the Maus Haus, Down Below.

Roberto's (*High*) — New classy restaurant Down Below offering North Italian Cuisine. Robert Maus went to Italy and worked in a restaurant in Milan for a year, then came home, changed his name to Roberto, and opened the restaurant.

Robin O'Dell Catering (*Sang*) — New business in Pickax, owned by Celia Robinson and Pat O'Dell.

Roundhouse, The (*Whistle*) — Home of Floyd Trevelyan in West Middle Hummock. It's a "long, low contemporary building with wide overhangs and large chimneys," stained a "gloomy brownish green." The steps are formed from railroad ties. Inside, it's poorly furnished. Downstairs is a room which contains Floyd's six model trains, complete with buildings, roadways, rivers, hills, train depot, and a thousand feet of track.

Safe Harbor Residence (*Stars*) — Home for widows of commercial fishermen in Fishport. It's a three-story frame Victorian-style house, formerly a residence of a shipping magnate, then a boarding house for sandpit workers, then a summer hotel, then a private school. The Scotten, Hawley, and Zander families bought it as "a retirement home for widows of commercial fishermen."

Sand Giant (*Stars*) — Original explorers in the Mooseville area claimed to hear "rumbling inside the dune" and to see "a large gray shape moving among the trees on the summit." They decided that a giant lived in a cave inside the Dune. When settlers started cutting down the ancient trees, a giant sandslide killed everyone in the lumbercamp. People said the lumbermen had offended the Sand Giant. The Giant also protested when workers began to ship sand from the Dune for various construction purposes. The Sand Giant objects once again and a sinkhole opens up and causes the east end of the Dune to slide into it.

Sand Giant's Gnomes (*Stars*) — Youthful maintenance crew that cleans and summerizes houses in Mooseville.

Sawdust City High School Summer Camp Fund (*Whistle*) — Club that enables seniors to spend a week studying nature and ecology.

Say Cheese (*Underground*) — Photographer John Bushland's modest cabin cruiser.

SC & L Line (*Whistle*) — Sawdust City and Lockmaster railroad line that still hauls slow freight up from Down Below.

Scotten Fisheries (*Cheese*) — Moose County family business run by four Scotten brothers. It was started by their grandfather.

Scottie's Men's Store (*Post Office*) — Business in Pickax where Qwilleran buys a new tie at an "exorbitant price." (*Shakespeare*) — Owner Bruce Scott, a.k.a., Scottie, has a brogue "when talking to good customers." (*Glue*) — The store looks like a Cotswold cottage. (*Ghosts*) — Scottie sells Qwilleran a dark suit and paisley tie, by burring his *r*'s. (*Whistle*) — Qwilleran buys a kilt from Scottie's.

Scottish Bakery (*Cheese*) — Business in Pickax that features afternoon tea with scones, cucumber sandwiches, shortbread, and a "death-defying triple-chocolate confection" called Queen Mum's cake.

Scottish Night (*Wasn't*) — Qwilleran attends this annual celebration at the Lodge Hall. (*Thief*) — Qwill wears his new kilt to the celebration on January 25, the birthday of Robert Burns. Bagpipe, haggis, and trays of Scotch circle the room twice, then dinner is served: forbar bridies, taters, and neeps, and Pitlochry salad.

Seagull Inn (*Breakfast*) — Bed-and-breakfast on Pear Island, featuring brass beds and a billiard room.

Senior Care Facility (*Shakespeare*) — Modern facility for the elderly, adjacent to the Pickax Hospital. (*Wasn't*) — The facility offers a "Pets for Patients" program in which Yum Yum and Bootsie participate. (*Closet*) — It's the site of a presentation of "The Big Burning of 1869." (*Whistle*) — The new Pals for Patients hires part-time companions for the sick or elderly.

Senior Towers (*High*) — Residence for the elderly, Down Below.

Shipwreck Museum (*Stars*) — Museum in Mooseville. There's a new exhibit of petroglyphs from the Ogilvie ranch.

Shipwreck Tavern (*Brahms*) — Business in Mooseville that can get lively on Saturday nights. (*Underground*) — It's the town's "noisiest and most popular bar," which occupies what appears to be the wooden hull of a ship. (*Stars*) — The Main Street business is constructed like a beached boat; the interior is "as dark as a ship's hold."

Sip 'n' Nibble (*Cheese*) — Wine and cheese shop in Stables Row in Pickax, run by Jerry Sip and Jack Nibble. It carries assortments of wine and cheese unknown to Moose County. (*Thief*) — Qwilleran depends on this shop for Christmas gift baskets of wine, cheese, and other treats.

Skyline Towers (*On/Off*) — Apartment building Down Below where Sylvia Katzenhide lives.

Sloan's Drug Store (*Sang*) — Moose County business owned by Phoebe's parents, Mary and Orville.

Smitty's Refrigeration (*Glue*) — Pickax business on South Main Street.

Smooth Sailing (*Stars*) — Twenty-four-foot sailboat in the Fourth of July parade.

Smugglers' Cove (*Breakfast*) — Restaurant at the Pear Island Hotel.

SOCK (*High*) — Save Our Casablanca Kommittee. This group has been formed to save the Casablanca, an old apartment building scheduled for demolition.

Sorbonne Studio (*Danish*) — Business owned by Jacques Boulanger. The interior is an "awesome assemblage of creamy white marble, white carpet, white furniture, and crystal chandeliers." The carpet looks like meringue.

Sorta Camp (*On/Off*) — Junktown antique business owned by Sylvia Katzenhide.

Split Rail Farm (*Cheese*) — Kristi Waffle's renovated goat farm, where she makes cheese to sell at Sip 'n' Nibble.

Spoonery, The (*Cheese*) — Lori Bamba's new restaurant, which offers dozens of types of soup, including Mulligatawny, Scotch broth, Portuguese black bean, eggplant and garlic, sausage gumbo, butternut squash soup with garlic and cashews, borscht, and tomato-rice. (*Thief*) — She also serves Asian hot and sour sausage soup.

Spudsboro Gazette (*Mountain*) — Newspaper in the Potato Mountains, similar to the *Moose County Something.*

Spudsboro Golf Club (*Mountain*) — Club in Spudsboro with a new chef who introduces a lighter menu. The club doesn't admit Taters.

Squunk Water (*Glue*) — Water from a village in Moose County, from a "flowing well, whose waters are said to be therapeutic." In 1919, the sheriff confiscated smuggled liquor and poured it on the dump in Squunk Corners. "That's why

Squunk water is so good for you." (*Underground*) — Gary
Pratt fills containers with Squunk water and retails "the pre-
cious stuff at an incalculable markup." (*Thief*) — It's reputed
to be the "fountain of youth." (*Stars*) — Squunk water was
reportedly discovered by Haley Babcock's grandfather when
Haley was ten.

Stablechat (*Cardinal*) — Newsletter in Lockmaster, a collection of steeplechase news and horsey gossip.

Stables Row (*Cheese*) — A block-long stone building on a
back street in downtown Pickax that was a ten-cent barn in
horse-and-buggy days. Now it's been remodeled to accommodate several shops.

Stephanie's (*Post Office*) — New restaurant owned by the
Lanspeaks. They name it after their cow. The whole place is
done in dairy colors: "milk white, straw beige, and butter yellow." (*Shakespeare*) — The restaurant occupies an "old stone
mansion in an old residential section." It has the best food,
but the chef has a mental block. (*Wasn't*) — Stephanie's
closes.

Stilton Hotel (*Red*) — Location of the Medium Rare
Room. (*Shakespeare*) — Qwill and Junior Goodwinter stay at
the Hotel Stilton when they go Down Below for Arch Riker's
retirement dinner.

Suitcase Productions (*Closet*) — Name of the production
company for *The Big Burning of 1869.*

Sully's Saloon — See *Trackside Tavern.*

Summers, Bent & Frickle (*Cardinal*) — Lockmaster law
firm.

Suncatcher (*Stars*) — Cabin cruiser spotted on the lake. It
belongs to Owen and Ernestine Bowen.

Tacky Tack Shop (*Cardinal*) — Store in Lockmaster with gaudy sweatshirts, T-shirts, and posters.

Tait Manufacturing Company (*Danish*) — Family owned firm organized Down Below in 1883 to make buggy whips. Later the company produced car radio antennas.

Tanks and Tees (*Sang*) — A shabby business located behind the Shipwreck Tavern in Mooseville.

Teahandle, Burris, Hansblow, Maus and Castle (*Danish*) — Law firm in the Midwest city. (*On/Off*) — It's the most prestigious law firm in town, of which Robert Maus is a partner.

Tech-Tiques (*On/Off*) — Basement antique stop in Junktown run by Hollis Prantz.

Theatre Club (*Glue*) — Amateur group in Pickax. The group is working on a production of *Arsenic and Old Lace*. A previous production was *The Boys from Syracuse*. The club was founded a hundred years ago and named the Pickax Thespians. Later members thought it sounded "like deviant sex," so the name was changed to the Theatre Club. (*Cardinal*) — The club's current production is *Henry the VIII*. (*Wasn't*) — The club produces *Macbeth* in September. (*Whistle*) — The group's next production is *A Midsummer Night's Dream*. They replace the fairies with little green men. (*Thief*) — The group presents *Hedda Gabler*. (*Stars*) — The club is doing summer theater in a barn near Mooseville. The first production is a comedy, *Visit to a Small Planet*. The next is *Life with Father*.

Three Weird Sisters (*On/Off*) — Antique store in Junktown run by Cluthra, Amberina, and Ivrene.

Tipsy's Tavern (*Glue*) — Restaurant in North Kennebeck in Moose County. It's a very popular log cabin restaurant with good food. The "exterior logs are dark and chinked." The interior has rustic furniture and a "portrait of a white cat with black boots and a black patch." (*Ghosts*) — The restaurant started in a small log cabin in the 1930s. It now occupies a large log cabin, where "serious eaters" converge for "serious steaks, freshly peeled potatoes, boiled carrots, and cole slaw." (*Tail*) — The tavern sits high and dry on the summit of a hummock. It's a "sprawling roadhouse of log construction, with dining rooms on several levels.

Tiptop (*Mountain*) — A small country inn on Big Potato Mountain that was converted into a home for the Hawkinfield family. It's on the top of the mountain, with a "fabulous view from every window, and gorgeous sunsets! Wide verandas, eight bathrooms, large kitchen, your own private lake!"

Toddwhistle's Taxidermy (*Glue*) — Business located in North Kennebeck and owned by Wally Toddwhistle.

Toledo Restaurant/Toledo Tombs (*Danish*) — The most expensive restaurant Down Below. (*On/Off*) — It delivers Christmas Eve dinner for Mary and Qwilleran. (*Red*) — Still the most expensive restaurant in the Midwest city.

Toodle's Market (*Cardinal*) — Market in Moose County with a deli. (*Wasn't, Closet, Whistle*) — Qwilleran buys food for the Siamese here: red salmon, smoked oysters, caviar, chicken liver pâté, or tenderloin. (*Cheese*) — From a family with an old respected food name, Mrs. Toodle runs the business with assistance of sons, daughters, in-laws, and grandchildren. (*Tail*) — Food demonstrators hand out samples of food and little paper cups of coffee.

Toodle Family Restaurant (*Shakespeare*) — Pickax restaurant.

Top o' the Dunes Club (*Brahms*) — Private club on the lake near Mooseville with "substantial vacation houses."

(*Underground*) — It's a "private community of summer people." The social enclave has a variety of people, from Captain Phlogg to Mildred Hanstable.

Tourist Development Association (*Brahms*) — Office in Mooseville that purports to develop tourists instead of tourism.

Trackside Tavern (*Whistle*) — Bar in Sawdust City, the site of a fatal knifing. It's "strictly a male hangout" that's a hundred years old. It has knotty pine walls, mounted deer heads, wide pine floorboards, and a wood-burning stove.

Trevelyan Construction (*Whistle*) — Firm developed by Floyd Trevelyan into the largest construction firm in Moose county, then sold to XYZ Enterprises.

Trevelyan Farm and Orchard (*Ghosts*) — Farm in Moose County with a cider mill. They throw in "bruised apples, windfalls, worms, and everything," to make a delicious cider.

Trevelyan Plumbing and Heating (*Underground*) — Business in Moose County. For the Fourth of July Parade, the company sponsors a flatbed with old fashioned bathroom fixtures, with Grandpa Trevelyan sitting in a bathtub, smoking a corncob pipe.

Tubes (*Whistle*) — Amateur softball team composed of hospital personnel.

Tuesday Afternoon Women's Club (*Wasn't*) — Club in Kennebeck that plants a tree in the village park.

Turp and Chisel (*Backwards*) — Art club that originated Down Below forty years earlier. Now it occupies the top floor of the best hotel. There's a lounge, a dining room, and a very busy bar. The game room, paneled with old barnwood, offers everything from darts to dominoes.

Typos (*Whistle*) — Moose County amateur softball team composed of newspaper staffers.

Vacation Helpers (*Breakfast*) — Service business on Pear Island that will "sit with the baby, wash your shirt, bake a birthday cake, sew a button on, cater a picnic, address your postcards, mail your fudge, clean your fish." It's run by Shelley, Mary, and Midge. They make a delicious meat loaf, which Qwilleran orders for the cats.

Valley Boys' Club (*Mountain*) — Club in Spudsboro.

Vance the Village Smith (*Mountain*) — Craft store in Potato Cove.

Viewfinder, The (*Stars*) — Bushy's new boat. It has an open cockpit, two-person helm station, four berths, and galley with refrigerator, stove, and sink.

Villa Verandah (*Danish*) — a.k.a., Architect's Revenge. High-rise apartment building, shaped like a bent waffle, in the big city Down Below.

Westside Gallery (*Backwards*) — Art gallery Down Below.

Wheels for Meals (*Cheese*) — Bike-a-thon sponsored by the Pedal Club to benefit the hot-meal program for shut-ins in Moose County.

Wickes Animal Clinic (*Mountain*) — Spudsboro veterinary clinic run by Dr. John and Dr. Inez Wickes.

WPKX (*Post Office*) — Pickax radio station. The newscasters have a style that Qwilleran calls "Instant Paraphrase," because they tend to repeat themselves when giving the news. They tend to repeat ideas when it's time for news.

(*Shakespeare*) — The station keeps forecasting the Big One, but the sun keeps shining. (*Glue*) — The radio provides headline news: "twenty-five word teasers sandwiched between two hundred word commercials." (*Cardinal*) — WPKX has a talent for garbling the news to give the wrong impression.

XYZ Enterprises, Inc. (*Shakespeare*) — Company in Pickax that developed the Indian Village apartments and condominiums on the Ittibittiwassee River. The firm owns a "string of party stores and a new motel in Mooseville." It's owned by Don Exbridge, the X. The Y is Caspar Young, a contractor. The Z is Dr. Zoller, a dentist. (*Underground*) — The second largest contractor in the county is building the East Shore Condominiums on the lake. (*Breakfast*) — XYZ Enterprises develops the Pear Island Resort on Breakfast Island, spending "a fortune on wining and dining travel editors." A storm destroys the whole resort.

Yellyhoo Market (*Mountain*) — Ramshackle market in Spudsboro.

Yesteryear-by-the-Lake (*Breakfast*) — Bed-and-breakfast on Pear Island, featuring a cobblestone fireplace and a collection of toy trains.

Zoller Clinic (*Shakespeare*) — Dentist office in Pickax owned by Dr. Zoller. The clinic occupies a "lavishly renovated stone stable that had once been a ten-cent barn behind the old Pickax Hotel in horse-and-buggy days."

The Cats' Geography Book

Airport Road (*Shakespeare*) — Moose County road with abandoned shaft houses, slag heaps, ghost towns "identifiable only by a few lonely stone chimneys," and the "stark remains of trees blackened by forest fires."

Batata Falls (*Mountain*) — Former falls on Big Potato, now Lake Batata.

Bixby County (*Stars*) — County near Moose County, where there's a detention facility. Bixby Countians' taste is "raunchier" than Moose Countians. The county is "chiefly industrial and big on sports." Schools are not the best and unemployment is a problem.

Black Creek (*Ghosts*) — Creek that angles across the back of the Goodwinter and Fugtree properties.

Black Creek (*Cheese*) — Area not far inland from Mooseville. Once a boomtown during river and railroad traffic, the only things that remain are a bar, an auto graveyard, and a weekend flea market.

Black Creek Junction (*Whistle*) — Area south of Wildcat through which the Lumbertown Party Train passes before it wrecks.

Black Creek Lane (*Shakespeare*) — Road in North Middle Hummock where Senior Goodwinter's farmhouse is located.

Black Forest (*Whistle*) — Qwilleran's name for the dense evergreen woods between the former Klingenschoen mansion and his apple barn.

Bloody Creek (*Sang*) — Former thriving community. The only things that remain are a bridge and burial ground.

Boyerville (*On/Off*) — Town north of the Midwest city, where Mrs. McGuffey used to teach.

Breakfast Island (*Breakfast*) — Pear-shaped island several miles from the Moose County mainland. The north shore has treacherous rocks; the southern shore has sand. It used to be peaceful, but now it has a hotel and shops. It's called Providence Island by the settlers, Grand Island by the rich folks, Breakfast Island by the mainlanders, and Pear Island by the developers. (*Stars*) — The island has been restored to its wilderness state after a disastrous attempt at turning it into a tourist attraction.

Brrr (*Shakespeare*) — Coldest spot in Moose County. (*Glue*) — The village is on the lake. (*Stars*) — Brrr is the breeziest spot in Moose County in the summer, on a promontory with a good harbor. It has the Hotel Booze on its summit.

Buckshot Mine (*Post Office*) — Abandoned mine on Ittibittiwassee Road where eighteen miners were buried alive in 1913.

Canard Street (*On/Off*) — Street where the Press Club is located.

Chipmunk (*Shakespeare*) — Town in Moose County. (*Glue*) — It's the "slummiest town in the county." There are "cottages with sagging porches and peeling paint, sheet-metal shacks, trailer homes hardly larger than gypsy wagons, and larger houses advertising rooms to rent." (*Underground*) — The village was known as the "moonshine capital of the county" during Prohibition.

Dimsdale (*Post Office*) — Former thriving town in Moose County. Officially it no longer exists, but there are shanties of squatters back in the woods.

Down Below (*Brahms*) — Mooseville parlance for metropolitan areas to the south. They are thinking "not only of geography" when they use the term. (*High*) — Qwilleran is warned against respiratory ailments caused by pollution, violence, kitnapping, stress, and generally dangerous conditions when he announces plans to spend the winter Down Below. (*Whistle*) — It's the "polluted and crime-ridden centers of overpopulation" four hundred miles south of Moose County. (*Sang*) — It's the "mega-cities south of the Forty-Ninth Parallel."

Dumpy Road (*Underground*) — Road leading off Sandpit Road that dead-ends at Hogback Road. It has a "benighted colony of substandard housing" on the way to the Ittibittiwassee River.

Fishport (*Stars*) — Fishing village near the resort town of Mooseville.

Five Points (*Mountain*) — Intersection on the way to Hawk's Nest Drive in the Potato Mountains.

Flapjack (*Whistle*) — Old layover for the railroad, on the other side of Wildcat. It's an early lumber camp that has been converted into a public recreation park.

Fugtree Road (*Shakespeare*) — Road in North Middle Hummock.

Gingerbread Alley — See *Pleasant Street*.

Goodwinter Boulevard (*Post Office*) — Street in Pickax City. Old family mansions include those belonging to Penelope and Alexander Goodwinter, Dr. Halifax and his invalid wife, and Amanda Goodwinter. (*Wasn't*) — The Gage house, belonging to Junior Goodwinter's grandmother, is on Goodwinter Boulevard. The boulevard is a "broad, quiet avenue off Main Street with two stone pylons at the entrance." It has a landscaped median and old-fashioned streetlights, ending in a small park with an impressive monument commemorating the four Goodwinter brothers who founded the city.

Great Dune (*Stars*) — Huge sand dune that rises abruptly and towers over the downtown area, with a forest on the top. It has a sheer drop of about a hundred feet. Part of the Great Dune has gone Down Below to be used in concrete for highways, bridges, and skyscrapers—"like a little bit of Moose County in cities all over the northeast central United States." A sinkhole opens up behind Owen's Place and causes a gigantic sandslide of the east end of the Dune. The Sand Giant is blamed.

Hanging Tree (*Glue*) — Tree on Ittibittiwassee Road, past the Old Plank Bridge. A wealthy Goodwinter once dangled from a rope there.

Happy View Woods (*Danish*) — Middle-class residential area Down Below.

Hawk's Nest Drive (*Mountain*) — Road in the Potato Mountains where several expensive houses are located. Tiptop is at the top.

Hogback Road (*Underground*) — Dirt road near the Ittibittiwassee River where Little Joe Trupp's shack is located.

Horseradish (*Thief*) — Town on the lakeshore in Lockmaster County. Once the horseradish capital of the Midwest, it is filled with summer homes and country inns. (*Stars*) — Agriculture has given way to tourism. Lingering fumes still make "an invigorating atmosphere for vacationers."

Huggins Corners (*Underground*) — Area where Cecil Huggins's grandfather used to have a general store, on the Old Brrr Road.

Hummock Road (*Whistle*) — Road that forks off from Ittibittiwassee Road and leads to West Middle Hummock and beyond.

Inglehart Park (*Cardinal*) — Park located on the river in Lockmaster, named for Grummy Inglehart's family.

Ittibittiwassee Road (*Brahms*) — Road to the Ittibittiwassee River. Where Indians once had a village, there are apartments and condos. (*Glue*) — The Old Plank Bridge is located on this road. This new road, also called "Ittibittigraft," was built to accommodate Don Exbridge's condominiums. (*Ghosts*) —

The road leads past the Dimsdale Diner, on toward the Good-winter Farmhouse Museum.

Junktown (*On/Off*) — A blighted area off Zwinger Street, where Qwilleran lives. Cheap lodgings, bars, and antique shops occupy the old houses. (*High*) — People are buying the old town houses and fixing them up, and there are some first-class restaurants and antique shops. Junktown has new brick side-walks, new trees, and old-fashioned gas lamps.

Kennebeck (*Shakespeare*) — Bustling town northeast of Pickax. (*Cardinal*) — The first sign of Kennebeck is a tower-ing grain elevator. The watertower bears the silhouette of a cat. It's a prosperous community with a wide main street and curb-stones, plus senior housing, condominiums, and other signs of the times. In the 1930s, it was almost a ghost town until Tipsy's Tavern opened.

Lake Batata (*Mountain*) — Formerly a falls on Big Potato Mountain, now a lake.

Lighthouse Point (*Breakfast*) — Point on Pear Island. It's "a desolate promontory overlooking an endless expanse of wa-ter to the north, east, and west."

Little Hope (*Whistle*) — Small town in Moose County south of Pickax where Homer Tibbitt grew up.

Lockmaster (*Underground*) — Town sixty miles southwest of Mooseville, the county seat of Lockmaster County. It's lo-cated in hunting country with its "rolling hills, opulent horse farms, and miles of fences." It has an "air of sophistication" that Moose County lacks. (*Cardinal*) — In the nineteenth cen-tury, wealthy shipbuilders and lumber barons built residences as huge as resort hotels, lavished with "turrets, balconies, verandahs, bowed windows, bracketed roofs, decorative gables, and stained glass." Now they are rooming houses, bed-and-breakfasts, law offices, insurance agencies, a funeral home, a museum, and Bushy's photographic studio.

Lost Lake Hills (*Backwards*) — A fashionable "exurb" fifteen miles outside of the Midwest city's limits.

MacGregor Road (*Shakespeare*) — Moose County road where Polly Duncan lives.

Maple Street (*Stars*) — Road in Mooseville that dead-ends at the Great Dune.

Mayfus Road (*Cardinal*) — Road that intersects with Ittibittiwassee Road, site of Hixie Rice's accident.

Merchant Street (*Danish*) — Street in the city with old mansions, including Mrs. Allison's residence for "career girls" and the home of Mrs. Highspight, the psycatatrist.

Middle Hummock (*Shakespeare*) — Small area in Moose County.

Moose County (*Brahms*) — Pickax City is the county seat and Mooseville is a resort town. (*Post Office*) — Industries include commercial fishing, tourism, and a little farming and light industry. (*Shakespeare*) — In winter it's "not unusual to see cross-country skis in downtown shopping area." (*Glue*) — Typical terrain is "rolling pastureland dotted with boulders and sheep, dairy farms with white barns, dark stretches of woods, abandoned mines with the remains of shafthouses." (*Underground*) — Moose County has lush evergreen forests in the north near the lake. (*Ghosts*) — The county is a "remote rockbound outpost" comfortably distant from the "crime, traffic, and pollution of densely populated urban areas to the south." (*High*) — In Moose County, nothing ever changes unless it blows away in a high wind. Moose County has king-size mosquitoes, poison ivy, skunks, and hazardous deer crossings, but it affords a "comfortable life among good people." (*Mountain*) — There are no fast-food chains or garage sales. Moose County is "thirty years behind the times" but the "business community is pushing for tourism." (*Wasn't*) — The population is 11,279. (*Closet*) — The worst storm ever to hit Moose County shuts down everything for four days. (*Breakfast*) — "Prehistoric" in Moose County is "anything before the War of 1812." (*Stars*) — The "locals are all a little balmy, and the summer people soon get that way." Sheep farming supports many families in the county.

Mooseville (*Brahms*) — Small town four hundred miles north of everywhere. Qwilleran inherits a little place on the lake near this resort village that stretches out along the lakeshore. Tourist attractions include the museum, the flower gardens at the state prison, and the prison gift shop. (*Underground*) — Located thirty miles north of Pickax, the resort town is "burgeoning with leaf, flower, bird, sunshine, blue sky, rippling wave, lake breeze, and hordes of carefree vacationers." Mooseville is two miles long and two blocks wide. The north side of Main Street has "the municipal docks, a marina, and the Northern Lights Hotel." Across the street are "civic buildings and businesses made entirely of logs, or concrete poured to resemble logs." From the lake, Mooseville looks "as quaint as an Italian fishing village." (*Stars*) — Mooseville is squeezed between the lake and the Great Dune, where several sidestreets dead-end. The lake air is "salubrious," but there's also something "insidious" about it. Rumors of UFOs and the Sand Giant abound near Mooseville. The Chamber of Commerce encourages the gossip, hoping that flying saucers will put Mooseville on the map.

Mudville — See Sawdust City.

Muggy Swamp (*Danish*) — Exclusive residential area Down Below with French châteaux and English manor houses. (*High*) — The Wilburtons and other wealthy families live in this suburb.

No Man's Gully (*Thief*) — Dried-up riverbed leading from the millstream to the Ittibittiwassee. It floods during the winter's warm rain.

North Kennebeck (*Glue*) — Small town eight miles north of Chipmunk. It's a "thriving community with a grain elevator, condominiums, an old railway depot converted into a museum, and Tipsy's."

North Middle Hummock (*Shakespeare*) — Area where Senior Goodwinter lives in Moose County. It has been a ghost town for fifty years. (*Ghosts*) — It's located thirty minutes away from Pickax. The Goodwinter Farmhouse Museum is located here on Black Creek Lane. North Middle Hummock had been a thriving community in the old days when the mines were operating, but economic disaster after World War I reduced it to a ghost town.

Oak Street (*Stars*) — Mooseville street that dead-ends at the Great Dune.

Old Brrr Road (*Underground*) — Abandoned road that's "gone back to nature."

Old Plank Bridge (*Shakespeare*) — Bridge in Moose County that's the location of Senior Goodwinter's fatal accident. (*Glue*) — It's located on Ittibittiwassee Road.

Paddockville (*High*) — Town south of Lockmaster.

Park Circle (*Brahms*) — Circle with "several impressive buildings: a nineteenth-century courthouse, a library with the columns of a Greek temple, two churches, and a stately residence with a polished brass house number that was Aunt Fanny's." (*Shakespeare*) — The site of old stone buildings in Pickax City, Main Street divides and circles a small park.

Pauper's Cove (*Mountain*) — Small town on the way to the Potato Mountains where Qwilleran buys slippers.

Pear Island (*Breakfast*) — New resort that develops suddenly due to the efforts of XYZ Enterprises and the Klingenschoen Foundation. The island is also known as Providence Island, Grand Island, and Breakfast Island. The worst storm in forty years destroys all new construction on the Island.

Pickax City (*Brahms*) — County seat of Moose County, with a population of 3,000. It used to be mining country, located in a valley in the hill country. Magnificent houses reflect the "wealth of the mining and lumbering pioneers." The commercial section extends for three blocks. Stores, restaurants, a lodge hall, the post office, the home of the *Picayune*, a medical clinic, and several law offices are all built of stone "with more exuberance than common sense." (*Post Office*) — It's "four hundred miles north of everywhere," but only thirty miles from Mooseville. There's "one traffic light, fourteen mediocre restaurants, a nineteenth-century newspaper, and more churches than bars." Lanspeak Department Store "poses as a Byzantine palace." The gas station resembles Stonehenge. (*Shakespeare*) —

The *Picayune* headquarters resembles an "ancient Spanish monastery." It's "squeezed between the imitation Viennese lodge hall and the imitation Roman post office." The city is "bounded on the south by South Street, but on the north by East Street, on the west by North Street, and on the east by West Street." (*Glue*) — The public library is housed in a Greek temple. The Lodge Hall is a small-scale Bastille. Scottie's Men's Shop is a Cotswold cottage. (*Mountain*) — Streets of the mile-square town are laid out north and south and every turn is ninety degrees. (*Closet*) — Pickax has its first Christmas parade, with Qwilleran as Santa Claus.

Pickax Road (*Ghosts*) — Road that goes north from Pickax and intersects Ittibittiwassee Road.

Pine Street (*Cheese*) — Downtown street in Pickax where Lois's Luncheonette is located.

Pine Street (*Stars*) — Street in Mooseville that dead-ends at the Great Dune.

Pines, The (*Breakfast*) — Estate of the Appelhardt family on Grand Island, with a main lodge and other facilities.

Pioneer Cemetery (*Brahms*) — Abandoned cemetery near Mooseville, down a dirt road through a cobblestone gate. (*Underground*) — The old abandoned cemetery has been restored. Student history clubs are "restoring all abandoned cemeteries and cataloging the family graveyards."

Pirate Shoals (*Stars*) — Dangerous area out on the lake at Mooseville.

Piratetown (*Breakfast*) — Town on Pear Island where the islanders live. They call it Providence Village.

Pleasant Street (*Cheese*) — Residential street in Pickax, a neighborhood of Victorian frame houses lavished with fancy wood trim. The street's nickname is Gingerbread Alley. Polly's sister-in-law's ancestral home is here. (*Thief*) — There's talk of restoring the homes to their former glory.

Potato Cove (*Mountain*) — Ghost town that artists on Little Potato resurrected as a place to sell their handcrafts. It looks like the "set for a low-budget Hollywood western: crude buildings of weathered wood, spaced haphazardly along the road and connected with wooden sidewalks."

Potato Mountains (*Mountain*) — Mountains that are just being developed for tourists. Spudsboro is the county seat, located between two mountain ranges. The mountains are "sort of round and knobby, friendly mountains." The West Potato Mountains are in a national forest. On the east side are Big Potato Mountain and Little Potato Mountain. Big Potato is being developed. Little Potato is inhabited, yet still primitive. There are lots of artists who sell all kinds of crafts. There are two kinds of people living on Li'l Potato: Taters, original settlers who "still cling to a pioneer way of life"; and New Taters, artists and others who like plain living and are "militant about protecting the environment."

Providence Island (*Breakfast*) — Original name of Breakfast Island. The settlers gave it this name because "a divine providence cast 'em up on the beach after their ship was wrecked."

Providence Village (*Breakfast*) — Town on Breakfast Island, called Providence Village by the natives and Piratetown by others. It has a "small but well-built schoolhouse with outhouses for boys and girls" and an old general store and a church.

Purgatory Falls (*Mountain*) — Waterfall on Little Potato Mountain that "drops off a high cliff and down into a bottomless pit."

Purple Point (*Post Office*) — Point on the lake at Mooseville where big salmon are biting. (*Cardinal*) — The Hasselriches have a cottage here where Irma Hasselrich and Polly Duncan go birding in the wetlands. (*Closet*) — It's a "narrow peninsula curving into the lake to form a natural harbor on the northern shore of Moose County." When seen across the bay at sunset, it's a distinct shade of purple. The approach to the Point is "across a low, flat, uninhabited expanse called the Flats, a wetland in summer and an arctic waste following the Big Snow." (*Sang*) — The point extends two miles into the lake. It is a ribbon of sandy beach and vacation homes on the west and a strip of rocks on the east.

Rattlesnake Lake (*Red*) — Lake near the Midwest city.

River Lane (*Thief*) — Road in Indian Village where the condominiums are located.

River Road (*Red*) — Road where Maus Haus is located.

River Street (*Danish*) — Location of decorating studio called PLUG, PLanned UGliness.

Roaring Creek (*Stars*) — Creek near Fishport.

Rocky Burn (*Thief*) — River in Moose County.

Sandpit Road (*Underground*) — Secondary road in Moose County that leads from Pickax to Mooseville. (*Closet*) — Mooseland High School is located on Sandpit Road.

Sawdust City (*Glue*) — Small town in Moose County. (*Underground*) — It used to be the center of the lumber industry. (*Whistle*) — It's an industrial town at the mouth of the Ittibittiwassee River, founded by the Trevelyans. Some consider it "unprogressive and undesirable by Pickax standards," but it's larger (population 5,000) and has a thriving economy. Sawdust City was originally the county seat. Mud tracked from unpaved side streets gave the town the nickname of Mudville.

Seagull Point (*Underground*) — Outcropping of rock projecting into the lake near Brrr.

Shantytown (*Wasn't*) — Area located on the unpaved stretch of Ittibittiwassee Road. It's a "slum of shacks and decrepit travel trailers, rusty vehicles, and ramshackled chicken coops."

Smith's Folly (*Shakespeare*) — Abandoned town in Moose County. (*Glue*) — It was founded in 1856 by Eddington Smith's great-grandfather.

Snaggy Creek Cutoff (*Mountain*) — "Short cut" to Hawk's Nest Road outside of Spudsboro.

Spudsboro (*Mountain*) — County seat in the Potato Mountains. The Yellyhoo River runs alongside the main street. It's a strip city, "a few blocks wide and a few miles long, wedged between two mountain ranges." There are several winding but roughly parallel streets and a railroad track "built on a series of elevations—like shelves." On the residential section of Center Street are "Victorian cottages, contemporary split-levels, and middle-aged bungalows." The commercial end has stores, bars, gas stations, small office buildings, barbers, two banks, one traffic light, a newspaper office, animal clinic, and public library.

Squunk Corners (*Shakespeare*) — Village in Moose County. (*Glue*) — It's noted for a "flowing well, whose waters are said to be therapeutic." In 1919, the sheriff confiscated smuggled liquor and poured it on the dump in Squunk Corners. "That's why Squunk water is so good for you."

State Street (*Red*) — Prominent road in the city Down Below, where the Golden Lamb Chop is located.

Suffix Township (*Thief*) — Geographic area in Moose County, where Indian Village is located.

Three Pines Mine (*Post Office*) — Site of a cave-in five years ago in Moose County. The old shaft house is a "notorious lovers' lair."

Three Tree Island (*Underground*) — Small island with three trees, located in the lake near Mooseville. It has a "flat, sandy beach with a hump in the middle and a clump of trees," a dock and a "makeshift shack made of wood and corrugated metal."

Trawnto (*Wasn't*) — Small town in Moose County. (*Cheese*) — It's a quiet lakeside resort with "large old summer houses on a bluff." The settlers intended to name it Toronto, but they were misunderstood.

Trawnto Beach (*Cheese*) — Beach in Moose County.

Trevelyan Apple Orchard (*Cardinal*) — Site of Qwilleran's barn.

Trevelyan Drive (*Cardinal*) — Road leading south from Pickax to Wildcat.

Trevelyan Road (*Wasn't*) — Back road to Qwilleran's apple-barn house. (*Whistle*) — It wanders through the neglected apple trees and near the ruins of the old Trevelyan farmhouse.

Trevelyan Trail (*Cardinal*) — Dirt trail from the Klingenschoen estate to Trevelyan Road, winding through overgrown pastureland.

Tupper Road (*Glue*) — Moose County road where Toddwhistle Taxidermy Studio is located.

West Beach Road (*Breakfast*) — Road on Pear Island that is uphill all the way to Lighthouse Point.

West Middle Hummock (*Shakespeare*) — Small town in Moose County. (*Glue*) — It's about five miles from Chipmunk. (*Whistle*) — Hummock Road passes through "a blighted hamlet or two" before entering an area of "knobby hills, bucolic vistas, architect-designed farmhouses, and no utility poles," because all cables are underground.

Wildcat (*Glue*) — Small town in Moose County south of Pickax. (*Cardinal*) — The ramshackle town's sign claims the population is 95. The Cuttlebrinks founded the town. There are four structures: a "dilapidated bar, an abandoned gas station, the remains of an old barn, and a weathered wood building for Cuttlebrink's Hdwe. & Genl. Mdse. Establ. 1862." (*Whistle*) — Originally called South Fork, it was renamed for a "runaway train that was wrecked on the trestle bridge there in 1908."

Willoway (*Ghosts*) — Lover's lane under the willow trees that grow on the banks of the Black Creek near the Goodwinter Farmhouse. It's "notoriously romantic."

Woodland Trail (*Thief*) — Road in Indian Village where the apartments are located.

Yellyhoo River (*Mountain*) — River in the Potato Mountains, running alongside main street in Spudsboro.

Zwinger Street (*On/Off*) — A main street in the Midwest town where Qwilleran lives. Downtown it's a "boulevard of new office buildings, medical clinics, and fashionable apartment houses." Junktown consists of rows of old town houses and Victorian mansions that are "neglected and forlorn." (*High*) — Zwinger Street has become Zwinger Boulevard, a "continuous landscaped park dotted with glass towers, parking structures, and apartment complexes." It's known as Eat Street by the *Fluxion* food editor, and has a dozen ethnic restaurants not to be found in Moose County.

7

Crimes and Clues

Scottie told Qwilleran he "canna remember any dead bodies before you moved to town" (Cardinal). *It's true that Qwilleran becomes in-*volved in solving many murders and other crimes. He always seems to "get sidetracked into some kind of unauthorized investigation" (*Mountain*).

Indeed there are many violent deaths from a variety of causes—shootings, knifings, poisonings, car crashes, carbon monoxide, drugs, fire, drownings, beatings, bee stings, whittlin', and smothering.

But how could Qwilleran ever solve all the mysteries and murders without the help of his chief investigator Koko and assistant investigator Yum Yum? Qwilleran's description of Koko to Cokey Wright (*Danish*) was very apt: "Koko gives the impression that he knows more than I do, and he has clever ways of communicating. Not that he does anything uncatlike, you understand. Yet, somehow he gets his ideas across." He seems to sense "without the formality of cogitation." Koko possesses "an intuition that could put him on the scent of a crime." With "a sniff here and a scratch there" he digs up information that astounds people who have to "rely on brain-power alone" (*Underground*).

The Cat Who Could Read Backwards

The first victim of foul play is Earl Lambreth, the supercilious owner of the Lambreth Gallery. Earl's body is discovered in the gallery by his wife Zoe. He was stabbed in the throat with a sharp chisel from his workbench.

Qwilleran uses a piece of paper on a string to encourage Koko in his leaps and acrobatic feats. This prompts Qwill to think "ballet dancer," which leads him to remember that the Ghirotto painting of the ballet dancer is missing from the Lambreth Gallery.

The other victim of foul play is George Bonifield Mountclemens, the controversial art critic for the *Daily Fluxion*. Qwill returns home late, only to hear Koko's cry of desperation. Koko isn't satisfied until Qwilleran follows him upstairs. Qwill's moustache begins to quiver. He opens the back door and sees Mountclemens's body on the pavement of the patio below. Koko moves in circles, performing a private ritual. Back upstairs, "the cat arched his back, made long legs, and stepped lightly in a pattern of three ever-narrowing circles."

The next day, Qwilleran goes to his apartment to check on Koko, who is now an orphan. Qwilleran realizes that Koko is uncomfortable without his cushion, so they go upstairs to Mountclemens's apartment. Koko sniffs at a closet door. When Qwill opens it, he discovers racks that hold paintings. At one particular slot, Koko tries to insert his paw, yowling excitedly. When Qwill removes the painting, Koko snags a small dark object with his claws—Mintie Mouse! Qwill also discovers the missing half of the Ghirotto. When Qwilleran entertains the notion of keeping the Ghirotto and saying nothing, Kao K'o-Kung sits in front of the canvas, "giving Qwill a reproachful stare." Qwill decides to report the find to the police.

Qwill thinks Koko might have seen who killed Mountclemens, so he comes right out and asks Koko who did it. Koko leads Qwilleran to a heavy wall tapestry, which conceals a door leading to the downstairs rear apartment. There are many unframed canvases facing the wall. A portrait of a steely blue robot is signed O. Narx. When Qwill accuses Koko of a false alarm, "Kao K'o-Kung gave him a withering look, then turned his back and licked himself extensively."

Koko tries again. He entices Qwilleran back to the kitchen of Mountclemens's apartment, where he nuzzles the knife rack and dislodges one of the four remaining blades. As Qwill returns the blade, his moustache flags him, and he goes down to the patio where he and Koko look for clues. Back in the kitchen, Koko suddenly tenses with excitement, goes over to the tapestry, and paws it. They go back to the downstairs apartment, and Qwilleran realizes there are fewer canvasses and the two pictures of robots are missing. When he looks at the other paintings, he discovers that they are Scrano's. Koko examines the painting, and when he comes to the signature, he reads the letters from right to left: O-N-A-R-C-S. Suddenly O. Narx arrives. Qwill and Koko team up to take Narx out of commission. Koko flies wildly around the room, crashing into Narx, and Qwilleran hits Narx with the flashlight.

Mountclemens owned the Lambreth Gallery. Earl had kept two sets of books on Mountclemens's transactions and threatened to tip off the Internal Revenue Service. He also warned the critic to stay away from his wife. Mountclemens killed Lambreth, then planned to kill Narx, his partner who faked the Scrano paintings, but Narx killed Mountclemens instead.

The Cat Who Ate Danish Modern

Once more Qwilleran encounters death. Mrs. Tait is found dead by her husband, apparently of a heart attack. Mr. Tait also discovers that his jade collection has been stolen. The houseboy is the police's main suspect.

Koko's Dictionary Game keeps flushing out words that point to Tait, like *bald, sacroiliac, koolokamba*—"a West African anthropoid ape with the head nearly bald and the face and hands black"—*rubeola, frame,* and *ruddiness.* Twice within one week Koko finds *sacroiliac* and *sadism.* Qwilleran feels "a significant vibration in his moustache."

Koko howls impatiently, then runs to the Spanish chest that houses the stereo set, trying vainly to reach underneath. Qwill gives in and extracts several items, including a crumpled scrap of paper and Mintie Mouse. Koko sniffs at his toy, then whacks it back under the chest before sauntering away. But Qwill studies the crumpled paper and finds a name on it: Arne Thorvaldson.

As Qwilleran is looking over the photographs of Tait's home and jade collection, he hears "a wet, slurping, scratching sound" and discovers Koko licking the photograph of the Biedermeier armoire. He notices "a thin dark line down the side panel" that doesn't make sense in the design of the cabinet. When Qwill takes a set of photographs to Tait, he takes Koko on a twelve-foot leash of nylon cord. While Tait goes to get his wife's cat, Qwilleran investigates the armoire and discovers the secret panel with the missing jade inside. Tait attacks Qwilleran with a spike, but a white blur and a "shock of white lightning" rescue him. Twelve feet of nylon cord are wound tightly around the legs of Tait, who lies on the floor. The room is silent except for the "hissing of a female cat on top of the Biedermeier armoire."

The investigation into another death is going on at the same time as the crimes involving Tait. Koko leaps from balcony to balcony of the Villa Verandah, over to David Lyke's apartment, where he sits until Qwilleran and Odd Bunsen find Lyke, dead of a bullet wound in the chest. Since robbery is apparently not a motive, Qwilleran searches for a reason. Lyke made "nasty cracks" about his friends, but everyone thought he was wonderful.

Koko dribbles Mintie Mouse across the living room and scores a goal directly under the Spanish chest. Qwilleran fishes out his missing jade button and something almost pink. Evidently Koko ate some wool while in Lyke's apartment, then spit up the whole wad and hid it under the chest. It's a yellowish-pink wool with gold metallic threads, from Natalie Noyton's shawl.

Qwilleran realizes that Natalie had been in David Lyke's apartment the night he died, and she had killed him. She confirms his conclusion by taking her own life, after leaving an explanation in her diary. She was "hopelessly in love" with Lyke, but finally realized that he would never marry her after her divorce.

Koko is honored for his part in the investigations with his own press card, complete with a photo ID.

The Cat Who Turned On and Off

When Qwilleran visits Junktown, he learns that Andrew Glanz, an antique dealer, has recently died in an accident. Mary Duckworth says he fell from a ladder in his shop. His friends say he was very prudent and careful, and would never have been so careless. The drunk on the street says he was murdered.

Koko wanders into the hall, into the midst of a jumble of

furniture. He goes straight to the finial upon which Andy Glanz
was impaled. Koko sniffs it "with mouth open and fangs bared,
a sign of repugnance." Qwill experiences in the roots of his
moustache "a tingling sensation he had experienced several
times before" when there was "murder in the air."

Mrs. McGuffey tells Qwilleran that Andy was writing a novel,
"sordid fiction." The setting was a community of antique dealers similar to Junktown—involving "alcoholics, gamblers, ho-
mosexuals, prostitutes, dope peddlers, adulterers."

The second man to die is C. C. Cobb, while he was scrounging at the Ellsworth house on Fifteenth Street. Qwilleran and
Iris find him at the foot of the stairs. The police accept it as
an accident, but Qwilleran wonders.

Qwilleran visits Ben in his apartment and discovers a stiff
blond hair. It's "three inches long, slightly curved, tapering at
one end." Qwill identifies it as Yum Yum's because it's mottled,
white and gray, while Koko's are pure white. Koko leads Qwilleran and Mary to the lower bookshelf, where he disappears
between two volumes. They discover an Underground Railway
passage, built by the abolitionist who owned the house, which
the cats use to go back and forth from the apartment.

Koko grinds his jaw against the latch of the ashpit door of
the potbellied stove. It clicks open and Koko pries it further.
It's full of papers—Andy's book manuscript. It's an awful book,
but it gives Qwilleran ideas about what really happened to
C. C.

When Qwilleran arrives home, both cats are "sitting tall in
the middle of the floor, with the attentive attitude" that means
they have a message. Yum Yum is staring hard with her crossed
eyes. Koko stares "so intently that his body swayed with an
inner tension." Koko turns toward a small shiny object on the
floor, a small packet of drugs. Koko jumps to the desk, then
steps "precisely on the green button of Iris's portable tape re-

corder" and turns it on to reveal C. C.'s snoring. Qwill cuts it off.

Qwill invites Ben into the apartment to toast the season. Koko's backbone bristles, and he arches his back and bushes his tail. With "ears laid back and fangs bared," he hisses, then jumps to the desk to watch the proceedings. Koko turns the tape recorder back on, but Qwilleran yells at him, so he jumps up on the mantle near the coat of arms. The tape plays a conversation in which C. C. accuses Ben of selling drugs. Ben attacks Qwilleran with a poker, but the iron Mackintosh coat of arms somehow skids off the mantel, catching Ben in the neck and knocking him down.

Ben admits pushing C. C. down the stairs because C. C. was blackmailing him with the knowledge that Ben was pushing heroin. Later Ben confesses to killing Andy because he was afraid Andy would turn him in.

The Cat Who Saw Red

In the middle of his first night in Maus Haus, Qwilleran is awakened by a scream. Moments later he sees a light-colored convertible pull away from the building. The next day Dan Graham tells him that his wife, Joy, has cleared out. Although Qwilleran knows she wanted a divorce, he is surprised that she acted so soon. The more he learns, the more his upper lip experiences a "disturbing quiver." It tells him that "something dire had happened to Joy."

Saturday night Mrs. Marron sees a man come down the fire escape that leads to the Grahams' loft. He's carrying a big sack which he throws into the river. Qwilleran takes Koko out for a walk near the river. Koko stops to sniff a bright blue-green object on the edge of the gravel, a "small, glazed ceramic piece the size and shape of a beetle." Scratched on the underside are the initials J. G.

Upon returning to the apartment, Qwilleran hears a "sudden disturbance on the desk—a shuffling of papers, a clicking of typewriter keys, some skidding of pencils and pens, then a light clatter as Qwilleran's new reading glasses fall to the floor." Koko has discovered the top row of keys. He types "3" with one paw and "0" with the other. Qwill feels a "tremor in the roots of his moustache"—"30" is the old newspaper symbol for the end of a story.

When Dan brags about sending out three hundred invitations to his exhibit and buying champagne and "horses' duvvers" for everyone, Qwilleran wonders where he's getting the money. Qwill becomes more convinced that something has happened to Joy.

Early one morning, William fails to show up to go with Robert and Qwill to the farmers' market. His bed hasn't been slept in, but his car is in the carport. The night before, he had stopped by Rosemary Whiting's and told her that he "had something" on Dan Graham and was going to investigate. He said he was going to "visit Dan and sponge a nightcap."

Qwilleran hears a *thud* in his apartment. A book with a red cover is lying open on the floor. Koko's tail stiffens, and he begins to "step around the book in a strange long-legged dance," circling the book three times. Qwilleran feels a "chill in the pit of his stomach." Qwilleran has seen Koko perform that ritual before (*Danish*). Once before, the cat walked around and around and around, and the thing he circled was a body (Mountclemens).

Koko and Yum Yum like to tilt pictures in the apartment. Behind one, Qwill notices a wall patch that moves from side to side. He peers through the opening and looks down into the two-story kiln room. He sees Dan Graham "copying from a loose-leaf notebook into a large ledger."

Qwill and Odd Bunsen go to the pottery to take pictures for a feature article. Qwilleran takes Koko, so they can snoop around. Koko enters the pottery "with the confidence of one who had been there before." In the clay room, Koko is attracted to a trapdoor in the floor. Qwilleran pulls open the door, peering into blackness. A "strange sound came from Koko, teetering on the edge." It starts as a growl and ends in a shriek.

While Qwill, Odd, and Koko are in Dan's studio, Koko jumps to a table and gently noses a pot with a brilliant red Living Glaze. Then he wanders off and sharpens his claws on a loose-leaf notebook. Qwilleran recognizes Joy's handwriting in the notebook, which has descriptions of her Living Glaze.

Qwilleran's eyes fall to Koko's typewritten message from the night before: pb. The Latin abbreviation for *Plumbum*, chemical symbol for lead, which is used in making pottery. Dan gives Qwilleran a red urn coated with Living Glaze. Koko stalks the urn, and a "growl came from his throat, starting like a distant moan and ending in a hair-raising screech."

The red library book still offends Koko. He's pushed it to the floor twice. Qwill picks up the book and finds the answer to the puzzle of what happened to Joy. In ancient China an animal wandered into a kiln while it was being loaded. The animal was cremated, and clay pots emerged in a "glorious shade of red." Qwill theorizes that Joy's cat was Dan's first experiment, and Joy was his second victim.

That night Qwill is awakened by "the fall of a body, the crash of a chair, the crack of a head hitting the ceramic tile floor, the shattering of a window." On the floor is Dan Graham—"his legs sprawled across a tangle of gray yarn." The cats had been busy, and the room was "crisscrossed with yards and yards of gray strands, like a giant spiderweb."

Dan killed Joy because he wanted the credit for her beautiful color glazes. After William's body is found and examined, it's revealed that Dan Graham had spiked William's drink with lead oxide and put his body in the slip tank of the clay room.

The Cat Who Played Brahms

Qwilleran's expensive gold watch disappears at the cabin. His sleek gold pen Rosemary gave him for his birthday is missing. Later Rosemary's coral lipstick disappears.

When Qwilleran goes fishing with the Whatleys on the *Minnie K,* he catches something that "looked like the body of a man," but the skipper cuts his line, and no one believes him. He hears two voices, one with a "deep rumble and a British accent and another with a piercing twang and a flat inflection."

Koko perches on the moose head, "fussing and talking to himself" and trying to thrust his paw into a crevice behind the moose head. He tries harder, and a cassette tape falls out of the crevice. It has music, but also a message from a man who's warning someone to "bring up more stuff."

Buck Dunfield is beaten to death in his basement workshop with one of the big candlesticks he makes. Buck had confided to Qwilleran that he thought something was going on around Mooseville, and he was doing some investigating.

Qwilleran decides to take Koko for a walk. The appearance of the harness produces a "noisy demonstration" of "Siamese sounds denoting excitement." Koko makes a "beeline for the toolshed," which Qwill and Rosemary investigate. Koko paws industriously at the blanket on Tom's cot, uncovering a large manila envelope, which contains nearly twelve hundred dollars.

When Rosemary buys a variety of tulips from the prison gift shop, Koko removes the black ones and scatters them all over the floor, twice. Qwill's moustache sends him signals—the tulips had come from the prison gardens.

Nick Bamba reveals that inmates sometimes escape over the wall and pay men in the "ferry racket" to take them to Canada. When the escapees are a few miles out, there's a "big *splash*" and the bodies are never found. Qwilleran realizes that he had indeed snagged a body on his fishing trip on the *Minnie K.*

Penelope Goodwinter calls Qwilleran with bad news: Aunt Fanny fell down a flight of stairs and didn't survive. Qwill and Rosemary arrive at the cabin to find the two cats "howling in two-part harmony." A bar stool is knocked over and blood is on the white rug and Koko is licking his paws. Qwill figures that someone broke in and used a bar stool to reach the hiding place behind the moose head. Koko must have leaped on the guy's head from one of the beams and stabbed him with his eighteen claws.

Koko bats his catnip toy around the room until it disappears beneath the sofa. Qwill discovers one of his navy blue socks, Rosemary's coral lipstick, a gold ballpoint pen, his gold watch, and some folded bills in a gold money clip.

When Qwill chops up some turkey for the cats, Koko views the plate with distaste. He "arched his back and stepping stiffly on long, slender legs, circled the repast as if it were poison— not once but three times." He had performed this ritual twice before. Qwill decides that Koko is steering him to the turkey farm. Rosemary says the man at the turkey farm has a money clip like the one Qwill found in his cabin.

Upon arrival at the turkey farm, Qwill sees a "tall, hefty man" and smells an incredible odor. The man's face and neck are covered with raw scratches, and one ear is torn. When the man speaks, Qwilleran realizes it's the threatening voice on the cassette tape. When Qwill accuses him, the man grabs a knife and leaps over the counter. Tom comes to the rescue, pointing a gun at the farmer.

Tom confesses that the man, Stanley Hanstable, told him to buy whiskey for the prisoners. Hanstable smuggled it inside the turkeys he delivered to the prison. Stanley killed Buck because Buck was snooping into his ferry racket, in which he smuggled men out of the prison, then dumped them into the lake.

Qwill finds Koko howling inside the cabin. The cat insists on going outside to the small shed, where they find the body of Tom the handyman, a suicide. When Koko plays the Brahms tape, he hears Tom's gentle voice, confessing to pushing Fanny down the stairs because Stanley said that Tom would "get a lot of money to buy a nightclub." He was disillusioned when he got nothing and Qwilleran got everything.

The Cat Who Played Post Office

Qwilleran becomes interested in the disappearance of a young girl, Daisy Mull, who was a housemaid at the K Mansion for a few months five years ago. Upstairs in the carriage house is an apartment covered with "graffiti in every color available in a spray can." This was where Daisy lived when she was a maid. Giant flowers that look like daisies are on every surface, "intertwined with hearts, initials, and references to LUV." Qwill's moustache bristles as the flowers remind him of the tune Koko played on the piano: "Daisy, Daisy."

Koko leads Qwilleran and Melinda Goodwinter to the attic, where they find Koko on top of a large carton, scratching industriously. Qwilleran feels that "prickling sensation on his upper lip." There's a tag with Daisy Mull's name, and the carton contains various articles of winter clothing.

Later Qwilleran finds Koko crouching on a cheap suitcase with a tag that says "Daisy Mull." This one contains a collection of summer wearables, "tasteless junk jewelry," a fourteen-karat gold bracelet, and a sack with the Lanspeak's Department Store logo containing a "pathetic assortment of baby clothes." Later he finds a white envelope with ten new hundred-dollar bills inside.

Della Mull, Daisy's mother, is found dead in her trailer home, apparently a victim of accidental substance abuse. Qwill did not have a chance to talk with her.

Mrs. Cobb reports that things "move around mysteriously—mostly in the kitchen." Twice it is the kitchen wastebasket, and once it's an old suitcase. Later it's the step stool.

Koko plays the piano again: E, D, C—the opening phrase of "Three Blind Mice." Qwilleran feels the "familiar tickle on his upper lip." The clues elude him. Koko consistently sits on the third stair of the staircase.

Tiffany Trotter comes to talk about Daisy. They had been friends since ninth grade. Tiffany knew Daisy was pregnant, but she didn't know who the father was. Soon Tiffany, age twenty-two, is killed by a gunshot wound to the head.

Qwill realizes that Koko has never experienced the murals in Daisy's apartment. Koko's first reaction is to "flatten himself, belly to the floor." Koko paws the graffiti, trying to reach one set of initials: SG. Next he dives between the bed and the wall, poking something with one inquisitive paw. Qwilleran retrieves a notebook written in the distinctive, calligraphic handwriting of Daisy Mull. Mildred translates Daisy's diary. Within the diary, she mentions her new boyfriend, Sandy, who gave her money for an abortion.

Qwilleran wakes up in the hospital, with a brief loss of memory. Gradually he remembers that his bike accident was no accident. A truck suddenly swerved into the eastbound lane, "a murderous monster bearing down upon him."

That night Qwilleran hears a scraping sound in the kitchen. Another object has been moved. The cats' heavy metal commode filled with kitty gravel is in the middle of the floor. Behind it is Koko, "preparing to give it another shove with his nose."

At two A.M., Qwilleran hears a "prolonged wailing, shrill and mournful." Koko is "howling an unearthly lament that made the blood run cold." The next morning Qwilleran learns that Penelope had gone home and taken her own life by running the car in her closed garage, about two in the morning.

After lunch, Koko lugs in a long ivory envelope. It is a letter from Penelope in which she tells of Alexander's affair with Daisy, who had called him Sandy. Penelope asked one of Alex's boyhood acquaintances to convince Daisy to have an abortion and "leave town permanently in return for a generous regular support payment." He informed Penelope that Daisy was buried a thousand feet underground at the Three Pines Mine cave-in. Alex and the man agreed that the two witnesses must be silenced: Mrs. Mull by a drink with drugs in it and Tiffany Trotter by a "single perfect shot" in the head. They also tried to kill Qwill when he was riding his bicycle. She writes that when she confronted Alex, he became enraged, and she fears for her life.

That night Qwill is awakened by Koko, who throws his weight against Qwill's securely latched door. With "stentorian yowls that turned to shrieks," Koko races to the staircase. Qwill follows and hears the back door being slowly opened. He sees a "dark, bulky figure moving furtively through the entry hall." Koko leaps to the top of the seven-foot wardrobe, between two large, valuable vases. There's a confusion of sounds: "a thump, a clatter, a man's outcry, and a loud thud followed by the unmistakable crash of an enormous ceramic vase on a stone floor." Birch Trevelyan lies groaning on the floor, "one foot in the cats' spilled commode," which Koko had pushed to the middle of the floor.

Birch is the one who tried to run down Qwilleran on Ittibittiwassee Road. Qwill learns that Alex's plane crashed as he tried to escape. Qwill figures that Birch also doped Penelope's Scotch and carried her to the garage. After a "penetrating stare" from Koko, Qwilleran realizes that Penelope's death wasn't "a homicide set up to look like a suicide." It's a "suicide planned to look like murder" — in order to frame Alex and Birch.

The Cat Who Knew Shakespeare

Senior Goodwinter is killed on the old plank bridge. His car rams the stone rail, flips head over tail, and lands on the rocks in the river before catching fire.

The *Picayune* newspaper plant burns to the ground. Qwill's moustache quivers. If the *Picayune* is really in the financial trouble that Junior said, did Senior commit suicide? It's curious timing.

Koko is pushing books off the shelf again, on "a Shakespeare kick." Qwilleran finds *Hamlet* on the floor. Koko pushes *A Midsummer Night's Dream* off the shelf, then *King Henry VIII*, then *Hamlet* again. Koko pushes *Macbeth* off the shelf, along with *Julius Caesar*. Qwilleran reads the passage about bathing "our hands in Caesar's blood up to the elbows." In *Macbeth*, there was a conspiracy to murder the old king. A "tremor on Qwilleran's upper lip" alerts him. Was the *Picayune*'s double tragedy the result of a conspiracy?

Koko has been moving things around again. This time he wheels the iron herb garden around, moving it into a dark corner. Herb Hackpole welded the metal herb cart for Iris. As Herb and Iris are leaving after a visit with Qwill, they hear a loud crash. The mobile herb garden is in the middle of the floor. Nearby is a smashed clay pot. Uprooted plants are all over the room. Koko sits with "his chin on his paw" and his paw on *Hamlet*. Again.

As Qwilleran ponders the violent deaths of several Goodwinters, he wonders aloud whether Senior's death was an accident, suicide, or murder. At the last possibility, Koko responds with a "Yow!" and Qwilleran feels a "significant twinge in the roots of his moustache."

The evening of Iris and Herb's wedding, Qwilleran discovers the latest volume that Koko has pushed off the shelf—*Othello*. He remembers a couple of quotes: "Then must you speak of one who loved not wisely but too well," and "Kill me tomorrow; let me live tonight." The next morning, Mrs. Cobb comes back to the mansion, "her face haggard and drained of color." At the sight of Qwilleran, she bursts into tears and says she's made "a terrible mistake." Herb's "a monster." She enters the hospital, no visitors allowed.

The Klingenschoen Museum is destroyed by a fire set by an arsonist, who dies in the blaze—Herb Hackpole. Iris reveals to Qwill what Hackpole had told her on their wedding night. He was drunk and boasting about "doing heroic things." He knew Gritty Goodwinter, "who wanted to get rid of her husband and marry Exbridge." Herb did something to Senior's car to make it "go out of control and burst into flames." He also torched the *Picayune* building.

When Koko "uprooted the herb garden, did he perceive some semantic connection with Herb Hackpole?" Why did Koko concentrate on *Hamlet?* Koko gives Qwilleran a "meaningful stare," and Qwilleran remembers the plot of the play. "Hamlet's father dies suddenly; his mother remarries too soon; the father's ghost reveals that he has been murdered; the mother's name is Gertrude."

The Cat Who Sniffed Glue

Koko's first irritable commentary on a conversation is a loud "Yow!" when Andrew Brodie says that "Francesca really passed up a good chance when she didn't marry David Fitch."

Harley Fitch and his pregnant wife, Belle, are shot to death in their house. Harley's twin brother, David Fitch, and his wife, Jill, say they found the bodies when they went to pick up the couple for play rehearsal. The sheriff's department indicates they were the victims of a robbery.

Qwilleran returns to his apartment to find his writing studio with "signs of vandalism: desk drawers open, papers scattered about the floor, desktop ransacked, paper clips everywhere." Koko has been on a "glutinous binge," licking all the glue from the envelopes. Qwilleran knows that "Koko never does anything unusual without a good reason," but Qwill doesn't know the reason yet.

Koko continues sniffing books. Is he sniffing glue? Lately the cat has become interested in *Moby Dick* and *Captain Courageous*. He also keeps rubbing his jaw against a picture of an 1805 gunboat and tilting it. Harley Fitch's "consuming passion" was sailing his boat the *Fitch Witch* and making models of ships with "exquisite detail." And Koko is sniffing sea stories on the bookshelves: *Two Years Before the Mast* and *Mutiny on the Bounty*.

Yum Yum sits "on her haunches with forelegs elegantly straight, forepaws close together, tail wrapped around her toes clockwise." Koko follows suit, arranging himself in an identical pose. Qwill realizes they are "almost like twins." Later Qwill finds both of them sitting at the top of the stairs in identical attitudes.

When Qwill complains that all Koko does is "sniff bookbindings and hang around waiting for envelopes to lick," he hears a loud "YOW!" Koko has tilted the gunboat picture again. Qwilleran plans a visit to the decrepit antique shop in Mooseville, where a "bogus sea captain" had sold him the copy of the gunboat picture. He comes back disappointed, "grumbling at Koko for giving him a false clue." It doesn't occur to him that he might have misunderstood Koko.

At the Goodwinter Farmhouse Museum, Koko paws the air in front of three model ships contributed by Harley Fitch. Koko revives his interest in Shakespeare, sniffing *The Comedy of Errors* and *Two Gentlemen from Verona*.

Qwilleran accompanies Eddington Smith to the Fitch mansion to dust the library books. Koko makes a section of the wall swing open and hops through it. The secret door opens into a storage room, where Qwill is attacked by David Fitch, who is swinging what appears to be a club. Qwilleran blows a brass bugle, then swings it at the head of his assailant, who falls to the floor. Koko climbs on the man's chest and sniffs "nose to nose." Qwilleran realizes it's actually Harley, not David, because Koko is attracted to the spirit gum holding on his false moustache.

Qwilleran realizes that Koko had shown an instant attraction to Harley, Edd Smith, Wally Toddwhistle, and Pete the paperhanger—all men who regularly worked with adhesives. He also understands Koko's interest in Harley's model ships and books about the sea and twins. And he should have noticed when the Siamese started posing as identical bookends.

The Cat Who Went Underground

There are several deaths, which are eventually connected. Joe Trupp, Little Joe the plumber's father, is killed when the tailgate of a dump truck falls on him. Buddy Yarrow is drowned in the river when he presumably slips off the bank and hits his head on a rock. Qwilleran feels a "peculiar sensation on his upper lip—a twitch that "had always presaged trouble."

Qwilleran arrives home to find a "crumpled rug that is supposed to cover the trapdoor" in the floor and confetti. Koko has destroyed "an entire page of the newspaper with the story on page one about the drowning of Buddy Yarrow."

Qwilleran hires Clem Cottle to build the addition to the cabin. He drives home each nail "with three economical strokes of the hammer. *Bang bang bang.*" On the Fourth of July, Koko sits on the windowsill overlooking the building site, slapping his brown tail on the windowsill in episodes of three taps. *Tap tap tap.* Clem Cottle isn't in the Fourth of July parade, nor does he attend the reunion on Sunday, nor does he come back to work on Monday morning. Qwill finds Clem's truck, windows open and key in the ignition.

Qwilleran believes that carpenters are "dying and disappearing at an unusual rate," with "two accidents, one death from so-called natural causes, and a couple of disappearances." Joe Trupp was the first, then there was an underground builder, Mert, who was putting up Lyle Compton's garage. Then Buddy Yarrow drowned, Captain Phlogg died, and Clem Cottle disappeared.

Koko again attacks a copy of the *Moose County Something*. He destroys Qwill's column about Emma Wimsey and Punkin. Qwilleran has a strong urge to take flowers to Emma Wimsey at the Senior Care Facility. She gives her keepsakes to Qwill, including a Valentine candy box covered in "faded pink brocade" and topped with a "heart outlined in yellowed lace." Koko applies his inquisitive nose to "every inch of the old silk and lace," all the while tapping the table with his tail. *Tap tap tap.*

Koko gives an ear-shattering yowl and sniffs the trapdoor. Qwilleran hears a distant rumble, the "kind of noise that Koko made when he was busy with some engrossing task." Qwilleran finally eases down into the crawl space. Koko is in the center of the space, "digging industriously." With one hand Qwill grabs a protesting Koko and with the other hand a canvas shoe, connected to a leg. Koko has found Iggy, Qwill's latest carpenter, dead from a "smashing blow to the skull."

Qwilleran begins reading stories from the notebooks Emma

gave him. One explains a family tragedy. She and her husband had four sons and one daughter, Violet, who fell in love with a "rough fellow" and married him. Violet died when the second baby was born, and the older girl had to take care of the house and baby. The younger girl "shot herself with her father's gun" when she was twelve. The older girl is Little Joe, Emma's granddaughter. Big Joe had sexually abused both daughters after his wife died.

Koko once again sniffs the trapdoor and Nick realizes there's something else down there. Nick and Koko crawl into the space and talk to each other. Qwilleran squeezes down into the space. Nick and Koko have found marks on the joist, written in lipstick. There's a list of all five carpenters and the dates they were murdered. When Qwilleran confronts Little Joe, she tells him that "Louise" did it. She had "invented another self to do the killing" as the only way she could cope.

The Cat Who Talked to Ghosts

Qwilleran finds Iris Cobb's lifeless body on her kitchen floor after she calls him to complain of strange noises and something frightening outside the window. Iris's son reveals that she had gone to the doctor for indigestion and found out she'd had a silent coronary. Her letters indicate she is almost deranged by her fears.

But someone had turned off the lights and the microwave oven, and closed the door between the kitchen and the museum.

When Qwilleran and the Siamese move to the Goodwinter Farmhouse Museum, Koko goes to "the exact spot where Mrs. Cobb had collapsed." Koko "arched his back, bushed his tail, and pranced in a macabre dance." Qwilleran comes to the conclusion that Iris's death was murder.

Koko spends hours "gazing out the very window where Iris saw the frightening vision." He identifies a bed pillow from the Inchpot Centennial Farm, completely ignoring a similar pillow from the Trevelyan Farm.

Qwilleran says Koko is always talking to himself and staring into space. Roger MacGillivray says Koko's talking to ghosts.

Koko begins knocking books off the shelf again: *To Kill a Mockingbird* and *One Flew Over the Cuckoo's Nest*. When Qwilleran ignores Koko's book clues, Koko burrows under one of the Oriental rugs in the parlor. After Koko knocks *One Flew Over the Cuckoo's Nest* off the shelf for the second time, Qwilleran starts reading it.

In the meantime, Kristi Waffle's goats are poisoned by her ex-husband, Brent Waffle, who has escaped from a minimum security prison in Lockmaster.

After a visit to the barn when Vince Boswell tries to talk to him about printing presses, Qwilleran opens the door and Koko whizzes past his ankles. Qwilleran makes a flying tackle and grabs Koko before he can escape. As he asks Koko if he's "interested in printing presses," the idea flashes into Qwilleran's mind that maybe the unpacked crates contain something other than printing presses. Koko spends most of his waking hours watching the barn from the kitchen window. Qwilleran develops a theory that Boswell is "up to no good."

Qwilleran learns that the police found a body on Fugtree Road near the Black Creek bridge. The murdered man is Brent Waffle, who was hit on the head with a blunt instrument and dumped at the bridge.

Once again Koko burrows under an Oriental rug. Next Qwilleran finds him sitting on the dining table, guarding a large Bible and twitching his whiskers. The Bible has hand-written family records of the Bosworth family. Qwilleran un-ravels the family tree and discovers that Susan Exbridge, Larry

Lanspeak, and Vince Boswell/Bosworth are all descended from Lucy Bosworth, making them second cousins.

Koko manages to escape on his second attempt and disappears through the cat-hatch in the big barn door. Qwilleran hears a familiar rumbling growl "ascending the scale and ending in a shriek." He finds Koko hovering over something wedged between two crates—"a litter of squirming newborn kittens and a mother cat, bedded down on a piece of soiled cloth." The bundle of cloth is labeled LOCKMASTER COUNTY JAIL. Koko leads Qwilleran to a pile of straw, a bundle of something rolled to make a pillow, and "dried blood on the pillow and the straw." The police start a search for Vince Boswell/Bosworth.

Koko is hiding again under another Oriental rug. Qwilleran wonders why Koko tunnels under them in a neat, workmanlike way, when suddenly he has an idea. He goes back to the barn and finds "an arched tunnel of crumbling masonry," undoubtedly the "private stonework" escape tunnel built by Luther Bosworth for Ephraim Goodwinter. Koko and Qwill discover a small Halloween noise box, the source of all the noises that had frightened Mrs. Cobb.

Vince had been digging for gold coins his grandfather said were under the barn. That's why he killed Brent Waffle, who was hiding in the barn. At first he tried to frighten Iris away. When that didn't work, he gave Verona a white sheet and told her to stand outside the window and scare Iris. Then he smothered Iris with the featherbed pillow that Koko had identified in the museum.

Qwilleran realizes that Koko had twice knocked a novel off the shelf in which a character was smothered with a pillow. And Koko's habit of tunneling under rugs should have told Qwill something!

The Cat Who Lived High

When Qwilleran and the Siamese move into the Casablanca for the winter, Koko inspects an eight-foot bar situated in the middle of the floor in the huge sunken living room. As Qwilleran slides it across the carpet, Koko yowls as Qwilleran uncovers a large dark bloodstain. Koko "arched his back, elongated his legs, hooked his tail, and pranced in a circle"— Koko's death dance. Then "from the cat's innards came a new sound: less than a growl yet deeper than a purr." It sounds like "Rrrrrrrr!" Qwilleran learns that Dianne Bessinger had been murdered in her apartment, on the very spot that Koko located.

Koko examines the library sofa, sniffing and reaching down behind the seat cushions. Qwilleran finds an item of gold jewelry, "engraved discs linked together to make a flexible bracelet." One disc is engraved *To Dianne*. Another said *From Ross*.

Koko uncovers Scrabble tiles, which he scatters on the floor, making his new noise, "Rrrrrrrrr." Koko continues to make the sound, prowling restlessly and following Qwilleran everywhere.

Koko nudges the bloody butcher block painting in Qwilleran's apartment. "Standing on his hind legs with his head weaving from left to right like a cobra," he utters his "gagging guttural." When Qwilleran's moustache quivers, he takes the painting down from its hanger. Koko immediately sniffs the wall. With the aid of a lamp, Qwilleran reads faint letters that have been painted over: FORGIVE ME DIANE. There is a signature, two R's back to back—the confession. But "Dianne" is spelled with only one *n*.

Qwilleran realizes that Ross didn't paint the letters on the wall. Someone drugged him and threw him off the terrace, then painted the letters on the wall. Koko agrees: "Rrrrrrrrr," then slaps the table twice with his tail. There may have been *two* involved in the crime.

While walking Koko on the roof, Qwilleran looks down into the penthouse through the skylight. Someone on the roof could look down and see whatever was happening in the conversation pit, and Qwill asks himself if someone had witnessed the murder of Di Bessinger. Qwilleran believes that Di was murdered by someone hired to eliminate her, and Ross Rasmus was framed. His theory is that special-interest groups involving Rexwell Fleudd are resorting to criminal means to clear the way for the Gateway Alcazar office buildings.

Qwilleran arrives home after a dinner party to find the bedroom floor wet and the bathroom floor flooded. The sink is overflowing, the faucet is running full force, and Koko is sitting on the toilet tank, "surveying his achievement."

Koko prowls restlessly, "talking to himself in guttural rumblings and curling his tail into a corkscrew"—something he has never done before. Some of Koko's Scrabble clues include FOOT, ROOF, TOOT, and DODO. The word JOVE helps Qwilleran solve the murders.

Randy Jupiter comes to visit Qwilleran, and Koko devises "ways of tormenting the visitor." Koko jumps to the back of the sofa, then stops to sniff the guest's hair. He jumps to the cocktail table, where he bites the corners of record jackets Randy has brought. Next he has a catfit, scattering cassettes in all directions. Then he burrows under the rug once again.

When Qwilleran confronts Randy, Koko sits on the bar with "arched back, bushed tail, flattened ears, and bared fangs." When Jupiter pulls a knife, a "blur of fur passed between the two men and landed on the assailant's shoulder." A whiplike tail flicks twice. There's a yell of pain as the man puts a hand to his eyes. Qwilleran smashes a bottle on Jupiter's head.

Qwilleran learns that Fleudd has a past "history of dirty tricks." Scrabble words AGENT and HOAX and JOVE should have given him clues—JOVE is another name for Jupiter. In retrospect, he realizes that Koko is beginning to convey information by means of tail language, twisting his tail like a corkscrew—Randy is a bartender.

In the middle of the night, Koko wakes Qwilleran by "jumping on and off the bed, pouncing on his body, yowling, and growling." Next he races madly about, knocking things over, crashing into furniture. Qwilleran hears a "rustling, crackling, creaking" under the floor, and immediately sounds the alarm that there is a fire in the building. After they leave the building, a deafening explosion rocks the area. The sounds in the crawl space weren't flames, but someone planting a bomb, which destroyed the top floors of the Casablanca. The one-eared Raymond Dunwoody was experienced with dynamite, and he had been seen at dinner with Fleudd. Qwilleran realizes that Dunwoody and Jupiter were both undercover agents for Fleudd.

Koko's a hero—he saves an estimated two hundred persons.

The Cat Who Knew a Cardinal

Koko develops a friendship with a cardinal that comes to the window and sits outside. The male cardinal "called every morning and evening in company with his soberly dressed mate." There appears to be "mutual appreciation between the cardinal and the aristocratic cat." Koko sits almost motionless, except for the last three inches of his tail, which is "fluttering to match the fluttering of the bird's tail feathers." Qwill says they communicate telepathically.

During the cast party for *Henry VIII* at Qwilleran's barnhome, Koko sits on top of the *schrank* to stare peculiarly at the top of VanBrook's head during his visit with Qwilleran. Suddenly Koko "swooped over the principal's head and landed on a rug ten feet away," after which he yowled "loudly and imperiously."

After the cast leaves, Koko remains at the side window, peering into the darkness. Qwilleran hears a low rumble, then a growl that rises, ending in a "falsetto shriek." Koko never gives that "ominous pronouncement" without a good reason. Qwill finds a car whose driver is slumped over the wheel. Hilary VanBrook has been murdered, in what becomes known as the "Orchard Incident." Later Qwilleran realizes that Koko had been staring down at VanBrook's head as if he had known the man was going to be shot in the head.

Dennis Hough disappears without a trace. Qwilleran returns home a few days later to find the cats "shrieking and howling from the top balcony." In the afternoon sun, Qwilleran sees the shadow of a body hanging from an overhead beam—Dennis. Qwilleran finds a message on Dennis's answering machine from his wife, telling him never to come home. She has found someone else and is filing for divorce.

Koko keeps knocking typeblocks from the typecase: first a fish, a rabbit, and a rooster. Next Qwilleran finds a squirrel, a rabbit, an eagle, and a seahorse. Another time he finds the rabbit, a skunk, and a horse's head.

When Qwilleran returns to the guest room at the Bushlands' home, he discovers that all the red jelly beans have been scattered about the floor. Something is going on in Koko's mind, but Qwilleran can't see it. Koko shreds the *Stablechat*, published by S. W. O'Hare and edited by Lisa Amberton.

While Steve O'Hare, Fiona Stucker and her son, Robbie, are visiting Qwilleran, both cats take off as if shot from a cannon: up the ramps and across the catwalks, "circling up to the roof and then racing down again" to the first balcony. They "swooped down like dive-bombers, Koko landing on the back of the sofa behind Steve, and Yum Yum landing virtually in his lap." Koko stands on the sofa back "exactly as he came to rest:

legs stiff, back arched, tail crooked like a horseshoe.'' Koko shreds the next issue of _Stablechat._ Steve O'Hare kills Koko's redbird friend because he likes to take potshots at targets.

In VanBrook's library, Qwilleran finds a catalog of all the books. Some of the boxes are coded with a red dot. Qwill opens the boxes, but finds only books. Qwill takes a couple of books home. Koko knocks them to the floor, then pushes _Ivanhoe_ around with his nose, sniffing the edges. Qwilleran rifles the pages and finds them interleaved with ten-dollar bills, which he later learns are counterfeit.

He finds other papers including copies of old business agreements signed _William Brooks_ and a will, plus another document that causes a ''tingling in Qwilleran's upper lip.''

Edd Smith brings Qwilleran a copy of Qwill's book, _City of Brotherly Love,_ which he had found. They tour the barn, ending up at the uppermost catwalk. When Steve arrives, Qwilleran asks Edd to ''stay there and listen, out of sight.'' Koko sweeps up ''to the top catwalk, on the railing forty feet above Steve's head.''

Qwilleran confronts Steve, and when Steve pulls a gun, the apple tree wall hanging falls down on top of him. Qwilleran finishes him off by hitting him with a long, frozen rabbit from the freezer. Eddington says the cats were pulling the corners of the tapestry off the tacks, so he helped them. VanBrook had written a will naming Steve's stableboy, Robbie, as sole heir, but then changed the will after the boy quit school. Steve had hoped to kill VanBrook before he changed the will, but it was too late.

The Cat Who Moved a Mountain

The cats carefully explore the large mountain home Tiptop, which Qwilleran has rented. Koko is particularly interested in a Queen Anne chair, "passing his nose up and down the legs," and the frame of "a French door, which looked newly painted." Both had been repaired after the chair's legs had been broken and the French door damaged when J. J. Hawkinfield was murdered and "pushed off his own mountain."

On a visit to Potato Cove, Qwilleran meets Chrysalis Beechum, sister of Forest Beechum, who is in the state prison for the murder of J. J. Hawkinfield. She says he didn't do it, and Qwilleran's upper lip responds with a tingling sensation—always a sign of a hunch that things aren't as they seem. He begins to understand his negative reaction to Tiptop.

Koko takes particular care to sniff the bottle of sherry that Qwilleran brings into the house. Qwilleran assumes it's the glue behind the label that attracts him. Koko is tilting paintings again, this time one of mountains painted by Forest. As Qwilleran examines the cabinet under the painting, Koko "moved the mountain for the third time." Qwilleran finds "an old-fashioned black iron key about three inches long" hanging from the picture hook.

Koko is in the living room, "talking to himself as he always did when puzzled or frustrated." Koko tries to put his paw behind the large desk. Qwilleran claps a hand over his tingling moustache. He finds a door behind the bookcase. Behind it is J. J. Hawkinfield's office, where Koko points out a large scrapbook containing clippings of Hawkinfield's editorials in which he took potshots at everybody and everything.

No one actually saw the murder happen, but police say there was a struggle and then J. J. was pushed over the cliff. Qwilleran puts Koko into his harness and walks him around the veranda. At the repaired railing, Koko freezes with "tail stiffened, back arched, and ears flattened." He "pranced in circles with distasteful stares at the edge of the veranda."

Forest's lawyer was Hugh Lumpton, who didn't appear at the arraignment, nor did he put any witnesses for the defense on the stand. Forest was convicted mainly on the testimony of Sherry Hawkinfield.

One evening Qwilleran finds the cats hiding under a table with a stamped, addressed letter with "perforations in two corners." Koko is the culprit, because he leaves fang marks as evidence. The letter is addressed to Sherry Hawkinfield, who had been married briefly to Hugh Lumpton, court-appointed attorney for Forest.

Later Qwilleran goes back into J. J.'s hidden office. Koko demands that Qwill open the middle drawer of the desk, where he "pounced on the stamp and carried it away to sniff and lick in some dark corner." At the rear of the drawer, Qwilleran finds an unpublished editorial written by Hawkinfield. He learns about the "Hot Potato Fund," which is "purported to promote the local economy," but actually finances bootlegging.

Sherry Hawkinfield arrives at Tiptop, where the cats are "yawning widely and showing cavernous pink gullets and murderous fangs." Sherry screams that she's "deathly afraid of Siamese."

When Qwilleran accuses Hugh of murdering Hawkinfield, Hugh grabs the Queen Anne chair and swings it in the air. A burst of loud music from the second floor startles Hugh and gives Qwilleran the edge. Qwill grabs the iron candelabrum and rams it "into his attacker's midriff like a flaming pitchfork," then he hits Hugh with the heavy burl bowl. Qwilleran tells Koko to keep an eye on Sherry, and Koko keeps the terrified woman at bay with "a belligerent stance."

Qwilleran figures out that Hugh killed J. J. to protect himself and his father, who is the organizer of the bootleg operation. Sherry collaborated "because she wanted to inherit her father's estate." He realizes that Koko was trying to tell him something by tilting Forest's picture of the mountain, sniffing the case in front of the hidden office to reveal Hawkinfield's editorial, and sniffing the label on a *sherry* bottle.

The Cat Who Wasn't There

Qwilleran dashes home from the Potato Mountains because Polly Duncan has been followed by a strange man with a beard. Qwill spots a "youngish man with a bushy beard and a gray sweatshirt," driving a car with a Massachusetts license plate. The car registration lists him as Charles Edward Martin of Charlestown, Massachusetts. Qwilleran's moustache bristles whenever he thinks of the bearded stranger and the maroon car.

Mildred Hanstable reads the tarot cards for Qwilleran and warns about some kind of fraud or treachery. Koko agrees. Irma Hasselrich dies in her hotel room on the Bonnie Scots Tour, a victim of what Dr. Melinda calls cardiac arrest. Qwilleran discovers that Koko had been howling in the shower between nine-thirty and ten of the night that Irma died. "He had a sense of death that spanned the ocean!"

Bruce the minibus driver disappears, and so does Grace Utley's jewelry. Bruce is suspected in the death of Irma.

When Qwilleran returns home, he learns that Yum Yum has stolen a pack of Mildred's emery boards, one at a time. Koko "swooped in and snatched" one of Mildred's diet pills as she was getting ready to take it.

Koko stares at a copy of the *Moose County Something* that has a half-page obituary of Irma Hasselrich, then begins "a slow prance around the lead item." He circles several times "in a hair-raising ritual" that he has performed several times before. It means that "Koko's extra senses were detecting a discrepancy" that has escaped Qwilleran's perception.

Qwilleran returns to the apple barn to discover a scene of

havoc: torn newspapers everywhere, books on the floor, the telephone knocked off its cradle, and his coffee spilled. Koko is "in the throes of a catfit." He races around the main floor, then up the ramp where "he screamed like a banshee." Koko had shredded Irma's obituary, and he is "trying to communicate that she had not died of natural causes."

When Koko hears a tape of Qwilleran's notes from Scotland, he reacts excitedly to a reference to serial killer Dr. Cream, noted for "pink pills for pale prostitutes." Qwilleran assumes Koko had mistaken "serial" for "cereal."

While Lori and Nick Bamba are visiting, Yum Yum presents an emery board to Nick. Later Yum Yum presents Qwilleran with an emery board.

Bushy Bushland brings over prints of the pictures he took in Scotland. Koko licks the prints, deglossing three photos with his sandpaper tongue. Each photo is of Melinda Goodwinter.

When Qwilleran takes Yum Yum to the Senior Care Facility for the Pets for Patients program, she visits Mr. Hornbuckle, who was Dr. Hal's caretaker and driver. Mr. Hornbuckle says that Dr. Hal had sent his troublemaking son, Emory, away and "paid 'im money reg'lar iffen he di'n't come back." After the boy was reported killed in a car accident, the doctor continued sending money.

While watching *Macbeth*, Qwilleran becomes alarmed when his moustache starts tingling. He leaves the theater and hurries home, only to find the glass door panel shattered. Inside he sees blood on the earthen tile floor. Koko is sitting on top of the refrigerator, "methodically licking his paws with toes spread wide and claws extended." His radio/cassette player and all tapes from his trip to Scotland, plus interviews around Moose County, are missing. After the police leave, Koko utters "a loud wail from the pit of his stomach, ending in a falsetto shriek." Qwilleran immediately looks for Yum Yum, but can't

find her. She doesn't even come when he yells "TREAT!"
Someone has stolen Yum Yum!

Nick says he believes the bearded stranger called Charles
Edward Martin hangs out in Shantytown. Qwilleran and Nick
head for Shantytown, stopping by a travel trailer with the maroon car. Through a window Qwilleran sees red gashes on the
man's forehead. He also sees his radio and cassettes. Once inside, Qwilleran yells "TREAT!" and immediately hears
"NOW!"—Yum Yum's piercing shriek—from behind a small
closed door. It's a closet-size toilet, and "Yum Yum was perched
precariously on the rim."

Qwilleran realizes that the Boulevard Prowler was Dr. Hal's
son, Emory. Each time Qwill found one of the emery boards
Yum Yum had purloined, his mind had gone to that stray son.
Charles Edward Martin is really Emory Goodwinter.

Qwill realizes that Emory had to have a partner, because
Emory wouldn't know all the details about Qwilleran and Polly.
The obvious answer is Melinda, who had learned about
"TREAT!" on her last visit to Qwill's house. Emory confesses
that Melinda had a way to get rich quick: "Get rid of Mrs.
Duncan." The plot against Polly was murder, not ransom!
When that plan failed, Melinda plotted to kidnap one of
Qwill's cats for ransom.

The police pick up Bruce Gow in London, but the jewelry
had been smuggled out of Scotland. He admits the theft, but
not the murder of Irma. Polly had taken high-potency vitamin
C capsules to Scotland, but they were too large to swallow comfortably, so she gave them to Irma. Qwill's theory is that Melinda tampered with Polly's vitamin capsules, not realizing that
Polly had stopped taking them and given them to Irma. Melinda kills herself in a high-speed car crash into the Goodwinter
Monument.

The Cat Who Went Into the Closet

Qwilleran moves into the Gage mansion for the winter. The old house has many closets, which the Siamese enjoy immensely. Koko and Yum Yum slink into closets and bring out a wide variety of items, including: purple satin bedroom slipper, man's argyle sock, man's spat, brown shoelace, handkerchief embroidered *Cynara*, box of corn plasters, a jeweler's box with a man's gold signet ring, newspaper clippings, an inner sole, purple satin pincushions embroidered ERG, canceled check for $100 to Lena Inchpot, birth certificate for Lethe Gage, and a square paper packet of foot powder. He also sits inside a safe.

Junior's grandmother, Euphonia Gage, is found dead in her bed at the retirement village in Florida. The police believe it's suicide, but there is no apparent motive. The Park of Pink Sunsets provides limousine services and recommends doctors and lawyers and tax experts. Euphonia's will leaves nothing for her family and everything to the Park of Pink Sunsets. Mrs. Gage's lawyer is trying to contest the will, but has trouble finding any financial documents.

Koko investigates pictures that Celia Robinson has sent of Mrs. Gage and friends at the Park of Pink Sunsets. He "passed his nose over every one of the Florida pictures and flicked his tongue at a couple of them." As Qwilleran studies the pictures, he discovers that two look "vaguely familiar." Celia identifies them as Betty and Claude, and Hixie Rice identifies them as the two strangers that had been at the first showing of "The Big Burning of 1869" at the Gage mansion. They had also seen a video that Mrs. Gage made of her home and furnishings.

The ring has an intimate inscription inside the band, with the initials *ERG* for Euphonia Roff Gage and *WBK*. Koko finds a birth certificate for Lethe Gage, November 27, 1928, born to Euphonia Roff Gage, while Euphonia's husband was in prison.

Lethe becomes Lena and grows up with another family, then becomes Euphonia's housekeeper. The yellowed clipping from the *Pickax Picayune* announces the marriage of Lena Foote, daughter of Mr. and Mrs. Arnold Foote of Lockmaster, to Gilbert Inchpot of Brrr, on October 18, 1961.

Koko stages a catfit, first "delivering a trumpetlike 'Yow-w-w!' that pained the aural and olfactory senses." Anytime Koko stages a catfit, Qwilleran knows he's in the doghouse. He begins to realize how many of Koko's "finds" are related to feet.

Celia helps Qwilleran discover that Betty and Claude have "an associate who helps residents unload their valuables—and rips them off." Qwill puts everything together: Euphonia had a baby named Lethe. She paid a farm family to take Lethe, whose name was changed to Lena Foote, who was Nancy's mother. That means that Nancy is Junior Goodwinter's cousin.

While Qwilleran is snowed in at the Lanspeaks, he receives a call that his cat-sitter can't find the Siamese and had seen a van parked behind the house. Nancy Fincher takes him across the Flats on her dogsled, and Nick picks him up and takes him to Pickax. The electricity is off in the house. Koko is sitting in the one shaft of light from outside a window, "huddled against the chill but otherwise unperturbed."

Yum Yum is "in a hunched position with rump elevated and head low—her mousing stance—and she was watching the door of the elevator." Someone is trapped in the elevator! Nick calls the police—the ballroom has been ravaged, and light fixtures and murals have been taken down. The thief's time spent trapped in the elevator has made him a "screaming maniac." His electrician partner has disappeared.

Curiously, Pete, Betty, and Claude have disappeared from the Park of Pink Sunsets. Apparently Lena's foster parents told Gil Inchpot about Lena's biological mother, and he began blackmailing Euphonia. When Euphonia confided the trouble to Claude, Gil was murdered a few days later.

Qwilleran's moustache confirms a hunch: All the "sui-
cides" at Park of Pink Sunsets have been murders. "Rob 'em
and rub 'em out!" Betty and Claude are picked up in Texas
near the Mexican border. Pete is arrested at an airport in Ken-
tucky.

Qwill analyzes Koko's clues: the choice of *Robinson Crusoe*
as reading material; articles related to financial affairs; articles
suggesting links to the Foote family; a gold signet ring to suggest a ring of criminals. After the crimes are solved, Koko loses
interest in *Robinson Crusoe*, ignores the fifty closets, and never
sits in the safe again.

The Cat Who Came to Breakfast

There are several accidents on Pear Island: Fifteen guests
become ill through food poisoning and a man drowns in the
new hotel's pool. An elderly guest at the Bambas' bed-and-
breakfast falls and breaks a rib when one of the front steps
caves in. Nick suspects dirty tricks; Qwill's upper lip tingles.
Nick convinces Qwilleran to visit the island and "snoop
around."

When Qwill returns to his island cabin, the desk and floor
are littered with paper. Koko the paper-shredder has ripped
the month of June off the calendar, piece by piece. Qwilleran
doesn't understand why, although Koko shreds paper only
when he has a reason.

Noisette owns an antique store where she sells only antiques, reads French magazines, and avoids publicity. Qwilleran
automatically suspects "anyone in the business world who de-
clined free publicity in his column."

Another Pear Island vacationer is killed, shot while hang
gliding on the sand dunes. Qwilleran is impressed by the di-
versity of happenings: food poisoning, drowning, bad fall, ex-

plosion, and shooting. Qwilleran recruits Derek Cuttlebrink for undercover investigations into the incidents on Pear Island.

Yum Yum finds a half-crumpled piece of paper behind the cushion on the sofa. On the crumpled-up piece of music manuscript paper is a phone number, which Qwill calls. A man's voice answers, "The Pines gatehouse." Why would June Halliburton be calling the Appelhardt gatehouse?

Derek says the only people who got sick were those who ordered chicken gumbo. The guy who drowned in the pool had been drinking with a woman, and they spoke a foreign language. Andrew Brodie tells Qwill that the man who drowned was George duLac of Lake Worth, Florida. In the meantime, Koko has removed all the hazelnuts from the nut-bowl in the cottage.

In the middle of the night, the cats wake Qwilleran by howling and scratching urgently on the door. Qwill smells smoke, which is issuing from June Halliburton's cottage next door. June's death is blamed on asphyxiation due to smoke inhalation.

Prior to the storm, Koko and Qwilleran play a game of dominoes, where the number of pips represents a letter of the alphabet. Qwilleran spells words from Koko's choices. His dominoes spell *field* again, twice. A tremor comes across Qwill's lip. He realizes that he can use the same dominoes to spell *filed*. Qwilleran and Nick take Koko underneath the porch steps to look at the new construction. Koko digs for something in the sand—it turns out to be an old hacksaw blade. Qwilleran remembers more of Koko's words: *hack* and *blade*.

Qwilleran begins to rethink some of his other spellings. *Lake* and *leak* could be *kale*, the name of a local family. Koko's "Yow!" makes his moustache bristle again. June Halliburton was a Kale before she married briefly, and her father is care-taker at The Pines.

Qwilleran believes the "crimes are being committed by a

coalition" to stop the resort development. The wealthy summer people have the brains to organize a campaign, and the islanders have the personnel to carry it out.

Elizabeth overhears the gatekeeper, Elijah Kale, accuse Jack of starting the fire by saying Jack was married to two women and had to get rid of one. Jack Applehardt countered by saying he would tell the police about the explosion, shooting, and poisoning. The last group of dominoes that Koko knocks off spell *Elijah*. In the same game, Koko's dominoes spell *Jack* and *Kale*. Liz says that Jack had met a French woman in Florida and wanted to divorce June, but June refused.

Qwilleran learns from Dwight's letter that Noisette's last name is duLac, the same as the man who drowned in the pool. Jack's plots become clear to Qwilleran: Jack is married to two women at the same time. So he gets rid of one wife and helps the other to get rid of her husband. He and Kale masterminded the other accidents to harass the resort.

Qwilleran remembers other clues from Koko: He tore the month of June off the calendar, dislodged the tragedy mask that "looked like the dissipated Jack Appelhardt," and picked the hazelnuts—called *noisettes* in French—from the bowl.

The Cat Who Blew the Whistle

The state banking commission padlocks the Lumbertown Credit Union, pending a state audit. The president, Floyd Trevelyan, his secretary, Lionella Hooper, and millions of dollars disappear. Nella's story is that she was fired two weeks before the surprise audit, but stayed until after the Party Train ride.

Qwill begins reading *A Midsummer Night's Dream* to the Siamese, and Koko reacts with a "Yow!" whenever Qwilleran says Hermia's name. He wonders if Koko's responses have a secret meaning, or whether Koko "might be playing practical jokes; he had a sense of humor."

Koko watches and waits at the formal entrance to the apple-barn home, standing on his hind feet, resting his front feet on the sills, and peering through the glass toward the part of the orchard where Polly's house is being constructed.

Yum Yum provides a clue—a black felt-tip pen—which she frequently knocks to the floor. Qwill ignores the clue and buys a walnut English box to lock pens and pencils in, calling her "an incorrigible cat burglar." The box locks with a key, something the cats have not yet learned to operate.

Koko sits on the *Moose County Something* that has an article on the Mudville scandal and a large picture of the credit union president. Qwill feels the familiar tingling sensation in his moustache. Koko "slowly rose on four long legs, his body arched, his tail bushed." He "circled the newspaper in a stiff-legged dance"—his death dance. That means only one thing: Floyd Trevelyan is dead.

Challenged to a game of Book! Book! Koko chooses *The Panama Canal*. When Eddie Trevelyan visits Qwill's barn, Koko reacts negatively, coming forward "with mouth open and fangs bared, emitting a hostile hiss." His tail is stiffened "as straight as a fencer's sword."

Another crime is committed during a mysterious blackout, which coincides exactly with the time that Koko spends in the exact center of the portable pyramid that Derek, Fran, and Elizabeth set up in Qwilleran's barn. James Henry Ducker is the victim of a knifing at the Trackside Tavern in Sawdust City. Henry is the "Benno" who was helping Eddie Trevelyan. Qwilleran suspects the stabbing may have been drug-related.

Koko tries another clue: He knocks *Androcles the Lion* off the shelf. Koko jumps into Qwill's lap, a rare act for him, and starts to dig in the crook of Qwilleran's elbow, excavating with great zeal. He and Yum Yum sit on the fireplace with the three wooden duck decoys.

Koko stages a catfit, rushing madly all around the main floor of the bar, then throws himself at the front door, twice. Finally Qwilleran covers him with a rug and pins him down. Then Qwilleran becomes aware of the stop-and-go noises from the bulldozer, and he goes out to the building site. As soon as he arrives, he hears a man's scream, a thud, then silence. Eddie is pinned underneath the huge bulldozer. Evidently he was attacked by a great horned owl and lost control of the machine.

When Qwilleran returns home, the pencil box is on the floor and Koko is carrying a black-barrelled felt-tip pen in his mouth. Qwilleran ponders Koko's bizarre behavior: vigils at the window, sitting with the decoys, his reaction to "Hermia," digging in the crook of Qwill's elbow. He scolds Koko, and the cat knocks a book from the shelf: Dostoyevsky's *The Idiot*.

Koko sits on a playscript that Fran wants Qwilleran to read: *Lion in Winter*. Qwilleran begins to realize there's a leonine theme in Koko's choices. Is it a clue or is it a lion-sized ego? Is Koko's attention to black felt-tip pens designed to call his attention to Edward Penn Trevelyan?

Eddie dies from his injuries, but not before conveying to Letitia what he's involved in. Eddie was an accomplice in the murder of his father, Floyd. Nella was the mastermind, Benno killed Floyd, and Eddie helped bury him. Later Eddie and Benno—whose real name was James Henry Ducker—were arguing, when Henry pulled a knife and ended up dead.

Qwilleran puts together Koko's clues: the death dance on top of Floyd's picture in the newspaper and his infatuation with black pens and duck decoys. When Qwill opens the door to the house, Koko slams into his legs and darts down to the building site, where he starts digging at the edge of the slab. Qwill realizes that Koko's digging in the crook of his elbow is a clue to what happened to Floyd, whose body is found under the concrete.

Meanwhile, Nella Hooper has disappeared. Once again the name "Hermia" comes up, and Koko yows loudly. Koko nudges *Androcles and the Lion* off the shelf, along with Fran's playscript of the *Lion in Winter*. Qwilleran figures it out! Nella's name is really Lionella. When he looks up "Hermia" in the dictionary, he learns nothing new until he reads about "hermaphrodite." At the sound of the word, Koko produces an "alarming response" that starts as "an ear-splitting falsetto" and ends in "a menacing growl." The word refers to an animal with both male and female organs. Immediately he calls Andy and tells him to look for a man named Lionel, who is probably growing a beard.

Koko has "blown the whistle on the whole crew."

The Cat Who Said Cheese

For a game of Book! Book! Koko chooses *Stalking the Wild Asparagus.* Koko stalks Yum Yum, pursuing her all over the apple barn.

The New Pickax Hotel is ripped by an explosion, which results in minor injuries to Lenny Inchpot and several others, but death to a staff member. The homemade bomb was placed in the room of the mystery woman, Onoosh, who leaves town as soon as she hears about the explosion.

Koko reacts with a loud "Yow!" whenever Gruyére cheese is mentioned. Again he sneaks up behind Yum Yum and pounces, then chases her up the ramp.

Qwilleran receives a letter from Onoosh in Salt Lake City. She explains that the man who is threatening to kill her is the one who planted the bomb. When Qwilleran realizes that the man is stalking Onoosh, he thinks about Koko's behavior toward Yum Yum.

A downtown merchant is shot during the fireworks of the Great Food Explo. It's Franklin Pickett, from whom the bomber bought flowers in which he concealed the bomb. Lenny Inchpot was also a witness. The police find Lenny and send him to his aunt in Duluth for safety.

Koko still responds with a loud "Yow!" at the mention of Gruyére cheese. He starts yowling at the mention of feta cheese. When Qwill reads the cheese-tasting program to the cats, Koko yowls at every mention of the word *cheese*. When Qwilleran tests him by using the French word for cheese, Koko yowls at every *fromage*. He yowls at Brie, Gruyére, and feta.

Koko is also still knocking *A Taste of Honey* off the shelf. Koko sits in front of the refrigerator, which has a frozen turkey within, staring at the door handle. When Qwilleran opens the refrigerator door, Koko jumps over the bar and lands inside with the bird.

A fisherman is found dead in one of Scotten Fisheries' rental cabins on the bank of Black Creek, as a result of multiple bee stings. He is identified as Victor Greer.

During the cheese-tasting party at Qwilleran's, Koko howls at the mention of Brie. Late in the party, Koko has a catfit, skidding through cheese platters and cheese on the table, leaping to the punch table, and knocking over lighted candles. Finally he perches on a beam and licks his fur. Qwilleran apologizes and says he doesn't know why Koko had the fit, but he knows that Koko wants everyone to go home. Koko makes one last "Yow!" at the mention of feta.

When everyone has gone, Koko goes back to the kitchen and claws at the refrigerator. Qwilleran decides to prepare the turkey now and cook it in the morning. When he puts his hand inside the turkey, he feels something unexpected and calls

Chief Brodie. Brodie reaches in and pulls out a small handgun. The turkey came from Nick Bamba's Cold Turkey Farm.

When Qwilleran visits Elaine Fetter to write about mushrooms, she tells him she's writing a cookbook. Celia investigates and discovers Iris Cobb's stolen cookbook. Qwilleran puts an ad in the *Something*, announcing a $10,000 reward. Soon afterward, the cookbook is returned to Celia by Donald Fetter.

Qwilleran brings Aubrey to his barn when the man threatens to kill himself. Koko yowls at the mention of the man's name. Aubrey tells about his friend, Vic Greer, who saved him from drowning when they were in the Navy. Vic talked Aubrey into helping him to see his ex-wife when Vic was in Pickax. Aubrey didn't realize what Vic was doing until Vic gave him the handgun to hide in a turkey, then told him they had to kill Lenny. Vic got drunk and Aubrey took him to his cabin. The next day Vic was dead from the bee stings.

Qwilleran puts together all of Koko's clues: He stalked Yum Yum, the way Vic was stalking Onoosh, and he pushed *Stalking the Wild Asparagus* from the shelf. He kept pushing *A Taste of Honey* off the bookshelf, which pointed to Aubrey. He reacted to Brie, which sounds like Aubrey; Gruyére, which sounds like Greer; and feta, which sounds like Fetter.

Qwilleran tests Koko by saying *Gruyére, Brie,* and *feta,* but the cat doesn't turn a whisker. He continues his reading of *The Frogs*. When he gets to the phrase, "and sleeping is a wool blanket," Koko yowls. Qwill realizes that Victor Greer was covered with a wool blanket, and bees are antagonized by wool.

The Cat Who Tailed a Thief

There's a rash of petty larceny in Pickax—eyeglasses, gloves, videos. When Chief Brodie asks why Qwilleran doesn't assign Koko to the petty crimes, Qwilleran informs him that "Koko doesn't accept assignments. He conducts his own investigations." But Koko knocks a Russian novel entitled *The Thief* from the bookcase. Brodie says his grandmother in Scotland "could tail a thief with scissors, a piece of string, and a witch's chant."

Almost two thousand dollars is stolen from a cabinet in the Indian Village clubhouse, a collection of winnings that the bridge players donate to the Moose County Youth Center.

While on a trip Down Below, Willard Carmichael is fatally shot. Shortly thereafter, Koko starts hitting Yum Yum, without provocation. One evening he calmly stretches, walks over to Yum Yum, and bops her on the head. On another occasion, Koko raps her on the nose. Qwilleran scolds him severely—Qwill doesn't understand what's gotten into Koko.

Lenny Inchpot is arrested as the petty thief, based on an anonymous tip, which leads to stolen items in his locker at the clubhouse. Qwilleran suspects George A. Breze, who had suggested that Lenny had "cracked up." Breze is "suspected of everything, yet was never charged with anything." Celia Robinson discovers that Breze is not the petty thief.

Lynette Duncan, newly married to Carter Lee James, dies on her honeymoon in New Orleans, of "gastrointestinal complications." Koko begins to slap his tail from side to side, right to left.

Qwilleran becomes suspicious of Danielle, who had given the groom Carter Lee an X-rated kiss at his wedding. There are rumors that Danielle and Carter Lee aren't really cousins, and Gary Pratt says that when they ate in his café, they didn't act like cousins. One of the cats spits up a hairball on the newspaper with Lynette and Carter Lee's wedding photos.

When Tracy Kemple tries to overdose after Carter Lee marries Danielle, Qwilleran experiences increasing tremors on his upper lip. Koko stares at him and slaps the floor vehemently with his tail. Tracy admits giving Carter Lee one of the Kemple dolls, which was found in Lenny's locker. Qwilleran begins to suspect that Carter Lee is a fortune hunter who married Lynette for her money.

Yum Yum insists that Qwilleran open a drawer, where he finds Clayton Robinson's photos and a transcript of Clayton's tape recording of Carter Lee and Danielle. Danielle calls him "Chuck" and tells him she's going to steal one of the daggers from Mr. MacMurchie and give it to Lynette as a wedding gift.

Late one evening, Koko is nervous and unfocused, murmuring to himself and examining a leather-bound scrapbook that contains pictures of houses that Carter Lee claims to have renovated. Qwilleran shows the pictures to Amanda Goodwinter, who says that she knows who did some of the houses, and it isn't Carter Lee.

Koko pushes Melville's volume ten off the shelf, but Qwilleran ignores it. Koko lashes his tail like a bad loser. The K Fund can find no evidence that Carter Lee is involved with preservation or restoration. After Qwilleran plans a trap for Carter Lee, he realizes he should have taken Koko's book interest seriously. The Melville volume that Koko is interested in is *The Confidence Man.* Koko is also attracted to a book on an Ossian *hoax.*

While listening to the *Adriana Lecouvreur* opera—sung in Italian—Koko issues a "hollow, tortured wail" as Adriana is dying in the arms of her lover. She dies from flowers that were poisoned. Koko had made the same response while listening to the story of the Dimsdale Jinx, in which men were killed by poisoned pasties. Qwilleran realizes that Carter Lee poisoned Lynette.

Qwilleran writes a tall tale about a scam that supposedly victimized Pickax residents years ago. Carter Lee gets the point and tells Danielle to run. The levered door handle of the cats' apartment unlatches, and Koko teeters on the railing before dropping down on Carter Lee and gripping the man's head with his claws, riding on his head and howling.

Qwilleran and Wetherby chase Danielle and Carter Lee as they drive through the flooded county. The couple tries to cross a bridge, but the van goes over the guard rail. They are rescued and placed under arrest, Carter Lee for murder and fraud. Danielle, a kleptomaniac who was the real petty thief, turns state's witness.

Koko is still slapping the floor with his tail—right, left, right, left. He walks over to Yum Yum and hits her on the head with his paw. When Qwilleran yells at him to stop, Koko hits her again, adding a contemptuous "Yow-ow-ow." Qwilleran finally understands: Carter Lee hired a hit man to kill Willard!

The Cat Who Sang for the Birds

Once again Koko uses his extra whiskers—normal cats have forty-eight whiskers, eyebrows included, but Koko has sixty—to sense out a crime.

Qwilleran's first book purchase is a 1939 copy of Nathaniel West's book, *The Day of the Locust.* The first hint of crime is vandalism—somebody spray-painted the front of Mrs. Coggin's farmhouse with the word *witch.* Koko's choice for reading aloud is *The Crucible,* a book about the Salem witchcraft trials.

In the new gazebo, the cats enjoy watching the birds. Koko has begun a new bleating sound: *aaaaaaaaaaaaaaaa.* He also answers back the pileated woodpecker with a red topknot: *kek-kek-kek-kek.*

Koko jumps at the handle of the broom closet, a sign that he wants to go out. Koko and Qwilleran find the door to the Art Center open and blood on the floor. Jasper the parrot's cage is uncovered and his night blanket is splashed with blood. Someone had come too close to Jasper—someone who had stolen the nude drawings.

Another evening, Koko sniffs out the book *Fire Over London,* a World War II title, for reading. Later he awakens Qwilleran by thumping against his bedroom door and yowling. The Coggin farmhouse is burning, and Mrs. Coggin dies in the fire. Koko begins a mournful bleating like a sheep: *aaaaaaaaaaaaaaaaa*. Police Chief Roy Gumboldt says it was an accident. Others, experienced firefighters, say it looks like arson.

Koko licks one of Culvert's pictures of Mrs. Coggin, one where she is digging with her spade in the barnyard. Qwilleran and Rollo McBee think that she buried her money from the sale of her land in a coffee can—and Rollo finds a buried can. Hasselrich Bennett & Barter open it and discover one hundred thousand dollars.

Qwilleran returns home to find yesterday's *Something* in shreds and Koko bleating *aaaaaaaaaaaaaaaaaa*. Koko's choice of reading is *The Day of the Locust*.

There are rumors that the county is leasing a large section of the former Coggin land from Northern Land Improvement. Qwilleran suspects involvement of Chester Ramsbottom, a county commissioner. The owner of Northern Land Improvement company is Margaret Ramsbottom, Chester's wife.

Koko bites Qwilleran! Qwill is reading *The Birds Fall Down* by Rebecca West when Koko suddenly nips the thumb holding the book. Once again Koko selects *The Birds Fall Down* for Qwilleran to read. His next choice is *The Red Badge of Courage*.

There's another break-in at the Art Center—nothing taken, but someone used equipment and left the smell of cigarettes in the air and beer cans in the wastebasket. But some of the nude drawings were returned.

Celia Robinson asks Lisa Campbell Compton about a scandal involving the Campbells. Chester was once charged with watering the liquor in his bar, but put the blame on bartender Broderick Campbell, who was "a very upright young man." Broderick was sentenced to jail, but Ramsbottom got the sentence commuted and Brod went Down Below. Later Brod was found to be owner of a large motel and restaurant, presumably after accepting money from Chester to take the fall. Koko's reaction to the tape: *aaaaaaaaa.*

The City Council votes to buy four acres of Ramsbottom's land to expand the Pickax Cemetery—at $6,000 an acre.

While Qwilleran is showing his seventeenth-century compass to Thornton Haggis, Koko inches closer and twitches his nose. His whiskers curved forward. Soon the north star on the compass card was pointing to the kitchen—west! Nothing happens when Yum Yum sniffs the compass, but Koko again makes the north star point west.

Phoebe Sloan writes a letter to Qwilleran, saying that she's going to her grandmother in California. She tells him that she found a stack of Daphne's figure drawings among Jake Westrup's things—her boyfriend—drawings he had stolen. Phoebe returned them to the Art Center, and Jake abused her. It was Jake's gang who broke into the Click Club. She overheard Jake asking Chet for more money. Jake said that he wanted his cut from the million dollars Chet was getting from XYZ Enterprises for the river frontage. Chet reminded Jake that he lit the match on Mrs. Coggin's house, but Jake said he did it on Chet's instructions. During an argument, Phoebe told Jake what she knew, then ran to Sarah's apartment.

WPKX announces that Phoebe Sloan has been killed in an accident in the Bloody Creek Gorge. Qwilleran believes that she was murdered elsewhere by Jake and her body driven to the bridge. This proves to be the case. And Andy Brodie says that Chester Ramsbottom will be implicated in the Coggin incident. Koko's comment is, "*Aaaaaaaaa.*"

Qwilleran brings out the compass and once again Koko makes the North Star point to the library—to the west. Qwilleran realizes that two of the books that Koko has been knocking off the shelf were written by authors named West, pointing to Westrup.

Koko demands a trip to the Art Center, where he and Qwilleran hear an intruder running up the basement stairs. Unintentionally they stretch a leash between them and trip the intruder. Koko jumps on the man's back, digging in with his claws. Qwilleran taps him on the head with the totem pole. The escaped prisoner Westrup is captured. The K Fund buys the Coggin land to put it in conservation for agricultural use, as Mrs. Coggin had wanted.

Koko has been bleating like "a dirty old ram," although Qwilleran didn't make the connection with Ramsbottom. And he disliked the woodpecker with a red topknot. But now he has lost interest in red checkers, the antique compass, and books written by people named West. He sits in the gazebo, listening for birdsong, then "chattering an obbligato or mewling a melodic phrase of his own."

The Cat Who Saw Stars

When an unidentified backpacker is missing, all of Moose County is wondering and gossiping about what happened. Did the Hawleys have something to do with the disappearance? They report that a stranger named David asked permission to camp by Roaring Creek. Qwilleran feels a "nagging sensation on his upper lip" to visit the village of Fishport to investigate.

Besides the sensations from Qwill's moustache, Koko sits up late on the screened porch, looking toward the beach, seeing something that Qwill can't see. The next day when Qwilleran returns home, Koko insists on going for a walk on the beach. Or rather, a ride on Qwill's shoulder while Qwill walks on the beach. With a strange growl, Koko gets down on the sand, struggling up the ridge. Koko digs and digs in the sand, until he uncovers the face of a wristwatch. The body is identified by the Hawleys as the backpacker who visited them before he disappeared.

Chief Brodie said the victim was twenty-five, from Philadelphia, no next of kin. The coroner can't determine the cause of death, so the body has been sent to the state forensic lab. Brodie says the body was not decomposed after four days, "almost like he was embalmed."

Qwilleran buys a handcrafted copper sailboat by Mike Zander, a local commercial fisherman whose hobby is metalwork. He also buys a pedestal, a railroad tie, to go along with it, planning to display the work on the screened porch of the cabin. Koko immediately claims the pedestal, his "rightful eminence," gazing at the stars. Toulouse is also staring into space; Mildred says he's watching for Visitors.

Qwilleran notices that a young woman dressed in black walks along the beach, carrying a polished leather bag. Later when Qwilleran sees her at the Northern Lights Hotel, she's very "standoffish" and curt when he tries to speak to her. She visits the Hawleys and identifies herself as a partner of David, the dead backpacker, in Philadelphia. David worked with computers, but his hobby was UFOs.

Koko chooses a book from the shelf, Mark Twain's *A Horse's Tail*, about an army horse named Soldier Boy. The cats enjoy Qwilleran's sound effects.

Several people tell Qwilleran about Visitors and unexplained flying objects, but he's skeptical. Bushy suggests that spacecraft along the lakeshore blew sand up into a long ridge over the summer. He points out that the backpacker's body was found in the ridge of sand.

When Qwilleran sees the sheriff's helicopter circling over the lake, his moustache begins to quiver. A young woman is helped off a cabin cruiser and taken to the hotel, and Qwilleran investigates. The woman is Ernie Bowen, whose husband,

Owen, has just drowned while they were out on the lake. Ernie said she was below taking a nap when the violent rocking of the boat awakened her. When she went up on deck, Owen was gone. Qwilleran's moustache gives him a "nagging sensation" about the story. When Unc Huggins says that Owen was "a horse's tail," Qwilleran realizes that Koko knew about Owen's death before and after it happened, as evidenced by Koko's interest in *A Horse's Tail.* Although anyone else would think the connection very far-fetched, the idea is commonplace for Qwilleran.

When Qwilleran hangs the wagon wheel over the mantel, he notices a crack along the length of the top of the mantel. It's just perfect for holding postcards upright, so he puts the cards from Polly there. Polly and Mona have seen four plays: *Oedipus Rex, Macbeth, Major Barbara,* and *The Importance of Being Earnest.* One card has a portrait of George Bernard Shaw; the other a caricature of Oscar Wilde. Koko investigates the dozen cards, making a gentle fang mark on two cards: the portraits of the two Irish playwrights.

Mrs. Bowen is staying in her hotel room and having meals sent up—including dinner for two and some champagne. Word is out that she plans to reopen the restaurant with a whole new menu. She's trying to sell her cabin cruiser, the *Suncatcher.* During a ride on Bushy's new boat, Qwilleran and Bushy had seen the *Suncatcher* tied up next to the *Fast Mama.*

Once again Qwilleran finds the Shaw and Wilde postcards on the floor. And Tess notices that one of the five potato skewers Qwilleran had hung on the wall is missing. Koko keeps knocking one of them down.

Qwilleran meets Phil Scotten, whose dog, Einstein, is a retired G-dog, trained to sniff drugs. Qwilleran and Phil take him on the *Suncatcher.* He inspects everything, then sits down—what he was trained to do when he detected drugs. Shortly afterward, the police search the cruiser carefully.

Qwilleran tries to figure out Koko's obsession with the two postcards that Polly sent, one of Wilde and one of Shaw. When he returns home to find them on the floor again, he reads the messages. The Shaw card has a note about seeing *Major Barbara.* The Wilde card has a note about seeing *The Importance of Being Earnest.* Qwill's moustache tingles! Barb Ogilvie and Ernestine Bowen. Both women had lived in Florida. Was Owen the married man in Barb's life?

A gigantic sinkhole opens up in back of Owen's Place, and the east end of the Great Dune crumbles, covering the rear of the restaurant. Ernie is behind the building in her RV. She dies when her RV drops into the sinkhole and is buried under the sand.

Koko seems to be trying to prevent Qwilleran from leaving the Mooseville cabin. He climbs to the rafters of the cabin, just before several important events: a phone call from Polly, a call from Junior, and a meeting with Barb Ogilvie. Barb admits to Qwilleran that she had been dating her boss, Owen Bowen, in Florida, not knowing that he was married. She left Florida to return home to Moose County. Barb says that Ernie figured out that Owen was involved in a Florida drug ring, and Owen threatened her. While the couple was out on the lake, Ernie used a potato skewer to stab Owen in the ear, then roll him over the railing.

8

The Women in
Qwill's Life

*There have been several women in Qwill's life, but no one quite
serious until Polly Duncan. In the meantime, he has enjoyed the com-*
pany of a variety of women. Koko has a habit of dealing with
the women he doesn't approve of. He's a "self-appointed chap-
erone with his own ideas of social decorum" (*Red*).

MIRIAM

In *Backwards*, Qwilleran reveals that he is divorced from an
executive. In *On/Off*, he receives a letter postmarked Connecticut, another "graceless hint for money." His ex-mother-in-law
"puts the bite" on Qwilleran once in a while. His ex-wife,
Miriam, is in a Connecticut sanitarium again. In *Red*, he explains that she was once a very successful advertising woman.
Qwilleran sent a couple of hundred dollars of his $1,000 prize
to Miriam because she's sick.

In *Brahms*, Qwilleran reveals that Miriam suffered a nervous breakdown, and he tried to pickle his troubles in alcohol. In *Post Office,* Arch reminds Qwill that he and Miriam were married in Scotland and divorced about ten years ago. The reason his marriage failed was that Miriam "tried to direct his life," but "he was his own man."

In *Underground,* Qwilleran's family consists of "an alienated ex-wife in Connecticut, some hostile in-laws in New Jersey, and two Siamese cats." In *High,* Qwilleran reveals that he "started drinking heavily" and his "ex-wife cracked up."

The Cat Who Could Read Backwards

Sandra Halapay is a rare beauty with almond eyes, straight hair, and a "rippling laugh" that delights Qwill. He takes Sandy to lunch a couple of times, but there's nothing serious between them—Sandy's married.

Zoe Lambreth has a soft voice, "like caressing fingers," and Qwill's mustache tingles when he first hears her. Zoe invites him to visit the Lambreth Gallery, which makes Qwill "pull in his waistline" and think about going on a diet. After her husband's murder, she calls to ask for a confidential talk, and Qwill invites her to his apartment. Qwill wonders how long it will be before he can "conventionally invite her out to dinner."

Qwilleran is nervous because it's been a long time since he has entertained a woman in his apartment, especially one who looks like Zoe. He tries not to stare at the "provocative indentation just below her kneecap." Later Zoe invites Qwill to have dinner at her house. Qwill doesn't return home until after midnight, but when he does, he is in a most congenial mood. When Zoe reveals the connection between her late husband and Mountclemens, Qwilleran becomes disillusioned. He feels he has fallen for that "helpless-female act." After the facts clear Zoe from involvement, Qwill takes her out to dinner.

The Cat Who Ate Danish Modern

Qwilleran is womanless, but being pursued by Fran Unger, the women's editor. The trouble began when he danced with her at the Photographers' Ball. Now he can't get rid of her. Once when Fran calls Qwilleran, Koko acts jealous and cuts the connection by standing with "one foot planted firmly on the plunger button."

Qwilleran meets Alacoque Wright and is entranced. He makes a date with Cokey right away and leaves with "a lilting sensation in his moustache." He takes her to the Press Club, where they eat upstairs because the atmosphere is quieter. Cokey mixes a special drink with cream, ginger ale, and freshly grated ginger. It's like Cokey—"cool and smooth, with an unexpected pepperiness." She wins his heart when she reveals that she loves cats.

One Saturday Qwill takes Cokey to the ballpark, dinner at a chophouse, then a party at the Villa Verandah. They ride there in a taxi, holding hands. While riding up the elevator, Qwilleran gives her a quick private hug.

Koko reacts negatively to Cokey while she's in Qwill's apartment. After Cokey throws herself down on the luxurious rug (causing Qwill to "comb his moustache violently"), Koko prowls through the shaggy pile of the rug, then springs at Cokey's head and tries to take a nip. The psycatatrist tells Qwilleran that he'll have to call Cokey something else, because Koko thinks Qwilleran is using his name and he's very jealous.

Cokey invites Qwill to her apartment for dinner. Qwilleran is touched by the woman and her surroundings, and "for one brief moment he had a delirious urge to support this girl for life, but it passed quickly." He arrives home earlier than he expected. Cokey chased him out because they both have to work the next day.

The Cat Who Turned On and Off

Qwilleran has just received a note written in brown ink from Cokey, canceling a date for Christmas Eve because she's found another man.

Qwill meets Mary Duckworth at her antique store, the Blue Dragon. She has "large dark eyes, heavily rimmed with black pencil," but without expression. She's about thirty, "an age to which Qwilleran was partial." He begins to regard her as a prospect for Christmas Eve at the Press Club. Qwilleran is fascinated by the young woman who is "disarmingly candid one moment and wary the next—lithe as a willow and strong as an oak," alternately compassionate and aloof.

When Mary comes into Qwilleran's apartment, Yum Yum disappears, but Koko stands his ground, "arching his back and bushing his tail as he glared at the stranger." His reaction is "not hostile—only unflattering." Later Mary brings a heat lamp for Qwilleran's sore knee, and Koko looks her over from "an unfriendly distance." Qwill and Mary are close—their lips are very close. There's a breathless moment, then a sudden major catfight. After the commotion, Mary becomes nicely emotional, and it becomes "a gratifying evening." She even accepts his Christmas Eve invitation.

Cluthra invites Qwilleran over to Skyline Towers, and he takes Koko for protection. Koko starts out on Qwilleran's lap, but disappears against the coloring of the "paisley sofa surrounded by paisley pillows." Cluthra invites Qwill to come over to the sofa, but she begins to sneeze repeatedly. Koko buries his nose in her ostrich feathers, and Cluthra's eyes start watering. The visit ends abruptly, with a great sense of escape for Qwilleran.

After Mary learns the truth about Andy, she's distraught, and Qwilleran comforts her after she collapses in tears. Koko rises to the daybed, stands on his hind feet, stretches his neck, and rubs the doorjamb. He turns off the light, and the apartment is thrown into darkness.

The Cat Who Saw Red

Qwilleran goes to the Gourmet Club at Maus Haus, where he's surprised to meet his old flame, Joy Wheatley Graham. Qwill knew her in Chicago when they were kids and he was "the boy next door." They were engaged a long time ago, until she suddenly left town.

Joy has developed a sharp tongue, which she uses on her husband, Dan. Qwilleran thinks it looks like domestic trouble. Joy throws her arms around Qwill and tells him she's thought about him very often. Later when she visits Qwilleran's apartment, she gathers Koko in her arms, and he permits it, much to Qwilleran's "surprise and pleasure." Koko is a "man's cat and not used to being cuddled."

Joy explains that her leaving town suddenly had nothing to do with Qwill, but dissatisfaction with her life. She went to San Francisco where she worked in restaurants, then supervised the kitchen on a large ranch that was a pottery school where she learned her art and met Dan. They have lived in California, then Florida, then California again before Robert Maus asked them to take over the pottery at Maus Haus.

She sits on the arm of Qwilleran's chair, leaning toward him and whispering, "You were my first." Qwill replies that she was his first. Suddenly there's a loud "Yow!" from the top of the bookcase, and a book crashes to the floor. Cats fly in all directions, breaking the spell.

Joy tells Qwilleran that she's getting a divorce because she knows she can do better on her own. Qwill lends her $750 because the "sight of his childhood sweetheart with wrinkled signs of age in her face" fills him with sadness and affection.

The next day when Dan tells him that she's taken off, Qwill is surprised, but his instinct tells him to have faith in Joy because he has "never really stopped loving Joy Wheatley." Later he understands that it's the *memory* of Joy Wheatley that he loves, when she was age nineteen, not the current Joy Graham.

Arch gives Qwilleran the assignment of going to Rattlesnake Lake to judge a cake-baking contest. When he complains about the long drive in a company car, Rosemary Whiting volunteers to go with him and take her car. Her brown eyes fill with "an expression that he can't quite identify." He realizes that she's very attractive. They plan to leave in the afternoon, have dinner at the inn, judge the contest on Sunday, then return home. Rosemary has a pleasant voice, and Qwill finds "her company relaxing." She remarks that "it would be nice if they could have adjoining rooms."

After dinner and dancing, Qwilleran is suddenly overcome by exhaustion. Rosemary volunteers to massage his neck and shoulders. He feels "so relaxed . . . so sleepy" that he falls asleep. It's noon when Qwill wakes on Sunday. Back home at the Maus Haus, Qwill gazes at Rosemary with admiration, drops the suitcases, and kisses her. They are interrupted by an outburst from Mrs. Marron.

Late one evening Qwill invites Rosemary to his apartment where he tells her about the love letters addressed to Helen Maude Hake. Telling Qwill that she'd "never in my life received a love letter," she curls up among the pillows on the bed and reads the letters. Her eyes grow moist because the letters are so lovely. Suddenly Qwilleran pitches the cats into the bathroom and slams the door. It's midnight when Rosemary leaves.

The Cat Who Played Brahms

Qwilleran greets Rosemary Whiting with a "kiss that is more than a perfunctory social peck." The Siamese sit "in stony immobility." He explains to her his plans for his summer vacation in Mooseville.

Melinda Goodwinter is the green-eyed doctor at the walk-in clinic at the Cannery Mall. On the whole, Melinda is "enjoyable company," although she "referred to his age too frequently."

Rosemary calls and tells Qwill she can come up for a week, and Qwilleran is "speechless with joy." He misses her in more ways than one. She's not as young as some of the women he has been seeing, but she's "an attractive brunette with a youthful figure," and she's comfortable to have around. Koko and Yum Yum react to her presence "without feline wariness but also without overt friendliness." Rosemary brings the cats some "catnip tied in the toe of a sock," which Koko especially likes to bat and chase around.

After a prolonged good night, she goes to the guest room and dislodges the two cats from their favorite bunk. Everyone is awakened in the middle of the night by a "horrendous screaming." It turns out to be an owl, swooping down on a rabbit and carrying it away, but Rosemary tells Qwilleran that she'll "feel a lot safer in his room." He doesn't mind.

Rosemary buys some tulips in a variety of colors from the prison. Koko pulls the black ones out and scatters them all over the floor. When he does this a second time, Rosemary locks him in the bathroom. Rosemary says she thinks Koko wants her to go home. When Rosemary announces that she's leaving Mooseville, Koko responds with a "YOW!" that sounds "so much like a cheer that both Qwill and Rosemary looked at him in dismay."

Qwill's not entirely sorry to see her move to Toronto. Rosemary is "not tuned in to his sense of humor" and she's "certainly not tuned in to Koko." She treats him "like an ordinary cat." Qwilleran bids her a friendly farewell, but with "none of the warmth and intimacy there had been a week ago."

The Cat Who Played Post Office

Penelope Goodwinter piques Qwill's curiosity; she's a challenge and a "fascinating enigma." She has a "dazzling smile and provocative dimples, but they are used solely for business purposes." When he asks her out to dinner, she declines.

When Qwill wakes up in the hospital, he sees Dr. Melinda Goodwinter's "green eyes and long eyelashes." He asks if she's his wife, and she replies that she's "working on it." They've been dating for two months.

Melinda asks Qwilleran out to dinner at Otto's Tasty Eats. They go back to the Klingenschoen mansion, where they sit close on the leather sofa, listening to romantic music. Qwill's "mournful eyes met her inviting green gaze and the world stood still." This moment is interrupted by a simulated cat fight. Soon Qwilleran leans closer again and there's a "sense of pleasurable propinquity." The clock starts to strike eleven times, and Koko walks in and utters an "imperious 'YOW!'" He turns and leaves, then a moment later they hear another insistent yowl. Qwilleran finds Koko "in the vestibule, staring at the front door." Qwill thinks Koko is looking for the mail. Koko stalks into the library a second time. Staring hard at Melinda, he says, "Nyik nyik nyik YOW!" and again marches to the front door.

The third time Koko makes his entrance, "scolding and glaring at the guest," Melinda follows the cat, who is "stopping at intervals and looking back to make sure she is following." In the vestibule he stares "pointedly at the door handle." Melinda says she thinks he's telling her to go home. Qwilleran apologizes and replies that Koko likes lights turned out at eleven. Qwilleran escorts her to her car in the garage and stays there for an unspecified amount of time. He returns, "preening his moustache with satisfaction."

Qwilleran asks Melinda to be his hostess at a dinner party he's giving for his friend, Arch Riker. When Arch Riker comments that Melinda is a remarkable young woman, then asks if those are her own eyelashes, Qwilleran responds that "everything is absolutely real." He's checked it out. After the dinner party, Qwill buys a gold necklace from Diamond Jim's and drops it off at the clinic for Melinda.

The Cat Who Knew Shakespeare

Melinda Goodwinter leaves Pickax and goes to a hospital in Boston, where she will be able to specialize, saying she never really wanted to be a country doctor.

Qwilleran now has "something going with the head librarian," Polly Duncan. Polly is "not as young and slender as the career women Qwilleran has dated Down Below," but she's an "interesting woman with a voice that sometimes made his head spin." She is reserved and always insists on going home early.

Polly knows Shakespeare forward and backward. She's from New England, but has lived in Pickax for twenty-five years. In college she married a Pickax native and they came to manage his family's bookstore. Her husband died very young, a volunteer firefighter killed by a falling timber in a barn fire. At least Koko doesn't order Polly out of the house, as he has done with other female visitors.

Qwilleran receives an invitation from Polly to come to her cottage for dinner—roast beef with Yorkshire pudding. The Big One hits as Qwilleran is on his way to Polly's. His car goes off in a ditch during the blizzard, and he barely makes it through the dark and snow to her cottage. The phone is dead, and soon the electricity goes out. Qwill sleeps well, "but not because of tramping through the snow or eating too much roast beef."

The Cat Who Sniffed Glue

Francesca Brodie, an interior designer who's remodeling the carriage house, makes a play for Qwill. Her strategy is "all too transparent." She asks for a key to Qwill's apartment to "supervise workmen and the delivery of merchandise." She brings wallpaper-sample books and catalogs and sits close to him on the sofa. She times these visits at the cocktail hour, and Qwilleran offers her a drink or two, after which "a dinner invitation was almost obligatory." However, Qwill is beginning "to feel more comfortable with women of his own age who wear size 16." Polly is "rediscovering love, and her responses are warm and caring." Clerks in Lanspeak's Department Store, who have sold him items of clothing in Polly's size, are happy to see him come in.

But Qwilleran's friendship with Polly Duncan begins to fail. She has been "noticeably cool since he joined the Theatre Club and hired a designer." Suddenly there are "no idyllic Sundays at her cottage in the country, no berry picking, morel gathering, nutting, birding, reading aloud, or other delights."

After the Fitches are murdered, Qwill calls Polly to talk about the news and invites her to dinner. They enjoy dinner, but conversation later doesn't go well. She's critical when he tells her he's going to give up on writing a novel and stick to journalistic writing. She calls it "disposable prose" instead of "something of lasting value." With a brief good night, she leaves in her cranberry-red two-door car Qwill gave her for

Christmas. He realizes that it was too good to last. Once loving and agreeable, Polly has become critical.

Francesca comes over to discuss wallpaper for his apartment. While she and Qwilleran are sitting together on the sofa, Yum Yum grabs Fran's ankles with needlelike claws. She also pilfers Fran's lighter and puts it in her sandbox. Qwilleran has always felt comfortable with Polly, but he's never felt entirely comfortable with Fran.

Qwilleran goes to Mrs. Cobb's home for dinner and realizes how much he misses his former housekeeper's cooking. She's looking "prettier than usual in her pink ruffled blouse." When she cries after he gives her a real silk scarf, Qwilleran feels a "surge of compassion for her." Life had been agreeable when Mrs. Cobb was his housekeeper and cook. Yum Yum catches a mouse at "an auspicious time," saving him from "an amorous slip of the tongue."

Polly and Qwilleran begin "rediscovering their old camaraderie." He hopes for a reconciliation. Qwilleran is once again reading aloud to the cats and "spending weekends at Polly Duncan's cozy house in the country."

The Cat Who Went Underground

When Qwilleran decides to spend the summer at the log cabin in Mooseville, his only regret is that Polly will not be there to share it with him, since she's going to England on an exchange program. He's going to miss their "animated discussions" at dinner and "weekends at her country hideaway that made him feel twenty years younger."

He invites Mildred Hanstable to the Fish Tank restaurant after they judge the Fourth of July parade. After dinner they go to her cottage, where she gives him a wonderful shoulder rub, and "his thoughts flew across the Atlantic to Polly."

Qwill learns that Polly's doctors have advised her to cut her visit short because of a "bad case of bronchitis and asthma." He's glad she is coming home!

The Cat Who Talked to Ghosts

At the Dingleberry Funeral Home during visiting hours for Iris Cobb, Polly exchanges glances with Qwilleran "across the crowded room." They are "always discreet in public."

Polly is given a Siamese kitten by the librarian in Lockmaster. Her gushing over the kitten is more than Qwill can stomach. There will be "no more relaxing country weekends at Polly's cottage"—not while Bootsie is vying for Polly's attention. He can't believe that Polly can be "reduced overnight to a blithering fool." Never mind that he calls Yum Yum his "sweetheart."

Qwilleran invites Mildred Hanstable to dinner in order to learn more about Kristi Fugtree Waffle. When dating Polly, who is "not attuned to fashion," Qwill wears what is readily available and clean. Mildred teaches art as well as home economics, and she has an "eye for color, design, and coordination." For Mildred he tries harder. He wears a camel's hair cardigan over a white open-neck shirt, and tan pants, an ensemble that "enhanced the suntan he had acquired during recent months of biking."

Qwilleran invites Polly to his carriage-house apartment for dinner. There is a "warm moment of greeting that would have titillated the Pickax grapevine."

The Cat Who Lived High

Qwilleran is looking forward to moving to the big city for the winter, but will miss Polly Duncan. He has spent "many idyllic weekends" at her cottage. When he leaves, she asks him to call her as soon as he arrives. He had hoped for "less wifely anxiety and more amorous sentiments."

Amberina, who now calls herself Amber, suggests Qwilleran and she go to Roberto's for dinner. Amber is divorced and makes several comments about Qwill's wealth and divorced status. One evening is enough of Amber's company. Qwilleran wonders if Mary Duckworth has romantic memories of their previous association, when she had relaxed briefly on "one unforgettable Christmas Eve."

Qwilleran begins to miss Polly more than he thought he would. He wears the bottoms of the "valentine-red pajamas" that Polly gave him last February. When he's with Polly he doesn't reveal his true feelings because he's tongue-tied.

Winnie Wingfoot catches his eye with her model's figure and angel's face, enhanced by "incredibly artful makeup." She also has a "model's walk and an heiress's clothing budget." But Qwilleran misses Polly.

The Cat Who Knew a Cardinal

Qwilleran and Polly are still seeing each other, but Polly becomes disinterested. She goes to a wedding in Lockmaster and isn't the same when she returns. She's distracted, and she starts wearing brighter colors. She talks about dancing with everyone—but Qwilleran and Polly have never danced. Qwilleran sees a picture of Polly in an "electric blue dress," dancing with a "man with a red beard" and a "green plaid sports coat." She looks entirely too happy. Qwill discovers that he is Steve O'Hare.

Everything is pointing toward a rift in the intimate relationship between Qwilleran and Polly. They have been "close friends" for two years, "sharing confidences, giving each other priority, consulting on every question that arose."

Mildred Hanstable is recently widowed and one of Qwilleran's favorite women—and cooks. Susan Exbridge is a handsome and interesting woman—more fashionable than Polly—but she's "too aggressive and theatrical for his taste," and she "never sat down and read a book."

When Qwilleran and Polly finally get back together, it's their first dinner together in ten days. And they have missed two weekends. But Polly says they belong together, and the last two years have been "the best of her life." They go back to her place (for coffee).

The Cat Who Moved a Mountain

After Qwilleran decides to spend the summer in the Potato Mountains, there's a farewell dinner with Polly Duncan at the Old Stone Mill, followed by a "sentimental parting at her apartment."

Upon arrival at Spudsboro, Qwilleran feels the need to converse with someone back home—and Polly naturally comes to mind. After their conversation, Qwilleran wonders "why he was here alone when he had been so comfortable in Moose County among friends."

Qwilleran learns that Dr. Melinda Goodwinter is moving back to Pickax to take over her father's practice after the death of her parents. Qwilleran is nervous. Before Melinda left for Boston, she had been determined to marry Qwilleran.

After Qwilleran solves the murder of J. J. Hawkinfield, he

calls Polly and learns of her harrowing experience of being followed by a strange man. Qwilleran tells her he'll leave Spudsboro immediately and head for Pickax—because he loves her!

The Cat Who Wasn't There

Qwilleran cancels his vacation arrangements in the Potato Mountains and returns to Moose County "at a speed that discommoded the two yowling passengers in the backseat and alerted the highway patrols of four states." He dashes to the library as soon as he arrives, rushing upstairs to Polly's office. A "fervent and lingering handclasp was as amorous a greeting as they dared" in public. In private, however, they engage in a "warm, silent, meaningful embrace that would have astonished the library patrons."

Amid his worry about Polly, Qwilleran is concerned about his inevitable encounter with Dr. Melinda Goodwinter. He's "unsure how to handle their reunion." She is very aggressive, and her previous efforts to "bulldoze him into marriage" had been embarrassing. She's "still carrying the torch for him, Polly or no Polly."

On the Bonnie Scots Tour, Melinda goes to Qwilleran's room with an unconventional proposition: She wants Qwilleran to marry her for three years, after which he will have his freedom, and their children will assume the name of Goodwinter. She wants sons to carry on the family name, and besides, she's broke. Qwilleran tells her she's out of her mind, "suddenly suspecting that the strange look in her eyes was insanity." Qwill tells her that if he marries anyone, it will be Polly. Qwill resents "being hounded by an overzealous female." Besides, Koko has never liked Melinda.

The Cat Who Went Into the Closet

Polly moves into the carriage house of the Gage mansion, and Qwilleran rents the Gage mansion for the winter. He envisions "cozy winter evenings and frequent invitations to dinner and/or breakfast."

While Qwilleran is working on *The Big Burning of 1869*, he and Hixie Rice spend a lot of time together, since she's producing and directing the docudrama. It's a difficult time for Polly, who tends to be "jealous of women younger and thinner than she." But he's "happier than he had ever been in his life," content in "loving an intelligent woman of his own age."

For Christmas, he buys Polly a lavaliere and earrings: "fiery black opals rimmed with discreet diamonds."

The Cat Who Came to Breakfast

Polly's college roommate invites her to Oregon, and Qwilleran tells her that "life will be dull and devoid of pleasure and excitement." Although various people hint that Qwilleran and Polly ought to marry, Qwill declares that they are "happily unmarried until death do us part."

While Polly is in Oregon, Qwilleran goes to Pear Island, where he's pursued by June Halliburton. Previously on the mainland, June had come to Qwilleran's house with the Comptons, but she didn't stay long because of a headache. Qwill knows that actually it was "Koko giving her the whammy" by staring at her forehead.

As the days go by, no mail comes from Polly. Qwilleran is beginning to be uneasy, fearing that Polly might decide to stay in Oregon. He can't imagine life without her. Finally he receives a short postcard that says she has made a very important decision. Qwilleran is afraid that means she's not coming back. As it turns out, Sarah has been helping Polly design her own house. Qwilleran offers her two acres on the corner of his property in town.

The Cat Who Blew the Whistle

Polly is very involved in building her new home. She's an "independent person" who likes to make her own decisions. As a librarian, she's "efficient and briskly decisive." She advises her younger assistants with "kindness and common sense." In solving her own problems, however, she melts into "a puddle of bewilderment."

Qwilleran is concerned because all Polly talks about is her new house. He's frustrated by "too much of Polly's house and not enough of Polly." She's worrying too much and exercising too little. Dinner dates are "becoming more of an obligation than a pleasure."

One evening Polly calls and asks to be taken to the hospital. Dr. Diane calls it a mild heart attack. Polly has coronary bypass surgery in Minneapolis, and convalesces at the Duncan homestead with her sister-in-law.

The Cat Who Said Cheese

Polly is recovering nicely at Lynette's home. When Qwilleran goes to visit, they cling together in a "voluptuous embrace" until Bootsie protests.

When people start a sentence, "Why don't you and Polly—" Qwill replies that their cats are incompatible, and that they're happily single.

Polly is returning to work, half-days, and Qwilleran takes her to Boulder House Inn in Trawnto for dinner and overnight. They have adjoining rooms upstairs, Polly with a four-poster bed and a fireplace and Qwill with a refrigerator, an overstuffed sofa, and a chess set.

The Cat Who Tailed a Thief

Qwilleran buys a condo at Indian Village to live in during the winter months. Polly lives in the same building. His Christmas present for Polly is a terra-cotta suede suit with a silk blouse. Her present to him is a 1924 set of leather-bound books by Herman Melville and an opera recording, *Adriana Lecouvreur.* He and Polly walk hand-in-hand, "romantic grist for the gossip mill."

Qwilleran makes a serious mistake by criticizing "Bootsie" as an inappropriate name for a "noble, aristocratic animal like a Siamese." He doesn't know that one "should never question a person's choice of a name for a pet, no matter how intimate the friendship." After thinking about his advice, Polly decides to rename the cat Brutus. They spend a weekend of reading aloud, listening to music, and "doing all the things they enjoyed."

The Cat Who Sang for the Birds

Qwilleran contracts with artist Paul Skumble to paint Polly's portrait. He begins to feel uneasy, afraid that Polly is becoming too entranced by the artist. Paul has a "talent for charming the socks off his female subjects." And Paul gives Polly a handkerchief that had belonged to his grandmother.

Paul paints a beautiful portrait of Polly—but neither Paul nor Polly gives Qwilleran anything to worry about in their relationship.

The Cat Who Saw Stars

Polly Duncan is away for a whole month—on a trip to Ontario, Canada, with her sister Mona. They're seeing Shakespeare in Stratford and some Shaw plays in Niagara-on-the-Lake. He already misses the nightly phone conversations and "would miss their weekends even more." She sends Qwilleran a postcard every day, because he complained that on previous trips, he rarely heard from her. He orders a special hand-woven vest for Polly from Barb Ogilvie.

Wetherby Goode's cousin Dr. Teresa Bunker, a corvidologist, shows up with luggage at Qwilleran's cabin to discuss possible collaboration on an animated feature about crows. He puts her in the Snuggery. Qwilleran finds her "well read, well spoken and not a bad-looking dinner date." He's anxious for her to leave so he can return to Pickax, until she begins to cook fabulous meals for him.

Qwilleran plans his reunion with Polly. He will avoid talk of the *Suncatcher* and *Fast Mama*, because Polly becomes alarmed when he becomes enmeshed in an investigation.

Sunday afternoon, Tess and Qwill are on the lake porch. A few minutes later, Janelle from Safe Harbor arrives, bringing the framed sampler. A few minutes later, Barb Ogilvie arrives, bringing the vest for Polly. A few minutes later—Polly arrives to find three young women on the porch with Qwilleran! Polly leaves. Tess leaves. Janelle leaves. Barb leaves. A few minutes later, there's a terrific squall on the lake that bombards the shore.

The next day, unable to return to Pickax because the roads are flooded, Qwilleran has the Pickax florist deliver a mixed bouquet to Polly, with the card signed "the grocer boy." When she calls to thank him, she says she was shocked to see that "aggregation of youthful pulchritude" on his porch, but she won't ask for an explanation. Qwilleran replies that he won't ask about the professor who talked her into staying longer in Quebec City.

When Mildred asks why Qwilleran and Polly don't get married, he replies that she drinks tea and he drinks coffee. He has missed Polly greatly, for many reasons: "her loving smile, soft voice, merry laugh—and their shared interests." She brings him a vest made in the Mackintosh clan tartan.

9

Gracious Abodes

Architecture and unusual houses and apartments are part of the background of Koko's adventures. Qwilleran lives in a wide variety of abodes, from a cheap, plastic hotel to a many-room mansion filled with expensive antiques. "Home is where I hang my toothbrush and where the cats have their commode (*Ghosts*)."

The Cat Who Could Read Backwards

In the beginning, Qwill lives at an old, cheap hotel with plastic floors and plastic-covered armchairs. The coffee shop features cold plastic plates. In fact, the whole place is plastic-coated.

After making the acquaintance of Mountclemens, the newspaper's art critic, Qwill moves into one of Mountclemens's apartments, which has a living room with a bed and a kitchenette. There are gas logs in the fireplace, and the floor is covered with red carpeting. It has what Mountclemens calls "ambience." Qwill calls it lots of junk. Except for the painting over the mantel—one of Monet's less successful works. Qwill's one complaint is the low level of lighting.

The Cat Who Ate Danish Modern

Qwill is evicted by the new owner of Mountclemens's house, but finds a place that links him to the new world to which he's assigned: the architecture and design beat. He moves to Harry Noyton's apartment while Noyton is out of the country.

It's a *pied-á-terre* Noyton uses for entertaining, located in the Villa Verandah, an eighteen-story apartment building that looks like a "bent waffle." The Villa is "curved around a landscaped park" with a balcony view of the other balconies. It's "too sunny, too windy, too dirty," and is known as "Architect's Revenge" by its residents.

Noyton's apartment is "soft, comfortable, but rugged." Harry calls it Scandihoovian. David Lyke describes it as "tastefully done in wall-to-wall money." The floor is made of tiny squares of dark wood (imported from Denmark) with a velvety oiled finish, covered with a rug of "genuine goat hair from Greece." It has high bookshelves, which Koko likes, and gold bathroom faucets. Qwilleran likes the trio of sofas covered in natural tan suede. There's a green chair, which is Danish, Finnish dining chairs, and a leather-topped desk.

The Cat Who Turned On and Off

Qwilleran is now living in one room in a third-rate hotel, Medford Manor. Qwill's room has a double bed with limp fringe on its cotton bedspread, an armchair, a cluttered dresser, and a closet. The two Siamese like to climb inside the bedsprings.

While working on an assignment, Qwilleran learns that the Cobbs have an apartment on the second floor of their antique store, The Junkery. He moves into the rear apartment, "a large square room with four tall windows and a frightening collection of furniture." There's a pair of "high-backed gilded chairs with seats supported by gargoyles," a patterned rug "suffering from age and melancholy," and a "crude rocking chair made of bent twigs and tree bark." The daybed is "built like a swan boat, with one end carved in the shape of a long-necked bad-tempered bird." The wall behind the bed is papered with the "yellowed pages of old books, set in quaint typefaces."

A second room has been subdivided into a kitchenette, dressing room, and bath. The large dressing room has "a solid bank of built-in bookshelves filled with volumes in old leather bindings." Mrs. Cobb adds "a reading lamp sprouting out of a small brass cash register," a floor lamp made from a musket, a rolltop desk, a cupboard for books, an old-fashioned Morris chair and ottoman, and a potbellied stove.

Qwilleran discovers that the Cobb mansion was built by William Towne Spencer, the famous abolitionist, in 1855. There's a secret Underground Railroad passageway, which the cats quickly discover.

The Cat Who Saw Red

Qwilleran goes to the Maus Haus for a Gourmet Club meeting and ends up moving in. Number Six is a studio apartment two stories high, and "half the outer wall was window, composed of many small panes." The furniture is massive, "almost medieval in appearance—heavily carved and reinforced with wrought iron." There's a big lounge chair in "bold black-and-white plaid," built-in bookcases, and a white bearskin rug. The rent is higher than Qwilleran has been paying on Zwinger Street, but he tells himself that the "sophisticated cuisine is appropriate to his new assignment."

The Maus Haus is the home of Robert Maus on River Road. The houseboy explains that it's sort of a "weird boarding-house." It used to be an art center known as Penniman Pottery until Robert Maus took it over. The gigantic stone house resembles an "Egyptian temple that had been damaged in transit and ineptly repaired." It has Georgian chimneys and factory windows.

The Cat Who Played Brahms

Robert Maus sells Maus Haus, so Qwilleran has to move. He plans to spend the summer at a small cabin belonging to Aunt Fanny on the lake near Mooseville, which is four hundred miles north of everywhere.

The picturesque cabin is "perched on top of the highest dune and dwarfed by hundred-foot pine trees." Its logs and chinking are dark with age. A screened porch overlooks the lake, and another faces the woods. There's a huge fieldstone chimney.

Inside, a knotty pine ceiling soars to almost twenty feet at the peak, "supported by trusses of peeled log." The walls are whitewashed exposed logs. Above the fireplace is a moosehead "with a great spread of antlers, flanked by a pickax and a lumberjack's crosscut saw." It's not all rustic: It has the latest type of telephone, a microwave, a whirlpool bath, and several shelves of books.

When Qwilleran becomes Fanny's heir, he must live in the Klingenschoen Mansion in Moose County for five years in order to inherit the fortune. The Klingenschoen home is a "large, square fieldstone mansion, with a carriage house in the rear." The high-ceilinged hallway has a grand staircase. There's a formal drawing room and dining room, a paneled library, a "breakfast room smothered in chintz," and an "airy room with French windows, wicker furniture, and ancient rubber plants." There's an "English pub in the basement that was imported from London." The third floor was supposed to be a ballroom, but it was never finished.

The library has "four thousand leather-bound books, unread; four closets filled with Fanny's spectacular wardrobe; the Staffordshire collection in the breakfast room, the envy of three major museums; and Georgian silver in the dining room."

The Cat Who Played Post Office

The K mansion is situated on Pickax Circle, a "bulge in Main Street that wrapped around a small park." The mansion has eighty tall, narrow windows. It's the most impressive edifice in town, and the costliest. It has priceless French and English antiques and art objects worth millions. There's a circular driveway in front and a side drive to the carriage house in the rear, also built of "fieldstone with specks of quartz." Qwilleran calls it "Alcatraz Provincial" or the Bastille.

The rooms are huge. It has a "high-ceilinged foyer with grandiose staircase; a dining room that could seat sixteen; the drawing room with its two fireplaces, two giant crystal chandeliers, and ponderous antique piano; the solarium with three walls of glass." The breakfast room has "William and Mary banister-back chairs surrounding a dark oak table, and yellow and green chintz covering the walls and draping the windows." In the library the "warm colors of Bokhara rugs, leather seating, and thousands of books" offer a "wraparound coziness."

The massive front door has a brass handle and escutcheon, a brass doorbell, and a brass mail slot. The kitchen has a "butler's pantry, a food storage room, a laundry, a half bath, and a walk-in broom closet." The whole service area is floored in square tiles of red quarry stone.

Qwilleran chooses a bedroom suite that is "eighteenth-century English with Chippendale highboys and lowboys and a canopied bed." Every bedroom has a canopied bed, sitting room, dressing room, and bath. There are four suites, each done in a different period: French, Biedermeier, Empire, and Chippendale. The French suite has an early eighteenth-century "Norman bonnet-top armoire." The Old English suite has side curtains on the bed. The Biedermeier has flowers painted on everything. The Empire has enough sphinxes and gryphons to cause nightmares.

The dining room is lighted by "twenty-four electric candles mounted on two staghorn chandeliers." It has dark linenfold paneling, Austrian chandeliers, and German furniture. The drawing room furnishings include chandeliers, oil paintings, and a collection of Chinese porcelains.

The carriage house has four stalls for automobiles and two apartments upstairs. The first apartment has drab walls and shabby furniture. The walls and ceiling of the second apartment are "covered with graffiti in every color available in a spray can." Giant flowers that look like daisies are on every surface, "intertwined with hearts, initials, and references to LUV."

The Cat Who Knew Shakespeare

The Klingenschoen residence has "crystal chandeliers by the ton and Oriental rugs by the acre." The solarium has a stone floor, a "forest of ancient rubber plants," and some wicker chairs.

Qwilleran decides to turn the Klingenschoen mansion into a museum, and he and the cats move into a remodeled carriage-house apartment. There are "four arched doors to the stalls, a cupola with a weather vane on the roof, and a brace of ornate carriage lanterns at each corner of the building." Qwill's sitting room has easy chairs, good reading lamps, and a music system. The other rooms are his writing studio, his bedroom, and the cats' parlor.

The K mansion is completely gutted by fire.

The Cat Who Sniffed Glue

The carriage-house apartment now has "oatmeal-colored, oatmeal-textured" handwoven Scottish tweed on the walls, along with a framed print of an 1805 gunboat. The cats have their own apartment, including a private bath with "his and her litter pans." Their room is furnished with television, soft carpet, cushions, baskets, scratching posts, and wide window-sills facing south and west.

The mansion itself fronts on Main Street facing the park. It's being remodeled as a theater for stage productions. The interior has been redesigned to provide "amphitheater seating, a thrust stage, a professional lighting system, and adequate dressing rooms." It will seat three hundred and will be the new home of the Pickax Theatre Club.

The Cat Who Went Underground

Although Qwilleran's legal address remains 315 Park Circle, Pickax, he decides to spend the summer at the Klingenschoen cabin, three miles to the east of Mooseville. It's seventy-five years old and has "acres of woodland and half a mile of lake frontage." The private drive "meandered through the woods, past wild cherry trees in blossom, through a stand of white birches, and up and down over gentle dunes covered with giant oaks and towering, top-heavy pines." It has "whitewashed log walls, an open ceiling crisscrossed with log trusses, oiled wood floors scattered with Indian rugs, two white sofas angled around a fieldstone fireplace, and an incomparable view from the bank of north windows." A hundred miles across the water is Canada.

The Cat Who Talked to Ghosts

After the death of Mrs. Cobb, Qwilleran and the Siamese move into the Goodwinter Farmhouse Museum apartment until another manager can be found. The kitchen has shelves displaying "antique pewter plates, porringers, and tankards; the overhead beams were hung with copper pots and baskets"; wrought-iron utensils hang around the fireplace. In the parlor are an Austrian dower chest and a large pine wardrobe—the Pennsylvania German *Schrank* that came from the Klingenschoen mansion. Chairs are covered in dark velvet, "the better to show cat hairs," and the "polished wood floors were scattered with antique Orientals, good for pouncing and skidding."

The bedroom has a monster of a bed, a "priceless General Grant bed that was made of rosewood a century ago for a World's Fair." The headboard looks like the door to a mausoleum, and Qwill has a nightmare that it falls on him.

The original section of the Goodwinter farmhouse is built of "square logs measuring fourteen by fourteen inches, chinked with mortar made of clay, straw, and hog's blood."

The east and west wings were added later, and the whole structure is "covered with cedar shingles, now weathered to a silvery gray." It has wide floorboards, "extravagant use of milled woodwork," and "six-over-six windows," many panes being the original wavy glass.

The basement originally had a dirt floor and was used "for storing root vegetables and apples in winter." It now has a concrete floor and modern heating and laundry equipment. The stone walls are a foot thick.

There's also a classic style barn with a gambrel root. The weathered wood barn perches high on a fieldstone foundation that becomes a full story high as the land slopes away to the rear. A grassy ramp leads up to huge double doors, large enough to accommodate a fully loaded hay wagon. A man-size door called the eye of the needle is cut into the larger door.

The Cat Who Lived High

Qwilleran moves to the Casablanca apartment building in the Midwest city Down Below while trying to decide whether the Klingenschoen Fund should buy it and renovate it.

Qwill's penthouse apartment is 14-A, which is actually on the thirteenth floor. The foyer is furnished in contemporary style, with doorways and arches leading to other areas. French doors overlook a large room with a "lofty ceiling and a conversation pit six feet deep"—the former swimming pool. There is an "enormous onyx cocktail table stacked with art magazines; an eight-foot bar; and an impressive stereo system with satellite speakers the size of coffins." Around the rim of the former pool are "indoor trees in tubs, some reaching almost to the skylight twenty feet overhead." Art is everywhere: "paintings on the walls, sculpture on pedestals, crystal and ceramic objects in lighted niches."

The Casablanca is a huge, old apartment building "between Junktown and the reclaimed area where new office towers and condos are going up." The exterior is white glazed brick in a "modified Moorish design." The walls are built two feet thick at the base, tapering to eighteen inches at the top. It looks like a refrigerator—white with a "dark line across the facade at the ninth floor."

The building has lost most of its grandeur. The lobby is narrow, a "tunnel-like hall with a low ceiling and a lingering odor of disinfectant." There are fluorescent tubes for lighting and well-worn, but clean, vinyl on the floor. The walls are covered with something that looks like sandpaper. The manager's office has a window of "thick, bulletproof acrylic." There are two elevators, Old Red and Old Green.

The Countess, owner of the Casablanca, lives on the twelfth floor and never leaves it. The burnished bronze elevator with scenes from *Don Quixote* and *Carmen* is her private elevator.

The Cat Who Knew a Cardinal

The latest scandal in Moose County is that Jim Qwilleran is living in an apple barn. The octagonal structure is built on a hundred-year-old fieldstone foundation, rising as high as a four-story building. Originally used for storing apples, pressing cider, and making apple butter, all that remains is a "wealth of empty space rising cathedral-like to the octagonal roof." On a warm and humid day, the interior still exudes the aroma of Winesaps and Jonathans.

The walls of the main floor are the original stone foundation, "a random stack of boulders held together by hidden mortar, craggy as a grotto." Ramps and catwalks spiral upward around the interior walls, with "balconies floating on three levels," and massive beams radiating under the roof. The Siamese love to race wildly on the timbers thirty or forty feet over-head. Some of the massive pine timbers are twelve inches square. Sandblasted to their original honey color, they contrast nicely with the newly painted white walls. On one of these ra-diating beams is the mark of the original builder: J. Mayfus & Son, 1881. High triangular windows preserve the "symmetry of beams and braces."

In the center is a contemporary fireplace, a "huge white cube with three chubby cylindrical white flues rising to the center of the roof." Furniture is arranged in conversation groups on Moroccan rugs on the earthen tile floor. In the lounge area are two sofas and a large chair upholstered in "oatmeal tweed." The tables are off-white cubes.

The library area has "deep-cushioned lounge chairs in pale taupe leather" arranged around one wall of the fireplace cube. White lacquered shelves are loaded with old books.

The first balcony contains Qwilleran's sleeping room and writing studio. On the second balcony is a guest room. The cats have their own apartment on the top balcony. There are comfortable carpets and cushions, baskets, perches, a scratch-ing post, and TV.

Qwilleran orders tapestries to decorate his barn-home. One is an eight-by-ten foot wall hanging for the railing of the high-est catwalk. The design is a "stylized tree dotted with a dozen bright red apples the size of basketballs." The second, smaller tapestry is hung on the wall of the fireplace cube, facing the foyer. It's a "galaxy of birds and green foliage."

The Cat Who Moved a Mountain

Tiptop is a "dark, glowering, uninviting building in a gray-green stain, the upper floor sided in gray-green fishscale clap-board." The first-floor windows are shaded by a "gray-green wrap-around veranda." Upper-floor windows and dormers have deeply overhanging roofs. A "gray stone arch inset with a mosaic of darker pebbles" spells out TIPTOP INN—1903. Eighteen stone steps lead up to the inn, and seven wooden steps lead up to the veranda.

The interior is dark. A wide central hall runs the length of the building and ends in French doors at the rear. Surrounding the hall are a "cavernous living room, a dining room that seated twelve, a hotel-sized kitchen." It's "depressingly gray: gray plush carpet, gray damask draperies, wallcoverings predominantly gray." The rooms are bleak, with no small or personal items.

The foyer has a group of "inviting chairs around a stone fireplace." There are "two old-fashioned hat-and-umbrella stands with clouded mirrors, a couple of tired umbrellas, and some stout walking sticks." A huge, unattractive chest holds the telephone, above which is a painting of the mountains. Qwilleran calls it "Musty Rustic."

The Cat Who Wasn't There

Qwilleran and the Siamese live in the nineteenth-century apple barn, which is "an octagonal structure four stories high, with large windows cut into the walls at various levels."

The Cat Who Went Into the Closet

Qwilleran rents the Gage mansion from Junior Goodwinter for the winter months. The house is made of stone, built to last forever. The furnishings are sparse, but the "closets were stuffed to the ceiling with odds and ends." Gage, a shipbuilder, was used to having everything built-in, and ship's carpenters built the house. The woodwork was the best on the boulevard. The foyer looks like "a luxury liner of early vintage." The basement ballroom is a "large, turn-of-the-century hall with Art Deco murals and light fixtures." On the main floor are the "coffered paneling of the high ceiling and the lavishly carved fireplaces."

The Cat Who Came to Breakfast

The Bambas' bed-and-breakfast, called the Domino Inn, has "seven rooms, two suites, and five housekeeping cottages." It had been a private lodge in the Twenties, owned by a family that was "nuts about dominoes." It's a "large ungainly building with small windows, completely sided with a patchwork of white birchbark." Wooden steps lead to a long porch with swings hanging from chains. The Domino Lounge has "a skylight about thirty feet overhead and balcony rooms on all four sides." The whole structure is "supported by four enormous tree trunks," almost a yard in diameter, with the bark intact.

The five cottages are "hardly larger than garages," and stained a somber brown. The doors are painted black with white pips, like the numbers on dominoes. Qwilleran and the cats are staying in Four Pips, which has a screened porch in back that is "minuscule and rather like a cage." It's the "smallest living quarters he had experienced since an army tent." It has "a tiny sitting room, snug bedroom, mini-kitchen, and pocket-size bathroom." The furniture and windows are covered with "yards of fabric in a splashy pattern of giant roses, irises, and ferns." It's a "rustic straitjacket with slipcovers like horticultural nightmares."

The Cat Who Blew the Whistle

The apple barn has a "fieldstone foundation two feet thick and as high as Qwilleran's head." The interior has a "series of balconies connected by ramps, surrounding a central cube of pristine white." The Siamese consider the spiraling ramps an indoor race track.

The formal entrance to the barn is a double door flanked by tall, narrow windows. They have sills "about twenty inches from the floor, a convenient height for a cat who wanted to stand on his hind feet and peer through the glass."

Indirect lighting accents the "balconies and the beams high overhead;" downlights create "mysterious puddles of light on the main floor;" a spotlight focuses on a "huge tapestry hanging from a balcony railing."

The Cat Who Said Cheese

The apple barn is topped with a cupola. Qwill's private suite is on the first balcony, the only area not open to the Siamese. There's a spiral metal staircase from the first balcony down to the main floor, which is a hundred feet across.

The Cat Who Tailed a Thief

Qwilleran and the Siamese aren't living in the barn this winter because it's impossible to heat evenly. Qwill buys a condo in Indian Village for the winter, Unit Four of Building Five on River Lane, and has it furnished by Fran Brodie. She buys old pine farm furniture and has it stripped to a honey color. The condo has a "lofty living room" with big windows overlooking the Ittibittiwassee River on one side. Opposite is a balcony with two bedrooms, and below are the kitchen and the dining alcove, which he uses as an office.

The Cat Who Sang for the Birds

Qwilleran and the cats are back in the barn after spending the winter in the condo. The small windows cut in the stone look like "crossbow ports in a medieval fort." Above the barn's fieldstone foundation, the walls are shingled with weathered wood. The eight-foot-high fireplace cube is a safe perch for the cats, "just beyond human reach." Thornton calls it the "Guggenheim of Moose County."

Qwilleran has a gazebo built behind the barn so the cats can "enjoy the fresh air and commune with the wildlife." It's a "free-standing octagonal structure screened on all eight sides." Kevin Doone develops an avian garden with trees and shrubs, birdfeeders, and bird baths. The Siamese enjoy watching the birds and other animals, and Koko even sings for them!

The Cat Who Saw Stars

Qwilleran's old cabin at Mooseville is perfect for short summer visits. Its remoteness is "more psychological than geographic." The beach is "Cat Heaven." The screened porch is "Cloud Nine." Qwilleran goes there for peace and quiet. The property is a "half-square mile of ancient forest on ancient sand dunes." The sandy drive curves among pines, oaks, maples, and cherry trees.

The old cabin is built of "full-round logs interlocking at the corners," and seems to be anchored to the ground by its huge stone chimney. There are three new skylights in the roof to let in more light. A sandladder leads to the beach; it's a frame of two-by-fours filled in with loose sand for steps.

The gable end above the fireplace once held a mounted moosehead. Later there were such things as axes and saws. Qwilleran buys a rusty iron wheel with sixteen spokes to hang on the blank wall.

Qwill has a new guest house, but it's not "too comfortable or too attractive" because he doesn't want to encourage visitors. He says it's "strictly for emergency overnights." The cottage is a "little larger than a dollhouse" and a "little more comfortable than a tent."

The Snuggery is the same size as the toolshed, made of the same green-stained cedar, and hidden in the woods. It has windows, indoor plumbing, and modular furniture. Blankets, rug, and a picture of poppies add bright red accents. Qwilleran decides it is good enough for one overnight, but not for two—his plan all along to discourage visitors.

10

A Companion's
Guide to Dining

CONNOISSEUR CATS

*K*oko and Yum Yum's meals are delicacies far beyond what Qwilleran fixes for himself. Koko prefers white grape juice, the best brand, naturally. Mountclemens (*Backwards*) feeds him beef cut into small pieces, "warmed in a pan of broth and sprinkled with sage or thyme." For breakfast, he often has *pâté de la maison* (or meatloaf, as Qwilleran describes it).

Qwilleran brings Koko some corned beef from the Press Club (*Danish*). From Lyke's buffet—laden with caviar, shrimp, and meatballs—Qwilleran chooses delicacies to take home to Koko. He buys cans of smoked oysters, fixes chopped chicken livers sautéed in butter with a side order of Roquefort cheese, and cooks veal kidneys in cream. Qwill buys Koko a filet mignon for saving his life.

Qwilleran brings home turkey from the Press Club (*On/*

Off). He also buys round steak and canned consommé, then cream cheese for Yum Yum and blue cheese for Koko. He buys fresh liver at the grocery and warms it in broth (*Red*). From the Maus Haus, Qwilleran brings jellied clams. He opens a can of lobster, a gift from Mary Duckworth, then later red salmon.

One day Qwilleran decides that the cats need to "face reality," and he buys a can of Kitty Delight, some Pussy Pâté, and a box of Fishy Fritters. The cats refuse to eat. Qwilleran returns home to a scene of havoc, the cats' protest against regular cat food. He gives up and treats them to lamb from the Golden Pork Chop and chub from the delicatessen.

Mildred Hanstable leaves Qwilleran some turkey, which he shares with the cats (*Brahms*). She also leaves meat loaf, which Qwilleran says he tricks the Siamese into thinking it's pâté de foie gras. They eat corned beef but "fastidiously avoided every shred of carrot" contaminating the beef. Breakfast is often canned crabmeat.

Qwilleran eats half of a pasty at the FOO, then takes the remainder home to the cats. He scoops out half the filling, mashes it "into a gray paste," warms it, then spreads it on a handmade plate. The Siamese "approached the food in slow motion, sniffed it incredulously, walked around it, withdrew in disdain, and looked at Qwill in silent rebuke, shaking their front paws in a gesture of loathing." Qwilleran dices some pot roast and adds grated carrot and a "sprinkling of hard-cooked egg yolks." The cats carefully avoid the grated carrot.

Mrs. Cobb prepares "sautéed chicken livers with a garnish of hard-cooked egg yolk and bacon crumbles" (*Shakespeare*). The chef at the Old Stone Mill, Tony Peters, invents a line of gourmet food for cats, "Fabulous Frozen Foods for Fussy Felines." Entrées include pork liver cupcakes and lobster nuggets in Nantua sauce with anchovy garnish. The Siamese "devoured the chef's innovation, with tails flat on the floor, denoting total satisfaction."

Old Stone Mill busboy Derek Cuttlebrink makes daily deliveries of such delicacies as veal blanquette (which the cats like) with Japanese mushrooms (which they don't) and fresh artichoke hearts (*Glue*). One day he brings shrimp timbales in lobster purée. Another time he brings bouillabaisse without the mussel shells. When Qwilleran offers it to them for dinner, they decline; it was the "same stuff they had been served for breakfast." They also enjoy poached salmon with capers, chicken liver pâté, boned frog legs, tenderloin tips, shrimp cocktail, and veal Stroganoff.

For breakfast, Qwilleran has a stale doughnut (*Underground*). For the cats, he opens a can of "Alaskan King crab, mixing it with a raw egg yolk and garnishing it with a few crumbs of fine English cheddar."

Mildred Hanstable makes homemade cereal, which the cats love as a treat. Qwilleran shares beef stew with the cats. They "gobbled the meat and licked up the gravy," but "left the carrot and potato and onion high and dry on the rim of the plate." From the Fish Tank restaurant, Qwill orders a freshly broiled lobster tail to take home to the cats.

After Mrs. Cobb's death, Qwilleran has access to her freezer, which contains a "two-month supply of spaghetti sauce, chili, macaroni and cheese, vichyssoise, pot roast, turkey tetrazzine, shrimp gumbo, deviled crab, Swedish meatballs, and other Cobb specialties" (*Ghosts*). The Siamese eat more of this supply than Qwilleran does. Derek continues to make daily visits with "sushi, shrimp timbales, braised lamb brains, and other delicacies."

One evening Qwilleran brings home a napkin full of veal, scallops, and squid from Roberto's (*High*). While Qwilleran's back is turned, the Siamese eat three days' worth of food. Qwill is aghast because Rupert gives the cats an old, stale jelly doughnut—and they eat it!

Qwilleran makes himself "a bowl of chili, a small pizza, and two corn muffins" (*Cardinal*). The cats distract him, and he returns to find that "the cheese and pepperoni had disappeared, and the chili was reduced to beans."

The Siamese have "fickle palates" (*Wasn't*). Qwilleran feels they can read labels. Their "preferences changed just often enough to keep him perpetually on his toes." The only constant is "no cat food!" Qwilleran takes home some haggis (meat-filled pastry) from Scottish Night at the lodge, which they eat with approval.

The two cats can "smell turkey through an oak door two inches thick," and yowl and prance eagerly when Qwilleran brings home a foil-wrapped chunk of turkey from Lois's kitchen. Another day, he brings them a sample of boozeburger from the Black Bear Café.

After the Christmas parade, Qwilleran shares the last piece of fruitcake with the cats (*Closet*). They "slobbered over it eagerly, being careful to spit out the nuts and fruits."

While on Breakfast Island, Qwilleran orders meat loaf from Vacation Helpers, but the cats refuse to eat any (*Breakfast*). The next time he serves the meat loaf, they shake their paws and walk away. Later Qwilleran discovers that the meat loaf had been made with two parts beef and one part rabbit. The cats gobble up the all-beef meat loaf greedily, yowling for more.

After a party, the Siamese enjoy "nibbling sausage and cheese and fastidiously avoiding the bits of mushroom and green pepper" left over from pizzas (*Whistle*).

When Qwilleran offers the Siamese fresh lamb, they decline to even sniff it, even after he reminds them, "There are disadvantaged cats out there who don't know where their next mouse is coming from!" (*Cheese*). The cats are becoming cheese junkies. Qwilleran gives each cat a tiny crumb of Gruyére cheese from Switzerland, which they savor at great length. He also provides Havarti for Yum Yum and feta for Koko.

The Siamese enjoy meatballs from Lois's Luncheonette,

gobbling them with gusto, but spitting out the onion (*Thief*). Lois offers codfish, but the cats turn up their "well-bred noses" at anything less than "top-grade red sockeye salmon" (*Sang*). They feast on canned crabmeat garnished with goat cheese.

When Qwilleran has Andy over after the Fourth of July parade, he serves Gorgonzola cheese and crackers, along with single malt Scotch (*Stars*). Yum Yum looks at Qwill so longingly that he gives her a bite of Gorgonzola. Tess cooks macaroni and cheese for lunch for herself and Qwilleran. When everyone leaves and Qwill is distracted by a sudden and violent squall, the Siamese eat the cheese, "horseradish and all," but not the macaroni.

CONNOISSEUR QWILLERAN

Restaurants and food are inextricably tied to Qwill's social and professional life, both when he's dieting and when he's not. Since "dicing, thawing, and pressing the button on the computerized coffeemaker" are his only kitchen skills, Qwilleran eats out a lot (*Whistle*).

The Cat Who Could Read Backwards

George Mountclemens's kitchen is haute cuisine. When he invites Qwilleran over for dinner, they begin with hot tarts, which have a flaky crust and a wonderful custard filling of cheese and spinach. Next comes thick, creamy lobster bisque, followed by chicken in "a dark and mysterious sauce." The next course is a Caesar salad, "a man's salad, zesty and full of crunch." The meal is completed with a bittersweet-chocolate dessert and small cups of Turkish coffee.

At breakfast, Mountclemens serves fresh pineapple, a ramekin of eggs with herbs and sour cream, and chicken livers and bacon en brochette. After Mountclemens returns from New York, he invites Qwilleran for a cup of Lapsang Souchong tea and a Dobos torte from a Viennese bakery.

The Press Club is a restaurant and more. Located in a sooty limestone fortress with bars on the windows (it was formerly the county jail), the noisy bar downstairs serves great corned beef sandwiches.

Sitting Bull's Chop House is located in the packinghouse district, which accounts for the odor which seeps into the dining room. It features "chopped sirloin that weighed a pound," cheesecake "four inches thick," and gigantic lamb chops.

The Artist and Model is a "snug cellar hideaway favored by the culture crowd." Diners listen to classical music while eating French Food in an atmosphere of "cultivated gloom." Qwilleran orders *ragôut de boeuf Bordelaise.*

The Cat Who Ate Danish Modern

The place to eat is Cokey's apartment. When Qwilleran comes for dinner, she serves "a mixture of fish and brown rice in a sauce flecked with green." The salad is crunchy and requires a great deal of chewing. Later comes "ice cream made of yogurt and figs, sprinkled with sunflower seeds." After dinner, Cokey pours cups of herb tea, her own blend of alfalfa and bladder wrack.

At the Press Club, Cokey orders brook trout "with a large garnish of parsley" and a small salad. Qwilleran orders "bean soup, a hefty steak and a baked potato with sour cream."

Qwilleran and Cokey attend a party at David Lyke's apartment. Qwilleran tries lobster salad, garlic-flavored potato balls, ginger-spiced beef skewers, and hot buttered cornbread with ham.

The Cat Who Turned On and Off

Mrs. Cobb is a terrific cook. She welcomes Qwilleran with "bubbling hot pie with sharp cheese melted over the top." On his first morning, Iris gives him bacon and eggs and buttered hot corn muffins. Her Christmas baking includes frosted chocolate brownies topped with walnut halves. On Sunday morning she brings a cranberry twist coffeecake. She invites him for dinner: pot roast simmered with garlic and celery tops, mashed potatoes with sour cream and dill, salad with Roquefort dressing, and coconut cake.

The Toledo Restaurant (the most expensive restaurant in town) delivers Christmas dinner for Mary and Qwill: oysters Rockefeller, pressed duck, Chateaubriand, and French strawberries.

The Cat Who Saw Red

The Gourmet Club meets at Maus Haus, home of attorney Robert Maus. The menu is "cream of watercress soup, jellied clams, stuffed breast of chicken baked in a crust, braised endive, broiled curried tomatoes, romaine salad, and crêpes suzette." Another evening, the dinner is roast beef, corn chowder, broccoli parmigiana, Parker House rolls, and bulgur.

The Toledo Tombs is a "subterranean restaurant" consisting of a "series of cavernous rooms, long and narrow, vaulted in somber black masonry." The building was once a sewer. The menu offers everything from "aquavit to zabaglione, and from avocado supréme rémoulade to zucchini sauté avec hollandaise." Qwilleran and Robert Maus order French onion soup with melted cheese, eels in green sauce, veal and mushrooms "aswim in delicate juices," braised fennel almandine, tossed salad with nasturtium seeds, "chestnut purée in meringue nests," and the demitasse.

The Golden Lamb Chop occupies a building that's a nineteenth-century landmark, having once been the depot for interurban trolleys. Now the interior has a "golden glow, like money." The menu includes vichyssoise or herring in sour cream, rack of lamb, baked potato with sour cream, and rum cream pie, banana Bavarian, pecan caramel custard, strawberry shortcake, and chocolate mousse.

The new Petrified Bagel is located in Junktown and furnished with junk. Qwill orders a "frozen hamburger, gently warmed, and some canned peas." The hamburger has been "grilled to the consistency of a steel-belted radial tire." William orders strawberry cheesecake for dessert and calls it the "best wallpaper paste I've ever eaten."

The Rattlesnake Inn is famous for its bad food, but what it lacks in quality, it makes up in quantity. The hors d'oeuvre table presents "thirty different appetizers, all of them mashed up and flavored with the same pickle juice." The menu offers a choice of ten steaks, all "uniformly tender, expensive, and flavorless." The shrimp cocktails are "huge and leathery." An assortment of rolls, biscuits, and muffins are served in ice cold bun-warmers. The baked potatoes wear "foil jackets firmly glued to the skin." The "asparagus tasted like Brussels sprouts and the spinach tasted like old dishrags." The specialty of the house is the dessert buffet with "twenty-seven cream pies made from instant vanilla pudding."

At a Friendly Fatties meeting, Qwilleran and Hixie Rice have cabbage juice cocktails, a thick soup made by dragging a "bouillon cube through hot water," melba toast, a main course that looks "like grape seeds stuck together with epoxy glue," Brussels sprouts that taste "like wet papier-mâché," and prune whip made of "air, water, coal tar, disodium phosphate, vegetable gum, and artificial flavoring."

The Cat Who Played Brahms

In Mooseville, dining out doesn't look promising. For a restaurant reviewer, it's "like being sent to Siberia." The Northern Lights Hotel serves "mediocre pork chops, a soggy baked potato, overcooked green beans," and then "gelatinous blueberry pie."

Pasties at the FOO are a "foot wide and three inches thick." They're filled with meat and potatoes and plenty of turnips. Qwilleran eats half of the first pasty, "lubricating each dry mouthful with weak coffee," then takes the remainder home to the cats (which they refuse).

The Nasty Pasty has pasties that are "flaky, have a little sauce, and less turnip." The restaurant is "small and designed for intimacy."

On the dinner menu at the Northern Lights Hotel are "Nova Scotia halibut, Columbia River salmon, and Boston scrod." Qwilleran labels his food "E for edible."

The Old Stone Mill is an "authentic old mill with a waterwheel" with an ordinary menu. Qwilleran orders the "mediocre pork chops, a soggy baked potato, and overcooked green beans"—the Moose County specialty. He suggests that Rosemary order the chicken julienne salad, which is "probably tired lettuce and imitation tomatoes with concrete croutons and slivers of invisible chicken, served with bottled dressing from Kansas City and a dusting of grated Parmesan that tastes like sawdust."

The Dimsdale Diner in Mooseville is a "boxcar punctuated with windows of various sorts." The interior is "papered with yellowing posters and faded menus dating back to the days of nickel coffee and ten-cent sandwiches." The specialty is goulash with cole slaw. The goulash is "macaroni and canned tomatoes and hamburger."

The Cat Who Played Post Office

The Klingenschoen mansion becomes a terrific place to eat when Mrs. Iris Cobb arrives as Qwilleran's housekeeper and cook. She cooks a lamb stew with dumplings for dinner, and her famous three-layer, cream-filled coconut cake for dessert.

The Old Stone Mill's specialty of the house is ravioli. They "buy it frozen and it's the only thing on the menu that the cook can't ruin." Qwill orders French-fried ice cream for dessert, "a cannonball of pastry reposing in a puddle of chocolate sauce."

Otto's Tasty Eats is a "veritable shrine to gluttony: twelve-gallon crocks of watery soup, bushels of torn iceberg lettuce, mountains of fried chicken and fried fish, tubs of reconstituted mashed potatoes, and a dessert table that is a sea of white froth masquerading as whipped cream." Qwilleran persuades the kitchen to "*broil* two orders of pickerel *without breading*." Melinda bribes the waiter to find some fresh fruit for dessert.

The Hotel Booze is a stolid, ugly stone building three stories high, in the "plain shoebox architecture typical of hotels in pioneer towns." The dim lighting in the dining room camouflages "the dreary walls, ancient linoleum floor, and worn plastic tables." But the restaurant serves a superb "twelve-ounce bacon cheeseburger with fries" that taste like actual potatoes. Qwill and Roger order the "Cholesterol Special" and pie made with freshly picked wild thimbleberries.

Mrs. Cobb outdoes herself at Qwilleran's dinner party. He asks Melinda to serve as hostess, and she plans a special menu of foods indigenous to the area—"terrine of pheasant and jellied watercress consommé," Chinook salmon croquettes, "lamb *bûcheronne* with tiny Moose County potatoes and mushrooms," salad of "homegrown asparagus vinaigrette," and a wild raspberry trifle.

The Lanspeaks' new restaurant, Stephanie's, is named after

their cow, and it's done in dairy colors: "milk white, straw beige, and butter yellow." Qwill and Melinda order champagne and some *pâté de caneton* as an appetizer, then trout almandine and asparagus. They receive broccoli instead and send it back, but the chef insists it's asparagus. This is followed by a tossed salad on a chilled plate, then Ribier grapes with homemade cheese and coffee "served with Stephanie's own cream."

The Cat Who Knew Shakespeare

Mrs. Cobb continues her delicious meals: clam chowder and escalopes of veal Casimir; baked ham, ginger-pear salad, and sweet potato casserole; butterscotch pecan meringues; beef Stroganoff and poppy-seed noodles with pumpkin pie for dessert; and "real buttermilk pancakes and real Canadian peameal bacon." When Junior Goodwinter comes for dinner, Mrs. Cobb cooks loin chops with big Idaho baked potatoes and fresh peach pie for dessert.

The Old Stone Mill has been renovated and has a new chef, after being purchased by XYZ Enterprises, Inc. Hixie Rice, from Down Below, is managing the restaurant. They replace "the dreary menu with more sophisticated dishes and fresh ingredients." Hixie recommends lamb shank with ratatouille.

The Cat Who Sniffed Glue

Food at the mansion goes downhill after Mrs. Cobb leaves. Qwilleran makes instant coffee and warms up two-day-old doughnuts for himself.

Tipsy's Restaurant is named after a cat. Gus, the founder of the restaurant, was a "cook in a lumber camp and then a saloonkeeper." During Prohibition he operated a blind pig Down Below. After Repeal, he came back to Moose County with a black-and-white cat named Tipsy and opened a steakhouse in a log cabin. In the main dining room hangs a portrait of Tipsy. The "pickerel tasted like fish," the "steak required chewing," and the "lemon-meringue pie was irresistible." (Read more about Tipsy and Gus in "Tipsy and the Board of Health," in *The Cat Who Had 14 Tales.*)

Stephanie's is "one of the best restaurants in the county." It occupies an old stone mansion. The interior has a "hospitable ambience created by soft colors, soft textures, and soft lighting." Qwilleran and Fran have herbed trout with wine sauce.

Food at the Goodwinter Farmhouse Museum is top quality. Mrs. Cobb invites Qwilleran over for pot roast, mashed potatoes, and coconut cake with apricot filling. The "pot roast was succulent; the mashed potatoes were superlative; the homemade bread was properly chewy; and the coconut cake was ambrosial."

The Hotel Booze in Brrr is famous for boozeburgers. Gary Pratt serves the "best hamburgers and homemade pie" in the county. The pie of the day is "strawberry made with whole berries and real whipped cream."

The Cat Who Went Underground

Mildred Hanstable, the home economics teacher and food writer, invites Qwilleran to dinner, where she serves "stuffed mushrooms and rumaki;" a casserole which was a "sauced combination of turkey, homemade noodles, and artichoke hearts"; a Caesar salad; and raspberry pie that leaves him "almost numb with contentment."

The Fish Tank is a restaurant in Mooseville known for fabulous navy grog. It's a new restaurant in "an old waterfront warehouse on the fishing wharves," famous for clam chowder and broiled whitefish.

The Hot Spot is "the cool place to go for hot cuisine." It occupies a "former firehall in Brrr with thirty tables jammed into space that once housed two firetrucks." Specialties include Mexican, Cajun, and East Indian dishes. Roger MacGillivray orders the Cajun pork chops and Qwilleran orders "industrial strength" enchiladas. After they receive the wrong food, they leave for the Black Bear Café in Hotel Booze and its famous boozeburgers and homemade pies.

In Lockmaster, the Palomino Paddock has a "hostess in long dress, several diners in dinner jackets, and a wine steward." Roger MacGillivray and Qwilleran order vichyssoise, then prime rib. Qwill declares it to be "real beef."

The Cat Who Talked to Ghosts

Currently Polly Duncan is cooking with lots of very hot curry, not Qwill's favorite. He likes Indian food, but "Polly was whipping a good idea to death."

Tipsy's is the place where "serious eaters" converge for "serious steaks, freshly peeled potatoes, boiled carrots, and cole slaw." There's a waiting line for tables every night. The beef has "world-class flavor," but requires diligent chewing. It's homegrown, like the potatoes, carrots, and cabbage. Dessert is "old-fashioned bread pudding with a pitcher of thick cream," followed by coffee "powerful enough to exorcise demons and domesticate poltergeists."

Dinner at the Northern Lights Hotel is "French onion soup, frog legs, Caesar salad, and pumpkin pecan pie."

The Cat Who Lived High

Roberto's is a classy restaurant opened by Robert Maus. "Walls, ceiling, and arches were an unbroken sweep of smooth plaster in a custardy shade of cream." The carpet and upholstery of steel-based chairs are "eggplant." Qwilleran and Amber order an antipasto, soup, and a veal dish. The antipasti are "breaded baby squid with marinara sauce, and roasted red peppers with anchovies and onion." The soup is a "rich chicken broth threaded with egg and cheese." Amber orders the "top-price rib chop with wine and mushroom sauce," with a bottle of Valpolicella. Qwilleran requests the "medium-priced *vitello alla piccata*, sautéed with lemon and capers." Dessert is gelato and espresso.

The Press Club isn't the same. The corned beef sandwich is not as good as it used to be. Qwilleran and Matt Thiggamon have French onion soup and roast beef sandwiches with horseradish.

A Japanese restaurant on Eat Street (a.k.a., Zwinger Boulevard) has an imposing chef in a stovepipe hat, two feet tall. His audience is speechless as he manipulates the "splash of egg, hill of sliced mushrooms, and mountain of rice." Steaks, seafood, and chicken breasts "sizzled in butter and were doused with seasonings and flamed in wine."

At his dinner party, Courtney Hampton serves cream of watercress soup, "crabcakes with shiitake mushrooms, baby beets in an orange glaze, and wild rice," a salad of artichoke hearts and sprouts, and a chocolate soufflé.

The Cat Who Knew a Cardinal

At Tipsy's Tavern, the menu is always "steak or fish, take it or leave it." The soup is bean, the vegetables are boiled homegrown carrots and tiny Moose County potatoes, boiled in their skins.

Lois's Luncheonette in downtown Pickax provides eggs, country fries, rye toast, and coffee for breakfast. For lunch at the Old Stone Mill, Qwilleran suggests cheese and broccoli soup that is "so thick you could use it for mortar." The avocado-stuffed pita is "messy but delicious." The "crab Louis salad is the genuine thing."

The Cat Who Moved a Mountain

The Spudsboro Golf Club has introduced a lighter menu. Qwilleran orders poached flounder, which is "lightly sauced and served on an oversized plate along with three perfect green beans, a sliver of parboiled carrot, and two halves of a cherry tomato broiled and sprinkled with parsley." He also has "mashed turnip flavored with grated orange rind." Dessert is a slice of "double chocolate fudge cake" and coffee. Colin Carmichael orders a corned beef sandwich and cheddar cheese soup.

The Five Points Café has a Father's Day special of turkey with cornbread dressing, cranberry sauce, and turnips.

Pasta Perfect is an Italian restaurant in Spudsboro in a "rustic roadhouse that appeared ready to collapse." It has several small rooms with high-backed booths for privacy. In the non-smoking room is a "painted portrait of an Indian chief smoking a peace pipe." The restaurant offers "fifteen kinds of pasta," fresh daily. For an appetizer, Qwilleran orders "smoked salmon and avocado rolled in lasagna noodles, with a sauce of watercress, dill, and horseradish." Sabrina orders "trout quenelles on a bed of black beans with Cajun hollandaise." For his entrée, Qwilleran has "tagliatelle in a sauce of ricotta, leeks, and ham." Dessert is almond ravioli with raspberry sauce.

The Cat Who Wasn't There

The Bonnie Scots Tour provides new and delicious foods for the travelers. The full Scottish breakfast consists of oatmeal, eggs, meat, fish, fruit, pancakes, scones, currant buns, oatcakes, bannocks, jams, marmalade; or dried apple slices, prunes, and figs with creamed finnan haddie and oatcakes. Dinners on the tour include fresh salmon or roast lamb with neeps (turnips) and tatties (potatoes); sheep's head broth, rabbit casserole, and clootie dumplings; cock-a-leekie soup with small meat-filled pastries called bridies, lamb stew with barley and neeps, and a dish of tatties and onions called stovies; or smoked salmon, lentil soup, brown trout, venison, and a dessert flavored with Scotch whiskey.

Arch, Amanda, Polly and Qwilleran visit a good Indian restaurant in Glasgow, Scotland. It has "white tile floors, tinkling fountains, hanging brass lamps, an assertive aroma of curry, and a background of raga music." They order samosas (meat-filled pastries), mulligatawny soup, and a main course of tandoori murghi and pulao, with a side order of dal. Amanda translates this to mean roast chicken with rice and lentils. Dessert is *gajar halva*, which Amanda insists is carrot pudding.

The New Pickax Hotel has a new chef who's serving things like chicken cordon bleu. The new selections are "french onion soup instead of bean, grilled salmon steak instead of fish and chips, chicken cordon bleu instead of chicken and dumplings, and roast prime rib instead of swiss steak." However, the chicken is Kiev, not cordon bleu, which the chef refuses to admit. Qwill and Polly leave to go to the Old Stone Mill.

The Dimsdale Diner is as dismal as Qwilleran remembers. The coffee is still the worst in the county. Thursday's special is "TOM SOUP, TUNA SAMICH and MAC/CHEEZ." The pasta is "cooked to the consistency of tapioca pudding" and "library paste could have tasted no worse" than the sauce.

At Linguini's, everyone eats whatever Mr. Linguini feels like cooking. One evening it's raw vegetables with *bagna cauda*, a dish of bubbling anchovy and garlic sauce; *zuppa di fagioli*, which Arch says is bean soup; *tortellini quattro formaggi*, pasta with four cheeses; and for an entrée, *polpettone alla bolognese*, which Arch says is meat loaf. Dessert is *zuccotto*, a "concoction of cream, chocolate, and nuts."

The Palomino Paddock is located in Lockmaster, in horse country. Their new chef offers grilled duck sausage with sage polenta and green onion confit for an appetizer. Soup is three-mushroom velouté. Specials are "lovely roasted quail with goat cheese, sun-dried tomatoes, and hickory-smoked bacon and also a pan-seared snapper with herb crust and a red pepper and artichoke relish." The waitress's favorite is "roasted pork tenderloin with sesame fried spinach, shiitake mushrooms, and garlic chutney." Polly decides on plain grilled swordfish, while Qwilleran orders fillet of beef. The house salad is a "botanical cross section of Bibb lettuce surrounded by precise mounds of shredded radish, paper-thin carrot, and cubed tofu, drizzled with gingered rice wine vinaigrette dressing and finished with a veil of alfalfa sprouts and a sliver of Brie." Dessert is "a delicate terrine of three kinds of chocolate drenched in raspberry coulis" and a demitasse that "smelled like almonds and tasted like a hot fudge sundae."

The fare for the evening at Scottish Night at the Lodge Hall is "haggis [meat pudding], tatties and neeps [potatoes and turnips], Forfar bridies [meat-filled pastries], Pitlochry salad, tea, shortbread, and a 'wee dram' for toasting."

The Cat Who Went Into the Closet

Tuesday at Lois's Luncheonette is always "hot turkey sandwich with mashed potatoes and gravy," but it's real turkey. The bread is baked every morning on the premises, and the potatoes are grown in the soil of Moose County. Her doughnuts are freshly fried each day—"old-fashioned fried cakes with a touch of nutmeg." Her buckwheat pancakes are served with Canadian bacon, maple syrup, and double butter.

The buffet table at the premier of "The Big Burning" has "stuffed mushrooms, bacon-wrapped olives, cheese puffs," and other dainty morsels. The "Fish House punch" is made with two kinds of rum and two kinds of brandy. The other punch is cranberry juice and Chinese tea with lemon grass.

Polly and Qwilleran visit Tipsy's and have broiled whitefish and king-size steak, respectively. The steak is an "old-fashioned cut of meat that required chewing."

For Thanksgiving, Qwilleran and Polly share dinner with Arch and Mildred. Polly has roasted a turkey and Mildred has made her famous mince pie. They also enjoy squash purée with cashews. Later, Polly prepares turkey leftovers in a curry sauce with mushrooms, leeks, and lentils.

Celia Robinson sends Qwilleran "rich, nut-filled, chewy chocolate brownies," and he has visions of moving Celia to Pickax to cook meat loaf and brownies and cater parties.

The Cat Who Came to Breakfast

The Corsair Room of the Pear Island Hotel features "Creole and Cajun specialities," including a gumbo described as "an incredibly delicious mélange of shrimp, turkey, rice, okra, and the essence of young sassafras leaves." For dessert, Qwill has sweet potato pecan pie. On other occasions, he has "jambalaya, a savory blend of shrimp, ham, and sausage" and "shrimp bisque and Cajun pork chops."

Breakfasts at the Domino Inn are so delicious that Qwilleran partakes of both entrée choices: pecan pancakes with maple syrup and turkey-apple sausages, and tarragon-chive omelette with sautéed chicken livers; souffléed ham and eggs with fresh pineapple, and waffles with ricotta cheese and strawberries; eggs Benedict with Hollandaise sauce, and johnnycakes with sausages and apple sauce; smoked salmon and scrambled eggs, and ham-and-potato cakes with chutney; ham biscuits with cheese sauce, and codfish cakes with scrambled eggs; pecan pancakes with homemade sausage patties flavored with fresh herbs, and brioches filled with creamed chipped beef; and French toast with apple butter and bacon strips, and poached egg on corned beef hash.

Harriet Beadle's café offers a variety of meals: vegetable soup, hot dogs with everything, meatloaf, and apple pie with ice cream.

The Cat Who Blew the Whistle

Cats and people both like Kabibbles, a snack made by Celia Robinson and exported from Florida. Mildred Riker says they're "croutons toasted with Parmesan cheese, garlic salt, red pepper, and Worchestershire sauce."

Dinner on the Lumberton Party Train includes jellied beef consommé and Chateaubriand so good that everyone agreed that "neither the meat nor the chef could have come from Mudville."

At the Palomino Paddock, a "five-star, five-thousand-calorie restaurant," Qwilleran enjoys "she-crab soup, an appetizer of mushrooms stuffed with spinach and goat cheese, a Caesar salad, and sea scallops with sun-dried tomatoes, basil, and saffron cream on angel hair pasta." Polly orders grouper.

The Cat Who Said Cheese

The Pasty Parlor is a designer pasty restaurant, run by a couple from Down Below. They offer four crusts: plain, cheese, herb, or cornmeal. Four fillings: ground beef, ham, turkey, or sausage. Four veggies: green pepper, broccoli, mushroom, or carrot, besides the traditional potato and onion, plus tomato, olive, or hot chili garnish.

Lori Bamba's The Spoonery offers dozens of types of soup, including Mulligatawny, Scotch broth, Portuguese black bean, eggplant and garlic, New Orleans gumbo, Viennese goulash, oxtail, turkey-barley, bouillabaisse, roasted peanut with garlic, sausage and white bean, chicken with rice and dill, plus one "boring soup each day for the fuddy-duddies."

The Old Stone Mill offers several specials: chicken breast in curried sauce with stir-fried veggies, roast rack of lamb with green peppercorn sauce, and "shrimp in a saffron cream with sun-dried tomatoes and basil, served on spinach fettucine." The meal ends with crème brûlée and apple pie with cheese.

The Boulder House Inn in Trawnto has delicious steak and trout. Served with the entrées are brussels sprouts with caraway, spinach and toasted almonds in phyllo pastry, and an herb-flavored soufflé. Dessert is poached pears stuffed with currants and pistachios and served with cherry coulis.

The Cat Who Tailed a Thief

Onoosh's Mediterranean Café is newly opened by Onoosh Dolmathakia. Willard Carmichael orders hummus for an appetizer; Qwill asks for *baba ghanouj*. Both have lentil soup with *tabbouleh* as the salad course, followed by shish kebab for Will and stuffed grape leaves for Qwill. Dessert is spicy walnut cake and dark-roast coffee.

The Nouvelle Dining Club is the new gourmet club in Pickax. The menu for the first monthly dinner is built around local products. Dinner includes smoked whitefish on triangles of spoon bread with mustard, broccoli coulis, black bean soup with conchiglie, roast tenderloin of lamb in a crust of pine nuts and mushrooms and cardamom, purée of Hubbard squash and leeks, pear chutney, crusty rolls, spinach and redleaf lettuce tossed with ginger vinaigrette and garnished with goat cheese, and baked apples with peppercorn sauce.

The Northern Lights Hotel in Mooseville has one waiter and one choice on the menu: fried fish sandwich with lumbercamp fries and cole slaw.

Weekly dinner at Polly's has changed. She is trying out seventeen low-calorie, low-cholesterol recipes for "glamorizing a flattened chicken breast." Although she calls a dinner *scaloppine di pollo appetito*, it's still flattened chicken to Qwilleran. The recipes include "flattened chicken" garnished with mushrooms and walnuts; ripe olives, garbanzos, and sun-dried tomatoes; or shallots, lemon zest, chopped spinach, and blue cheese. Qwilleran always thaws a burger for himself when he goes home.

The Cat Who Sang for the Birds

Qwilleran and Polly dine at Onoosh's Café. He has lamb shank with baked chickpeas; she has vegetarian stuffed grape leaves.

Polly and Mildred cook dinner for Arch and Qwill: fruit soup (a concoction of pear and raspberry), mushroom frittata (made with cholesterol-free eggs), and a warm salad of asparagus and yellow peppers.

Qwilleran meets Hixie at the Old Stone Mill. Its ancient waterwheel has been replaced by a reproduction of the original, which was destroyed during the spring floods. The specials for the evening are chilled gazpacho soup garnished with crème fraîche, quail stuffed with mushroom and prune duxelle, and roasted snapper with étoufée sauce and spinach.

Qwilleran meets Wetherby Goode at Chet's Bar and Barbecue. It's in a cinder-block building in Kennebeck. They have the choice of pork, beef, or turkey; sandwich or platter; hotmild, hot-hot or call 911.

Qwilleran and Polly dine at the Palomino Paddock near Whinny Hills in Lockmaster County. It looks like a working stable, with bales of hay and tack on the walls. There are no prices on Polly's menu, but the evening special is tenderloin of ostrich with smoked tomatoes, herbed polenta, and black currant coulis. Qwill tries the special; Polly orders a vegetarian curry.

The Cat Who Saw Stars

Arch and Mildred invite Qwilleran and the Comptons for dinner. Mildred offers butternut and roasted pepper soup, coddled pork chops, twice-baked potatoes, a broccoli soufflé, a pinot noir, old-fashioned Waldorf salad, and Black Forest cake.

The new restaurant in Mooseville is Owen's Place, run by Floridians Owen and Ernestine during the tourist season. Ernie, the chef, offers a "sophisticated menu and a good wine list." The lunch crowd likes the quiche, skewered potatoes, and the maitre d'. Skewered potatoes are the latest fad in food, Derek's idea. The skewer is a foot-long needle of twisted iron with a point at one end and a decorative medallion at the other. The baking time is supposed to be shorter and the potatoes better-tasting.

When Qwilleran goes to Owen's Place for lunch, he chooses

a "lamb shank osso bucco on a bed of basil fettuccini." The soup was a cauliflower and Gorgonzola purée served with chives. Other items on the menu include "veal loin encrusted with eggplant, spinach and roasted red peppers, with sundried tomato demiglaze."

Later when Qwilleran and Junior Goodwinter go to Owen's Place for lunch, they study the skewered potato: a 20-ounce Idaho potato, with a choice of one sauce (marinara, Bolognese, Alfredo, ratatouille, curried chicken, herbed yogurt with anchovies), one accompaniment (sautéed Portobello mushrooms, red onion rings, pitted ripe olives, garlic-pickled garbanzos, sautéed chicken livers, grilled tofu cubes), and one garnish (grated Parmesan cheese, toasted cashews, shredded carrots with capers, slivered fresh coconut, crumbled Stilton cheese, sour cream with chives). They order roast beef sandwiches with horseradish.

Arch and Qwill eat breakfast in the café at the Northern Lights Hotel. Qwilleran has "fried eggs with burnt edges, the sliver of ham, the warmed-over potatoes, all swimming in grease on a cold plate." Riker says he believes that Qwilleran just likes food, good or bad. Qwill retorts that he knows the difference, but adjusts. On another day, Qwill has a ham-and-cheese sandwich and a cup of cream of tomato soup. The ordinary food is expected by townspeople; it's "local color" to tourists.

Alice Ogilvie serves Qwilleran coffee and doughnuts, "real fried-cakes," Qwill's favorite.

Breakfast at the Rikers' is sometimes pecan waffles, apple-chicken sausages, and blueberry muffins. That's an advantage of being married to a former home economics teacher who is the newspaper's food writer. Arch and Mildred invite Qwilleran, Roger, and Lisa to dinner. Mildred serves zucchini fritters with a dill-yogurt dip for hors d'oeuvres, then squash bisque, lamb stew, crusty bread, and green salad.

Linguini's hasn't changed. It has the same broken locks on the restrooms but "the food is wonderful." Hixie has veal marsala, Fran has stuffed manicotti, and Qwilleran has lasagna.

Qwilleran takes Tess Bunker to The Northern Lights Hotel. They have Swiss steak, with "gravy thick as wallpaper paste," overcooked carrots, and potatoes that could be mistaken for shaving cream. He's hoping she'll leave soon, but extends her visit when she promises to cook "lamb shank with beans, lumberjack style." She picks fresh thimbleberries and makes pancakes for breakfast. For dinner, she prepares gazpacho and steak au poivre with skewered potatoes. For the next day's breakfast, she buys duck eggs from Grott's Grocery and makes mushroom omelettes and muffins. For lunch, she plans macaroni and cheese, made with cheddar from Grott's Grocery. When everyone leaves and Qwilleran is distracted by a sudden storm, the Siamese enjoy the cheese, but they eat around the macaroni.

Ernie is reopening Owen's Place. Her new menu of appetizers includes "miniature acorn squash with a stuffing of wild rice, fresh corn, and caramelized onion" and "grilled petite tenderloins of venison with smoked bacon, braised cabbage strudel, and a sun-dried Bing cherry demiglaze." Her menu of entrées includes "potato-crusted filet of salmon served with shiitake mushrooms, saffron risotto, and chive beurre blanc."

Qwilleran braves the downpouring rain for Mildred's gumbo and strawberry lemon cream pie. The gumbo is filled with chicken, shrimp, sausage, rice, vegetables, and spices.

11

The Quotable
Companion

"I have several girls here. Which one is yours?" Qwilleran, *Brahms.*

"Any small aperture is challenging to the feline sensibility. For a cat it is a matter of honor to enlarge the opening and squeeze through." Qwilleran, *On/Off.*

"I like cats. You can't boss them around." William, *Red.* "And you can't win, either. You may think you've put one over on them, but they always come out ahead." Qwilleran, *Red.*

"Did you ever try speaking to a cat about *anything?* He crosses his eyes and scratches his ear and goes right on doing what he was doing." Qwilleran, *Shakespeare.*

"Cats have a natural aptitude for care-giving." Qwilleran, *Cheese.*

"If a cat likes you, it means you have a princely character." Wally Toddwhistle, quoting his mother, *Glue.*

"Cats hate a closed door, regardless of which side they're on. If they're out, they want to get in, and if they're in, they want to get out." Qwilleran, *Underground.*

"Cats are perverse. They figure out what you want and then do the opposite." Qwilleran, *High.*

"I admit that [Koko] lives high, for a cat, but he saved my neck a couple of times, and I owe him." Qwilleran, *High.*

"The more you talk to cats, the smarter they become, but it has to be intelligent conversation." Qwilleran, *Breakfast.*

"Cats don't fight for their rights; they take them for granted . . . and if they don't get their rights, they quietly commit certain acts of civil disobedience . . . Tyrants!" Qwilleran, *Whistle.*

"Cats have a sly sense of humor. They like to make us look like fools, which we are, I guess." Qwilleran, *Cheese.*

"The dance of life should be created from moment to moment with individuality and spontaneity." Zoe Lambreth, *Backwards.*

"I have never been able to appreciate murder for revenge. I find murder for personal gain infinitely more appealing." George Bonifield Mountclemens III, *Backwards.*

"Our profession is above suspicion. You never heard of a newsman turning to crime . . . But journalists just go to the Press Club and drown their criminal inclinations." Qwilleran, *Danish.*

"Don't try to make bad news worse." Junior Goodwinter, *Whistle.*

"If you can't eat it, don't print it." On coffee mug, *Cheese.*

"If you want to test a guy's sincerity, serve him a bad cup of coffee. If he praises it, he's not to be trusted." Max Sorrel, *Red.*

"[Herb] can give up his smelly habit [of smoking]. You don't hear the Surgeon General issuing any warnings against *antiques.*" Mrs. Cobb, *Shakespeare.*

"An antique is worth only what someone is willing to pay for it." Qwilleran, *Glue.*

"We shape our buildings, thereafter they shape us." Eddington Smith, quoting Churchill, *Glue*.

"I'm going on eighty, you know. That's when life begins. Nothing is expected of you, and you're forgiven for everything." Inga Berry, *High*.

"All work and no play makes . . . money." Qwilleran, *Mountain*.

"Individuals who are attracted to islands are all a little odd, and if they spend enough of their lives completely surrounded by water, they become completely odd." Rev. Harding, *Breakfast*.

"Old legends never die. They only get made into movies." Qwilleran, *Breakfast*.

"One evil only leads to another." Polly, *Whistle*.

"Grief is a stubborn infection of the spirit." Osmond Hasselrich, *Cheese*.

"Daisies arrange themselves. One should never fuss with them." Polly, *Cheese*.

"Cheese belongs with a good meal and makes a bad one better." Jack Nibble, *Cheese*.

"Give Koko a taste of cheese, and he'll be your friend for life." Qwilleran, *Cheese*.

"One should never question a person's choice of name for a pet, no matter how intimate the friendship." Qwilleran, *Thief*.

"There's nothing wrong with a little local color to relieve the monotony of good English." Qwilleran, *Stars*

"Writers write—the way other people breathe." Junior, *Stars*.

"Work is a healthy way of coping with grief." Qwilleran, *Stars*.

"The male animal is as stubborn as a mule—and we all know about mules, don't we?" Ms. Gramma, *Stars*.

"Where is she? Where is that woman?" "I have four here. Which one do you want?" Qwilleran, *Stars*.

12

The Cat Who
Had 14 Tales

T ales *is a collection of short stories, some of which were writ-ten in the early '60s. Read them carefully and you'll find catly behavior* that reminds you of Koko and Yum Yum, and places and peo-ple described in *The Cat Who . . .* series.

Koko is not the first literary cat to claw an unabridged dictionary. "Phut Phat Concentrates" is about a Siamese who communicates by staring at his owners' foreheads until they get the message. His Sunday treat is creamed liver. Phut Phat scolds the phone when it rings and expresses his annoyance by sharpening his claws on *Webster's Unabridged.* He leaps to the top of a towering antique armoire. He leaps from the armoire onto the head of an intruder, ripping at the man's head with his razor claws.

In "Weekend of the Big Puddle," Percy (a "portly silver tabby") spends weekends in a rustic chalet on the north shore of Big Pine Lake in Michigan. A guest talks about the old days of lumberjacks and sawmills and saloons. The sawdust towns were destroyed by a huge fire. The two couples go to visit an old cemetery, and Deedee ends up with ivy poisoning. Percy talks to two visiting ghosts who mention the Tittabawassee River, an actual river in Michigan.

A "mechanical" cat is introduced in "The Fluppie Phenomenon." Sin-Sin is a seven-month-old Siamese kitten who visits her owner's sister and husband for a few weeks. She can let out a scream "with the decibel level of an ambulance siren." Once while left in the car, Sin-Sin steps on the push-button and opens a rear window, escaping to the roof of the car. She turns on a radio full blast and disturbs the neighbors. She disconnects the coffeemaker by clamping her teeth on the plug and yanking it out. Sin-Sin disconnects "all the lamps daily and the refrigerator occasionally." She enjoys turning on the television in the middle of the night. Sin-Sin likes to bump faucets and watch the water swirl, and she flushes the toilet by the hour. She also unties shoelaces. She opens the milk chute and admits the entire tomcat population of the neighborhood. Howard and his wife get custody of all four of Sin-Sin's offspring. They operate a "halfway house for wayward or unwanted cats, as well as a boarding school for the truly gifted and a placement bureau for upwardly mobile felines (Fluppies)."

"The Hero of Drummond Street" is a gray-and-white cat called Drooler, who finds a gas leak and saves the neighborhood from disaster. His picture is on the cover of a national magazine.

"The Mad Museum Mouser" is about Marmalade, an "overfed animal with bristling orange fur and a hostile glint in its squinting yellow eyes." He's the mouser for the Lockmaster Museum. Rhoda Finney—complete with hearing aid that doesn't work—welcomes a visitor to the museum and gives her a tour. Homer Tibbitt is the custodian. Marmalade is licking blood from his claws, evidently the result of attacking an invader who vandalized a room in the museum.

"The Dark One" is a Siamese who saves Hilda's life when her drunken husband is pursuing her. Dahk Won likes to sit inside the grand piano with its half-open lid.

"East Side Story" describes a romance between two cats, a little blind white Princess and a swaggering gray Prince Charming. It's told in the form of an interview with Mrs. P.G.R. as part of the Oral History Project of Gattville Community College.

"Tipsy and the Board of Health" recounts Gus and Tipsy's adventures before moving to Moose County. Tipsy lives in Nick's Market, hunting for mice. She likes to sit in the window and make passes at flies. When the inspector from the Board of Health tells Nick that no cats are allowed in a food store, Tipsy moves into Sam's drugstore. The inspector catches up with her, and her next stop is Gus's Timberline Bar, which is fixed up like a log cabin. The inspector catches up with her again, and Gus pays the fine for Tipsy and her offspring. Rather than give up Tipsy, Gus closes his bar and moves to North Kennebeck where he opens Tipsy's Tavern. This story is an interview with Mr. C. W. as part of the Oral History Project of GCC.

"A Cat Named Conscience" is an interview with Miss A.J.T. for the GCC project. Constance is a bank cat, black with white feet and green eyes. She is called Conscience because she can give a "reproachful-like" look. Mister Freddie the bank manager is found hanged in the barn behind the bank. He is blamed for the missing money, but it was the bank clerk Matt who stole the money and killed Freddie. Matt would meet Freddie's stepdaughter Abigail in a hotel and bring her presents. Abigail killed Conscience, who must have given the guilty Abby a "reproachful-like" look.

"SuSu and the 8:30 Ghost" tells the story of a Siamese cat's friendship with Mr. Van, an old man who claims to have been a cat in a former existence. He's an antique dealer who lives in the same apartment building. Mr. Van visits SuSu several times a week at eight-thirty. He plans to use his fortune to start a foundation named after SuSu, the Superior Suda Foundation, which will study "the highly developed mental perception of the domestic feline and apply the knowledge to the improvement of the human mind." After Mr. Van disappears, SuSu waits at the door every night at eight-thirty. SuSu conveys to her owners the message that Mr. Van has been drowned in the river. She's been talking to his ghost.

"Stanley and Spook" is the story of an unusual pair—Spook, a six-year-old boy who wears a Chicago Cubs sweatshirt, and Stanley, a beautiful cat with thick blond fur and a white bib. Spook has catly habits. Stanley is clumsy, for a cat.

"A Cat Too Small for His Whiskers" is about the Gang—two chocolate-point Siamese, a tortoiseshell Persian, and a red Abyssinian—and a cat too small for his whiskers. The little boy, Donald, finds the strange cat in the barn and calls him Whiskers because his whiskers are long and they change color. And Whiskers flies straight up like a helicopter.

"The Sin of Madame Phloi" is the cat story Lilian wrote to work through her anger at the person who pushed her Koko the First out a tenth-story window. Madame Phloi is a Siamese who can cock her head and melt hearts. She watches pigeons and listens to ghosts of deceased mice. When offered the wrong kind of cheese, she shakes a fastidious paw at it.

In "Tragedy on New Year's Eve," there's a sleek black cat who "helps" the woman he's visiting by pawing the paper as she writes. Shadow helps the woman figure out what really happened to Wally Sloan, then disappears.

13

The Lady
Who . . .

*F*ortunately, *Lilian Jackson Braun isn't like Qwilleran, who never finishes a book. To date, we have twenty-one wonderful books about* the crime-solving Siamese cats, Koko and Yum Yum, and their sidekick, James Macintosh Qwilleran, plus a collection of short stories, *The Cat Who Had 14 Tales.*

Lilian's own cats "aren't into crime," and neither is she. So just how did a young "spoem" writer become a best-loved, bestselling author of mysteries?

KOKO THE FIRST SETS THE STAGE

Lilian's long love affair with cats didn't start when she was a child, but after she was married.

"I had never had a pet in my life until I was married and living in an apartment. I received a Siamese kitten as a gift, and I called him Koko. He and I were devoted to each other. I adored him and he adored me," she said.

"When he was two years old, he was killed in a fall from a tenth-floor window. We lived in an apartment building on the tenth floor, and he somehow got out in the hall and went out the window. Well, I was distraught, but when my neighbors told me they had evidence that he had been pushed by an eccentric person who lived on that floor, then I was angry. I had nightmares for two weeks about friends and relatives falling out the window. I knew that to get over this, I would have to write something about it."

So Lilian wrote a short story in which she got her revenge. "It was not based on what actually happened in my case, but it was inspired by what happened. It was called 'The Sin of Madame Phloi,' and it is in my collection of short stories [*The Cat Who Had 14 Tales*]. I wrote it to get my revenge against this person who had pushed my pet out the window." The story was published in Ellery Queen's mystery magazine and made the 'Best Detective Stories of the Year' in the 1960s.

"They asked for more mysteries with a cat. So I wrote half a dozen more, and then a publisher asked if I would like to try writing a novel with a cat in it. So I wrote *The Cat Who Could Read Backwards*, and they asked for another, and then another."

But there's a big gap between book number three and book number four—eighteen years.

"By the time I had written the fourth one, tastes in mysteries had changed, the management had changed, the policy had changed. They wanted sex and violence, not kitty-cat stories. Sex and violence were not my style, so I just forgot all about *The Cat Who*. I had a full-time job on a newspaper and it was exciting, and I had a wonderful social life, so who needed it?" she asked.

"I forgot all about *The Cat Who* for eighteen years. By that time my husband had died, and I had married Earl Bettinger. One Sunday afternoon up at the cabin on the lake, it was rain-ing, and I said, 'You have never read the manuscript of the fourth novel, the one that was not published.' So he read it, and he said, 'I think its time has come. There are fifty-six million cats in the United States, and I think you should resubmit it.' So I did. Berkley Publishing took it as a paperback, gave me a contract for more, and the rest is history."

Lilian had never really read mystery stories, except when she was a teenager and read the complete Sherlock Holmes mysteries. She prefers nineteenth-century literature.

"When I wrote my first story, I was surprised when Ellery Queen's mystery magazine took it. I didn't think of it as a mystery. The stories that I went on writing for Ellery Queen I didn't think of really as mysteries. When I wrote my first novel, I thought, 'Well, let's see—how do you do this?' I may have gotten a book on how to write a mystery novel. But I don't follow all the rules. I don't think of them so much as mystery stories as character stories—life in a small town where things happen."

A LIFE OF WRITING

Lilian Jackson Braun has been writing "All my life: first for fun, then for an advertising job, then for a newspaper, and now for the *The Cat Who* readers." This life of writing began very early.

"When I was three years old, I asked my mother if she would teach me to read and write so I could correspond with my grandmother, who lived the long distance of twenty miles away. So my grandmother and I kept up a correspondence. In school, I wrote little stories."

Her mother contributed to Lilian's storytelling talent. "My mother had a very good idea for the family at dinnertime. Each one of us told what we had done that day, what had happened.

And if we could make it sound funny or exciting, all the better. My mother was a wizard at that. She could describe a trip to the grocery store and make it hilarious. And so I think I learned something from those evening recitations at the dinner table.'' She was the only child for nine years, then a brother and sister came along. ''It was a very happy family.''

There's at least one of her novels that we've never read.

''I was about twelve years old when I undertook to write a French historical novel. Needless to say I never finished it. Everybody got killed. They were sent to the guillotine, or they were killed in battle, and I cried a lot because all these tragedies were happening. My mother said, 'Why do you write things that make you cry? Why don't you write things that make you laugh?' I've been writing light, humorous fiction ever since, with the exception of 'The Sin of Madame Phloi' and the short stories that followed that. But even when I started writing *The Cat Who* novels, I thought, 'I want to give them the light touch. I don't want them to be gory.'

''Of course when you're writing about a cat who solves mysteries, you can't be entirely serious.''

Lilian's writing was published while she was still in high school.

''In high school I wrote for the school paper. I graduated at sixteen and had already sold things to national magazines. I was in my tomboy stage, crazy about baseball, and I had sold things to *Baseball Magazine* and *Sporting News*. It was a sign of the times that I felt obliged to use a pen name, a male pen name. I felt they would not run anything written by a girl, so I called myself Ward Jackson, Ward being my mother's maiden name and Jackson being my last name. It was a big thrill, you know, seeing your stuff in a national publication.''

After graduation, she went to the *Detroit Times* and showed them some of her little poems. ''Or spoems I called them— they were sport poems—and they said, 'Could you write one a day?' Of course you never say no, so I wrote six a week for the entire baseball season and part of the football season. To be sixteen going on seventeen and have a daily byline in a paper was a thrill. They were trying to syndicate, but decided the spoems were too topical to be syndicated. They were written about what happened yesterday."

So the young writer graduated from spoems to advertising.

"My mother suggested that I show some of my verses to the stores to be used in advertising, so I went to the first department store, and they said, 'We couldn't use these, but we could use a copywriter.' I said, 'What's that?'—that's how much I knew. And they said, 'Well, you write ads.' I told them I didn't know anything about that. And they said, 'Just come to work and you can learn all you need to know in three days.' I remember the first ad I wrote. It was for 'Ecru curtain material— 19 cents a yard.' "

Next was a job with another department store, where she stayed about fifteen years. "I was director of public relations when I left. The reason I left was I wasn't doing much writing anymore—it was mostly ideas. I had an urge to write."

After Lilian had worked in advertising for eighteen years, she made a change. "By that time I was married and I could afford to stop working. I stayed home for a few months and wrote short stories. I discovered that writing is a very lonely business if you're used to being in the workplace and going out to lunch every day with interesting people."

The *Detroit Free Press* invited her to come and talk to them about a special section. "I could never have written spot news, but this was more of a magazine format, feature articles, and that was my style. I said, 'I'm not interested in full-time work,' and they said, 'Come down and talk about it anyway.' So I went and talked about it. It was full time, and I took the job and stayed there thirty years. It was writing articles about decorating, antiques, art. It finally went into architecture, preservation, and so on. Qwilleran, writing his column and hunting for stories, was doing pretty much what I did.''

So Lilian wrote her own real-life version of *Gracious Abodes*. ''It was called the *Good Living Section*.'' She was kidded about it because her counterpart at the other newspaper said, ''I suppose that makes me the *Bad Living* editor.''

CATSPIRATION

Many of her ideas for *The Cat Who* . . . come from her background in the newspaper business and her experiences with her own cats.

''When I was asked to write a novel, I thought, 'Well, what would I write about? It's got to be something I know.' Newspapers are exciting. Then I thought, 'Who is the most hated person on a newspaper staff?' It's the art critic. And so I made the art critic my villain,'' she explained.

''People wonder why I have a male protagonist. The reason was that he was going to be a reporter who would be assigned to the art beat, although he knew nothing about art. And I had done that myself for the *Free Press*. I had taken a year to fill in for the art critic, although I'm no art critic, and I was even a little shaky about the subject of art. I thought that if I made my protagonist a woman, everybody would say, 'Oh, well, it's autobiographical,' and then they would start reading themselves into the book and identifying with certain characters and claiming that I had copied them. I made my protagonist a man with a large moustache.''

It occurred to Lilian that in fiction, detectives and newspapermen are always hard drinkers, so she made her protagonist just the opposite—an alcoholic who had licked his problem.

''When I wanted to invent a section for Qwilleran to work

on, I thought, 'What is the most ridiculous name I can give it?' *Gracious Abodes. Daily Fluxion* and the *Morning Rampage*—I thought those were funny, too.''

So where are Pickax and Moose County? Are they really ''four hundred miles north of everywhere?''

''No,'' she replied with a smile. ''Some people think it's Minnesota, some think it's Wisconsin, some think it's Michigan. Some people think it's Maine, but it couldn't possibly be.'' Qwilleran is described as the wealthiest man in the ''northeast central United States.''

''People want to know exactly were Pickax is, where Moose County is, and I say, 'It's in my head, and it's anywhere you want it to be.' I had a letter from a woman in Germany a few weeks ago. She's planning a trip to the United States and wants to include Pickax, and she wanted to know exactly where it is,'' Lilian said, smiling at the idea.

''Pickax is a composite. My places are composites. The Potato Mountains in *The Cat Who Moved a Mountain* are a composite of the Adirondacks, Poconos, Blue Ridge—all the mountains I have known. My characters are composites of people I've known.''

Her fans often write to say they know someone just like one of her characters.

''I had a letter from a librarian in a small town, Augusta, Michigan, and she said, 'All your characters are alive and well and walking around Augusta.' ''

Koko and Yum Yum are composites, too. Her own cats have been inspiration for her fictional Koko and Yum Yum, especially her second Koko.

''After I lost my first cat, my husband said, 'You've got to get another one right away.' He went right to the breeder to pick up another male kitten. I was at the office, and he called me and said, 'There are two of them here, a male and a female, and I really cannot decide,' so I said, 'Let's take both of them.'

I had learned that a single Siamese is apt to be neurotic and have bad behavior problems. Siamese are better in pairs. So that's how I got my second Koko and my first Yum Yum."

Lilian's second Koko lived to be eighteen. "I called him Koko the Great because he was so intelligent. A lot of the things that Koko in the book does, Koko the Great did. Like telling my guests when to go home. Eleven o'clock—that was his shut-off time exactly."

She recalled Koko the Second's behavior. "We would be having dinner, then after-dinner drinks, and he would have been absent all evening. At eleven o'clock, he would walk in with a very determined step, and he'd stand there, and he'd look at them. They'd said, 'Oh, there's Koko. Where have you been all evening?' And he'd say, 'Yow.' Then he'd turn around and walk to the front door, and look to see if they were following. He'd stand at the front door, and if they didn't show up, he'd come back and say 'Yow' again, and they'd say, 'Is he trying to tell us something?' So it worked!"

The Cat Who Played Post Office describes Koko's eleven o'clock ejection of Dr. Melinda Goodwinter from Qwilleran's home. Yum Yum joins him in an eleven o'clock dismissal of Dwight Somers in *The Cat Who Blew the Whistle*. Koko dismisses an entire room of people by throwing a late-night catfit in *The Cat Who Said Cheese*.

In *The Cat Who Sniffed Glue*, Koko likes to lick stamps and envelopes. This peculiar proclivity is based on Koko the Great, who once actually walked around with a stamp stuck on his nose.

"The one I have now is Koko III, not at all like Koko the Great. Even so, every day my cats do something that gives me an idea, and I run and write it down for future use."

Lilian's own Koko didn't actually play Scrabble or Dictionary. But he did try to sharpen his claws on her *Webster's Unabridged Dictionary*. He was not allowed to, but that gave rise to the word game episodes in the books. Koko the Great also liked to knock things off the table or off the desk. In the books, Koko knocks down dominoes, Scrabble tiles, books, or anything that appeals to him.

Lilian has had two Yum Yums. It was the second one who would steal her gold pencil and hide it under a rug. This behavior was inspiration for "Yum Yum, the Paw," who pilfers anything shiny and hides it under a couch or rug.

Lilian and her husband had a cabin in Michigan that was similar to the Klingenschoen cabin. *The Cat Who Played Brahms* has an accurate description of their own cabin, "except it didn't have a Jacuzzi. Otherwise it was quite similar. The location up on a dune, above the lake, that's quite similar."

So why do Qwilleran and Koko and Yum Yum pack their belongings and move around so much?

"I really have to have a change of venue for the cats so they can operate and do the things they do. That's why Qwilleran moves about so much. Some think it's because he's a gypsy at heart, but really it's more for my purposes."

In *The Cat Who Turned On and Off*, they were in a historic house that was a station of the Underground Railroad in pre–Civil War times, so that Koko could get in behind the books and go into the next apartment. In *The Cat Who Saw Red*, they lived at a pottery, with a peephole between the apartment and the pottery itself. "So all of those things are preplanned," she explained.

Lilian sneaks in tidbits from her many fan letters.

"I had a wonderful letter from a man in Cincinnati, who said, 'I love Polly Duncan. I would just love to be able to take her out to dinner, but I know I can't do that. I wonder if Polly has a sister in Cincinnati?' So when I wrote my next book [*The Cat Who Tailed a Thief*], Polly is talking about the Christmas presents that's she giving, and the one she's sending to her sister in Cincinnati. I put that in just for that man, and he's going to love it! I do a lot of in-jokes that way with people I know or people who have written fan letters. I sometimes name a pet after the pet of someone I know or someone who has written a fan letter."

In *The Cat Who Tailed a Thief,* Qwilleran collects names of cats from his readers—some of which Lilian has collected from friends and fans. She recently received a picture postcard from "Orlando," a beautiful bookstore cat lounging on a table with *The Cat Who Knew Shakespeare* and several of Shakespeare's works. Orlando just might appear in a future book.

LILIAN AND QWILLERAN

It's hard for avid fans to wait a whole year for a new book— a book a month would come nearer to satisfying their appetite. But it takes Lilian a year to write a book.

"For one thing, my eyes are not as fast as they used to be. They focus more slowly, so that slows up my reading and my writing. When I retired from the workplace, I thought 'I've been working from nine to five for fifty years; now I don't want any schedule.' Some days I work in the morning, other times in the afternoon, other times in the evening. When I feel like it, I can find the time."

Lilian and Qwilleran have similar writing habits. Qwilleran bought a typewriter with a broken *e.* "I still have an electric typewriter, although when I began writing in the sixties I had a manual typewriter, and it had certain faults that I used in *The Cat Who Turned On and Off.* Qwilleran had quite a bit of trouble."

Qwilleran balks when the *Daily Fluxion* puts in electronic machines. Lilian calls herself "very low-tech." She doesn't have an answering machine. "I don't know how to use our automatic coffeemaker. I don't want a word processor."

They both like to write in longhand. Qwilleran will probably never get a word processor. "Actually he's joined the lead pencil club. He likes to write longhand, on a legal pad, and so do I. I'm getting so that I write more and more of my chapters or scenes with a felt-tip pen and a legal pad. Like Qwilleran, I like to sit with my feet up. I have lounges all over the house. I think better with my feet up," she explained, using words similar to those of Qwilleran.

"When I first went to the *Free Press*, reporters and photographers would sit around with their feet on the desks, and in old movies about newspaper people, they always had their feet on the desks. I thought they just looked lazy, but I realize now they were thinking. You can think better with your feet up! That's my idea anyway."

The Cat Who Blew the Whistle has a description of Qwilleran's feet-on-the-desk thinking: "He could do his best thinking with his feet elevated, a legal pad in his left hand and a black felt-tip in his right."

"A lot of things have changed in newspapers. When Qwilleran first moved to Pickax, they had that old paper called the *Pickax Picayune*, and the owner set the type by hand—great fun writing that part of it. Now that the *Moose County Something* has started, it is quite different from the *Daily Fluxion*. In a small town, the newspapers are different. There's a sense of responsibility to one's community. Certain things are better left unreported. When I write these things, I think, 'Oh, my friends in Detroit are going to think this is all wrong.'"

Arch Riker had to come around to understanding that concept, after he retired from the *Fluxion* and went to the *Moose County Something*. "The chicken farm in *The Cat Who Went Underground* burned down, and they lost 5,000 chickens. Riker said if he'd been Down Below, he would have written 'World's Biggest Chicken Barbecue,' but he said all he could think of was how terrible it was for the farmer to have lost his entire year's work."

Lilian may use aspects of her own career as inspiration for Qwilleran's, but she sneaks in other facets of her life as well, including her interest in preservation [note the restoration efforts in Junktown and Pleasant Street in Pickax] and her tastes in food. There's a little bit of her in Rosemary Whiting, for example.

"I have been very much interested in cooking and ethnic foods and dining out all my adult life. I got into health foods, and it's a little in-joke with myself to have Qwilleran opposed to health food. He makes fun of health foods." So Rosemary was a little bit of Lilian—"And I had him make fun of her."

Lilian and her husband really have a very healthful diet. "I particularly like foods of India, curries [note Polly Duncan's interest in very hot curries!]. Earl was in India for six months with an acting company sponsored by the state department and they did Shakespeare and Sophocles. He learned to love curry and all the things that go with it. Right now I'm very interested in Middle Eastern or Mediterranean cooking—hummus, and tabbouleh, and baba ghanouj, and all of that. So I sneak that in where I can." [Visit Onoosh's Mediterranean Restaurant in *The Cat Who Tailed a Thief* and *The Cat Who Sang for the Birds*.]

One of Lilian's favorite family traditions at Christmas is to read a passage from Dickens's *A Christmas Carol*, the description of the Cratchits' Christmas dinner: "There never was such a goose!" [See *The Cat Who Went Into the Closet* for Larry Lanspeak's choice of Christmas reading.]

Lilian and her husband, Earl Bettinger, live full-time in North Carolina, with two Siamese, Koko III and Pitti Sing. For years she covered the furniture market in High Point, North Carolina, for the *Detroit Free Press*. "When I came down here, I thought, 'This is a wonderful state. This would be a wonderful place to live.' But I never really thought I would live here, until we decided to get away from the snow and ice and the ten-foot snowdrifts in Michigan."

Lilian and Earl read books on where to retire, and North Carolina was highly recommended. "So we flew down, rented a car, and made a circle tour of the state. We've never regretted moving here. It's a wonderful place to live."

Lilian enjoys attending book signings, especially at cat shows, where everyone loves cats. Earl was an actor until he retired several years ago. He's on the board of directors of a local amateur group, and he plays an occasional part.

THE CAT WHO . . . ?

The Cat Who . . . books are published in about fifteen countries, including Bulgaria, Hungary and Brazil. The books do very well in England, Holland, France, Italy, and Japan. Turkey and Russia have also expressed interest in the books.

And so thousands of her loyal fans all over the world eagerly await the next *The Cat Who* . . . mystery. What dastardly crimes will be committed? What clues will Koko try to communicate to Qwilleran? What new skills will Koko develop? What objects will Yum Yum the Paw pilfer? Where will they live next? Will Qwilleran and Polly stay happily single? Will Qwilleran finish a book? Will Koko and Yum Yum ever get along with Brutus?

14

The Cat Who Quiz

1. Artist from thirteenth century for whom Koko was named.
2. Former falls on Big Potato, now a lake.
3. Yum Yum's two earlier names.
4. Two books with "little green men."
5. Liz Hart's true name.
6. Who Polly would be if she could be any artist who ever lived.
7. Three other names for Breakfast Island.
8. Population of Pickax.
9. River in Spudsboro.
10. Lover's lane on the banks of Black Creek.
11. Pickax Theatre Club's summer theater near Mooseville.

12. Short story in which Tipsy first appeared (in *The Cat Who Had 14 Tales*).
13. Mechanical cat who could turn on televisions and flush toilets (in *The Cat Who Had 14 Tales*).
14. What LJB called her sports poems.
15. One meat that the cats have refused to eat on several occasions.
16. Pickax gourmet club.
17. Polly's sister-in-law in Pickax.
18. Polly's sister in Cincinnati (name and nickname).
19. Butterfly artist.
20. Schnauzer who likes *National Geographic* TV programs.

Answers:

1. Kao K'o-Kung
2. Batata Falls
3. Freya and Yu
4. *Whistle* and *Stars*
5. Elizabeth Appelhardt
6. Mary Cassatt
7. Pear Island, Grand Island, Providence Island
8. Three thousand
9. Yellyhoo
10. Willoway
11. Fryers Club Summer Stage
12. "Tipsy and the Board of Health"
13. Sin-Sin
14. spoems
15. lamb
16. Nouvelle Dining Club
17. Lynette
18. Desdemona, Mona
19. Phoebe Sloan
20. Cody